SEXTET

BOOKS BY JOHN MALCOLM BRINNIN

POEMS

The Garden Is Political
The Lincoln Lyrics
No Arch, No Triumph
The Sorrows of Cold Stone
The Selected Poems of John Malcolm Brinnin
Skin Diving in the Virgins

BIOGRAPHY

Dylan Thomas in America
The Third Rose: Gertrude Stein and Her World
Sextet: T. S. Eliot & Truman Capote & Others

HISTORY

The Sway of the Grand Saloon: A Social History of the North Atlantic
Beau Voyage: Life Aboard the Last Great Ships

CRITICISM

Emily Dickinson, *a selection of poems*
Casebook on Dylan Thomas, *a collection of essays*
William Carlos Williams, *a critical study*
Selected Plays of Gertrude Stein

ANTHOLOGIES

Modern Poetry: American and British (*with Kimon Friar*)
The Modern Poets:
An American-British Anthology (*with Bill Read*)

FOR CHILDREN

Arthur, The Dolphin Who Didn't See Venice

John Malcolm Brinnin

Sextet

T.S.Eliot & Truman Capote
& Others

DELACORTE PRESS/SEYMOUR LAWRENCE

Published by
Delacorte Press/Seymour Lawrence
1 Dag Hammarskjold Plaza
New York, N.Y. 10017

Manufactured in the United States of America
First printing

Designed by Rhea Braunstein

LIBRARY OF CONGRESS CATALOGUING IN PUBLICATION DATA

Brinnin, John Malcolm.
Sextet: T. S. Eliot & Truman Capote & others.

1. Brinnin, John Malcolm—Friends and associates.
2. Authors, American—20th century—Biography.
3. Authors, English—20th century—Biography.   I. Title
PS3503.R563Z474   818'.5203   [B]   81-7801
        ISBN 0-440-07785-0   AACR2

Foreword

"I have a passion for the truth," said Jules Renard, "and for the fictions that it authorizes." Teasing his readers, the great diarist at the same time names for them the distance between observation and its expression, intention and its consequence.

This sextet of reminiscences is based on a journal kept over a period of forty years. A number of entries taken from it have been incorporated into the text more or less intact. Others have remained where they were—bits of information, ephemeral as days, preserved out of habit and serving to tell me little more than where I was, what I did, and whom I saw:

8.14.40   Bennington. A walk along country roads with Red Warren. Much talk of conceptions of tragedy—fate & conscience, guilt & absolution. (These preoccupations of his—are they personal, or are they "literary"?) We saw a cat fishing a brook.

Dinner with A., who's in a sulk, one arm in a black silk sling. What's the matter, I ask. Swamp fumes and the Holy Grail, she says.

Back in my room, I find a note: *Carlos will be playing Bartok's Allegro Barbaro at nine or so. Come if you can. Katherine Anne will be there. R.P.W.* To the meadow house on the run, I'm introduced to Miss Porter . . . powdery white in a white dress, who talks as if under some obligation to ward off silence, until Carlos puts one steely finger on the keyboard.

9.19.80   Venice. Sleepless under a fool* moon, rise at four, make *espresso*. Below, in the courtyard, Milly Theale's gondola sits on silver stilts, moonlight reaching into the rotted upholstery of its slatted cabin.

In the library (still watching for the ghost of Henry James) I eke out words. . . . *Pipistrello!* Flapping like an empty glove, the little creature skitters from medallion to medallion overhead, hangs upside down for a minute, senses the open casement, dives zigzag into San Stefano.

Late morning, K. phones from Princeton to say Katherine Anne is dead. Her voice that Sunday morning (how many weeks ago?)—I'm dying angel . . . good-bye, and the click of the phone.

*(!)

What these and similar entries have to say that isn't impenetrably private has had to be coaxed out of them. When I began to keep journals, I was blessed with total recall, or plagued by it whenever one visual detail of a remembered experience would cause a hundred others to proliferate like the spawn of some runaway machine. In the course of writing this book, however, I found I could no longer claim that dubious gift and had to depend largely on what I'd already recorded. This was trustworthy, but many entries were too sketchy and elliptical to be of use. To lift them beyond mere memoranda, I expanded and reshaped them in the hope of making immediate what time had rendered remote.

Conscience—that flat-hatted tribunal I don't know and can't get rid of—has been my guide. Arriving at my desk whenever I did, it would sit, ruler in hand, ready to rap my knuckles when I'd try to use a spoken phrase I could not still clearly hear; quick to call Shame! when I'd start to impose on others opinions or ideas of my own. Its attempts to keep me honest have been a dreadful nuisance, but I believe they have been successful.

—JOHN MALCOLM BRINNIN

THE PICTURE OF LITTLE T.C.
IN A PROSPECT...

The Picture of Little T.C. in a Prospect...

Who can foretell for what high cause
This darling of the gods was born?
—ANDREW MARVELL

A T Yaddo * one June morning I got up at dawn, worked on a poem until ten, and decided to take a sunbath. Manuscript on clipboard, I climbed a dark stairs to a door that opened to my touch like the lid of a music box. The sounds I heard came from a harplike instrument, affixed to the door's other side, which twanged a limited diapason when struck by little leaden balls hung on loose wires. Stepping out onto a crenellated terrace level with the tops of pine trees, I took off my shirt and was about to remove my pants when another twanging of the lyre told me I'd been followed— by a stranger who stood waiting for the raucous jangle to stop.

"Oh, shut up," he said. "May I join you?"

We introduced ourselves. Spelling out the letters of his last name, C-a-p-o-t-e, he said his first name was Truman. Small as a child, he looked like no other adult male I'd ever seen. His head was big and handsome, and his butterscotch hair was cut in bangs. Willowy and delicate above the waist, he was, below, as strong and chunky as a

---

* A residence, not far from Saratoga Springs, New York, for artists—mainly writers who, upon application supported by prominent figures in their respective fields, may be invited to spend months there without cost. The largest unit of Yaddo is "the mansion"—a vast pile of Victorian brick furnished with the loot of Europe and the Middle East set among tinkling fountains in the glow of stained glass.

Shetland pony. He wore a white T-shirt, khaki shorts too big for him, sandals that fit as neatly as hooves.

He told me he was working on a novel, his first. He now had five chapters and a title. Did I like titles? What would I think of *Other Voices, Other Rooms?* His voice, odd and high, was full of funny resonances that ran a scale of their own: meadowlark trills and, when he laughed or growled, a tugboat basso.

Before I could respond, other questions came fast: Had I read stories of his in *Harper's* and *Mademoiselle?* Had I seen his picture in *Life?* The stories, he told me, were "drawn" from dirt-road Alabama where he'd been "sort of drug up by assorted relatives." Later, he lived with his mother and stepfather in New York City and went to "this private school for kids whose fathers had weekend visiting privileges and girl friends," then Connecticut and "a high school where everyone wore saddle shoes and thought I was a creep."

"College?"

"I never set foot in one," he said. "With an IQ that runs off the chart, why should I?" He began to write "as a mere child," he said, and by the time he was sixteen had "conquered technique." This information made me stare, but I kept a straight face. Would I care to listen to a chapter?

Led into a Gothic chapel-like tower room with tall windows on three sides, I sat on something that looked like a section of a choir stall while he read from yellow foolscap in a steady, barely inflected voice that seemed suddenly to belong to another person. His respect for every one of his own nuances was contagious; I found myself listening with as much care as he took to read. With no preface to cue me in, I grasped only that a character named Joel was being put through a series of small adventures meant to test his courage and sense of reality. The story didn't matter. What did was the quality of a prose that mixed hard observations with extravagant fancy, without ever losing a grip on either. There were too many shimmering "effects" and too much poetic "atmosphere," yet his eye for detail seemed to me as exact as Faulkner's, and much less portentous, or lugubrious. Most, I was struck by his concern for rhythm; when a paragraph got off on the wrong beat, he'd stop and start over. Surprised, I said only that I'd like to hear more of it sometime.

Photo by Lisa Larsen, Graphic House

"How about this afternoon?" he asked. "In your room—about five?"

He came at four, by which time I'd already taken a half-empty fifth of White Horse from the dresser drawer and completed my preparations: an ashtray in the shape of a lily pad, two toothbrush tumblers, Planters peanuts in a saucer kept for paper clips, a copy of Susanne Langer's *Philosophy in a New Key,* and the issue of *The Kenyon Review* with poems of mine in it—just in case conversation would lag.

It didn't. Our fellow inmates supplied more gambits than we needed. "Agnes Smedley—that woman who marched with the Red

The Picture of Little T.C. in a Prospect . . . / 5

Army in China," he asked, "is she a real communist, or only a Chinese one?" Did I know that, only a few weeks ago, Katherine Anne Porter left Yaddo to stay with friends because Carson Mc-Cullers's attentions got "moony and sticky"? That the new secretary in the office—the divorcée with the wolfhound and the Buick convertible—was suspected of being an informer for the FBI? Did I know Newton Arvin?

"Only by reputation."

"You think he's an important critic . . . like Edmund Wilson?"

Yes, I told him (the sound of the dinner gong came echoing upward through the Pre-Raphaelite gloom), he *was* an important critic, "like Edmund Wilson." We started down the grand staircase to the dining room, where Truman made a beeline for the place Arvin had been keeping for him.

Late that evening I was reading Dylan Thomas when a moth with a wingspread of perhaps seven inches lighted on my desk. Astonished, I studied it for a while, calculated its small chance of life in a rude world, and captured it whole between the pages of *The World I Breathe*.

A knock at the door: Truman. Everyone else, he said, was out on the town, or working. What about me? I opened my book and showed him the expired moth.

How did it get in? he asked.

"The same way you did," I told him.

We began to spend hours together every day, avoiding the "moping room" or the music room, where most of Yaddo's social life took place, in favor of sessions in the sun on his terrace or late afternoons in his sacerdotal tower or in the room—so big, bare, and sparsely furnished that it echoed—to which I'd been assigned.

He had not asked questions about Newton Arvin to satisfy an idle curiosity, I soon learned, but to hear how someone like me—more or less in the same academic game—(I taught at Vassar, Arvin at Smith)—regarded him. As these questions continued, I told him that I'd seen Arvin on professional occasions, and sensed that he was both amiable and retiring. But his total bearing, I had to say, so relentlessly caricatured the cloistered scholar as to make him a little forbidding. I had once met the woman from whom he was divorced, and I had read all of his books with profit. He was one of the few readers and rereaders of American literature whose insights were indispensable. None of this made me ready to accept Truman's word that Arvin was also a man of mellow charm and wicked wit who, in a few weeks at Yaddo, had made himself irresistible, particularly to Truman.

Prepared to see Arvin with new eyes, I joined him one morning when, clerkish with gold-rimmed spectacles, he wore a dark suit to breakfast, sat like a furled umbrella, and buttered his toast to the edges. He'd been reading Melville, he said, while he made a game of pretending to himself he never had. "It's the only way," he told me, "otherwise you're apt to see the beard and the whale and the customs house and miss the man."

Amen, I said to myself.

I soon found that Truman, in a crowd or tête-à-tête, could exist on no plane but that of intimacy—a necessity which most people did not at first see as a compulsion but as a gift. Glad myself to accept the gift, I began to understand the compulsion. At ease with him in private, I could not help observing that, in public, merely by entering a room he became a cynosure, a catalyst, the chemist's drop of volatile substance that changed the composition of any gathering from amity to effervescence. While instances of this, occurring daily, began to turn the social life of Yaddo into comedy, the journal I kept that summer records little but glimpses of my encounter with Truman which, I thought, would end when circumstance changed.

At home, in his tower [one journal entry reads], T. hands martinis to his guests—Yaddoites all, except for Mary Lou Aswell, an editor of *Harper's Bazaar* who's come from New York to see him. Then he sits in an ivory-colored bishop's chair holding a photograph of himself—the one taken in the same chair some weeks ago and enlarged to page size in *Life*.

"Look," says someone at the window, "you can see Agnes taking down her washing." To which someone else adds, "She's the only woman I know who can look chic in combat boots—except Dietrich."

T.'s attention is not diverted as he holds up the photograph, in turn, to Mrs. Aswell, to Newton, and to me. "I don't look *that* petulant, do I?"

Since each one of us has already exchanged glances, we make no further comment.

Into Saratoga with T. [reads the next day's entry], and I buy a raincoat. When we go on to the New Worden for a drink, a heavyset man in plaid shorts and a Hawaiian shirt who's seated at the bar swivels around, takes a long look in our direction, and says something we don't hear. Whatever it is, everyone along the bar turns around to look us over.

"Okay, okay," says the bartender, "who's for another? I'm going off duty."

"Forget it," says Truman. "I wasn't more than fifteen years old when I decided to be so obviously who I am and what I am that anyone who so much as asked the question would look like a fool."

He comes to my room late evening and sits on the desk. "When I go home, know what I have to face up to? A back room in a Park Avenue apartment house, a view of a brick wall. If I've got a story to finish, even a letter, I have to clear the coffee table to make typewriter space. My mother's an alcoholic . . . six years now."

"Your father?"

"Joe. He's a Cuban, he may be in Havana on business this minute. They're coming up to see me. You'll understand what I mean."

His eye falls on my leather-bound copy of Milton.

"What's that?" he says. "Looks like a prayer book." He picks it up, opens to a page marked with a red ribbon. "You actually *read* this stuff?"

"Of course. Don't you read Flaubert?"

"That's different, unless you mean you *filch* from it."

When the Capotes—Joe and Nina—came for a visit, I was invited along with Newton to meet them. Frail, dark, and pretty, she seemed tense; he was outgoing, a bit brusque, anxious to please. We sat on the liturgical furniture and made conversation while Truman, edgy as a preppie on Parents' Day, stared from one window, then another.

Early evening, when the others had gone, he and I sat, lights out, to watch the rising of an enormous harvest moon.

"Well," said T., "that's my family—a bewildered woman and a man who doesn't know he's bewildered. You see why I count on friends—anyone. When my father ran off, at least I had these aunts, these marvelous weird sisters. Then, for a long time, no one . . . until a schoolteacher. Miss Catherine R. Wood. She made me feel like an adult, we'd talk like adults, exchange books no one else ever read. She knew who Sigrid Undset was. She wore pearls, little strings of them. She looked like the Duchess of Kent . . . at least, I thought so."

There was a tap on the door. He wiped his eyes.

"Newton," he said.

Unwilling [says my journal for July 13] to sit in the general glaze of inattention that marks any group until Truman joins it, I quit the music room after dinner, but do not escape its pall.

Speculations: Beyond his intention (not beyond his awareness) Truman has engendered in almost everyone here a heightened sense of selfhood and, merely by his presence, charged the most ordinary of occasions with imminence. Spontaneous when others are cautious, he has a child's directness, a child's indifference to propriety, and so gets to the heart of matters with an audacity strangers find outrageous, then delightful. Yet nothing he says or does accounts for the magnet somewhere in his makeup that exerts itself like a force beyond logic; he's responsible for turning the summer into a dance of bees. His slightest movements throughout the mansion, about the grounds, or on the side streets of Saratoga are charted and signaled by sentries visible only to one another. Schemes to share his table at dinner are laid at breakfast, sometimes by single plotters, sometimes by teams united in shamelessness. There's always laughter at his table, echoing across the moat of silence in which the tables around it are sunk.

When I point this out, he sighs, says it's all too much, and makes his own schemes for privacy and avenues of escape. But his door remains wide open, and when he takes flight into Saratoga and some new hideaway, a party of familiar faces is there to welcome him.

His secret: More hungry for attention than anyone else, he's learned to bestow what he craves. For recipients, enchantment; for himself, a deeper longing, a bigger audience.

Talk at the dinner table I joined next evening was polemical. Ardents all, we ignored the freshets of hilarity that came from Truman and his companions across the room and pursued the question of whether the existentialism of Camus and Sartre was, from a Marxist point of view, a copout, a new *trahison des clercs,* or an unexpected shot in the arm for wavering political faith. Absorbed in the argument, I felt a hand on my shoulder. "Meet you at the back door," said Truman. "We're going to the flicks—Ida Lupino. My treat, I got my check from Random House."

His treat included a stinger at the Grand Union afterward.

"Do you like Newton—*personally?*" he asked.

"Very much," I told him. "Why wouldn't I?"

"Did you know that he's one of Carson's dearest friends?" he said. "Did you know that your pal Maya Deren was a student of his? He says she talked too much. She had another name then, a Jewish name. She was supposed to be passionate about French poetry, she had all these abstract ideas—communication and the artist, crap like that. I don't think Newton understands her sort of woman."

"What sort is that?"

"Women who preach ideas, especially about art. He's more comfortable with the sickies, the ones who've lost their fathers, or ditched them . . . who make *him* their father because he's smart and old and doesn't compete."

"They sound a bit like you."

"My dear Malcolm," he said, "I *don't* think Newton's interest in Miss Carson McCullers is anything at all like his interest in me. Do I have to tell you *why?*"

> The scent of pine grows heavier [I wrote in my journal], shadows on the lawn longer. When the one phone in the mansion rings, it rings for Truman. Today his pigeonhole at the mail desk is stuffed with business envelopes. Something's in the air, something I don't ask about.

That afternoon he told me. "One more day, I'll be sprung," he said. "I've just had a phone call . . . I'm going to New Orleans."

"Why New Orleans?"

"Cartier-Bresson. He's this photographer Mrs. Snow's imported from France. Very eminent. She wants me to do an article—impressions—to go with the pictures he's supposed to take. I used to live there, I was *born* there. Ten days, all expenses paid."

Suddenly the tower room was empty, the cabals of the breakfast table dispersed. Adrift, those of us left at Yaddo began to look for partners at Ping-Pong, Chinese checkers, croquet. Relieved of the nightly jostle for position, old friends met in an atmosphere of affectionate contempt. Truman was everywhere. To speak of him would have certified his absence. No one did.

In the course of talks in which we had mutually explored backgrounds and described friends, I had spoken to Truman of Ankey Larrabee. It was she who provided the next link in an association I had assumed was at an end when Truman took flight. "I'm back," he wrote from New York, "with, let me tell you, swollen ankles and fallen arches. But my article is finished." He went on to say that, at dinner with his friend Marguerite Young the night before, he had accepted an impromptu invitation to a party across the hall, where the first person he met was "your amazing Ankey." She was particularly sweet to him, he reported, adding that he did not find her the

The Picture of Little T.C. in a Prospect . . . / 11

Gorgon I and others had somehow led him to expect. Instead, he thought her hilariously amusing, slightly wacky, "an endearingly warm girl" who, to her credit he thought, did not begin to understand that she possessed the voice of an angel and, in spite of the Egyptian deity tattooed on her wrist, the presence of a duchess.

"Did they give you my holy room after I'd gone?" he wanted to know. "Have you muffled that goofy harp? I miss you, so write me, please, and please, let us meet soon."

The next mail brought a letter from Ankey. "What do you know?" she wrote. "A Friday night séance on Greenwich Avenue and there was Truman C. I had heard several heinous things about him from the Harvard-Algonquin set, but after I had meandered through a ten-minute monologue, I came to the conclusion that no one could listen in just that way and still have the initiative to *do*. He is so *small*, though. I had a feeling he might drift helplessly away at any moment, with a stricken look backward, before oblivion quite swallowed him up. These comments, I'm afraid, are inadequate: I really thought him vastly intriguing, thoroughly simpatico, and cuddly as a Pekingese. The fact that he whispers too much, and has no sense of humor (he was horrified when I said I'd heard you'd been expelled from Yaddo for wearing a bishop's cope to dinner) adds to his pastel charm. I'll bet you ten to one he doesn't live to reach his majority. Would iron pills help?"

Truman in a state of depression was something I had not conceived of when, for the first time, I visited him at home—an apartment on upper Park Avenue so scrupulously furnished without style, reference to period, or overtures to taste, good or bad, as to define a genre. After he handed me a drink, he produced a "surprise package"—a folio of photographs, including one by Cartier-Bresson, taken in the Vieux Carré: T., in a T-shirt, seated on a wrought-iron bench under big jungle-shiny leaves, looking winsome in a slightly evil way, or slightly evil in a winsome.

"Cheer me up," he said. "I'm losing the thread."

"Of what?"

"Book, life. . . . New Orleans started me thinking of things, mysterious, yet all perfectly visible. I can't get them out of my head.

I sit in this apartment. *You* see it. That lamp . . . my mother. I watch her. I wonder if she remembers what *I* do, the days she'd leave me by myself in a locked room. All the time I'm hearing the heartsick river boats you can see over the levee from Jackson Square. I'm boxed up, paralyzed. Do you think maybe there's something wrong with me that isn't just psychological?"

Even as his hands shook and his pallor made me wonder, I told him he looked all right, and tried without success to have him talk about his work with Cartier-Bresson. "How can I get in touch with Ankey Larrabee?" he asked—a question I could not answer until, a few days later, a letter from Ankey reported her new address. "I am still in poor condition from my rigadoon of a housewarming," she wrote. "Some individual (one of K.'s men, I fear) beat my head against a wall. Obviously a stranger to the group. I find, however, that concussion doesn't really keep one from the 'important' things. Yesterday I attended a garden party drinking fest at E.'s, where a lady photographer posed the company for some fly-by-night fashion

The Picture of Little T.C. in a Prospect . . . / 13

magazine. Since her pictures were meant to illustrate a story proving that ordinary people now live in the Village, I was promptly trussed upon arrival, and shoved into an old cactus pot.

"There's a rumor going around the San Remo and some uptown *boîtes* that Truman C. is sick—bad sick. It sounds like leukemia. For some reason, he's not in the hospital but at home. One of these days I'm going to take him the new issue of *Screen Romances* and Cocteau's treatise on opium—illustrated—just to see if he's capable of normal responses."

Truman's subsequent letter was not reassuring. "I woke up the other day with a left foot that had the shape of a balloon," he wrote. "Infected, deeply, and for reasons that baffle both me and my doctor. I have to stay in bed, but already that has compensations: Ankey came all the way uptown to see me yesterday and we had the whole afternoon together—I propped like a pasha on my bed, she at the foot of it leaning against a blue water-silk pillow, drinking rather a lot of bourbon and eating fried chicken. A wonderful girl, Ankey, and I love her; in fact, I can't remember when I have felt so charmed and exhilarated by anyone."

A writer who had not published a book, Truman was nevertheless an "item" in the purview of New York gossip columnists and his name had a way of turning up in circles he had never entered. Some particularly sober citizens I knew—unaware that I was acquainted with him—echoed rumor and swore it was fact. Between acts the other night, he'd been seen wearing an emerald on his forehead as he chatted with his escort, Lucius Beebe. He was, as "everybody" knew, the illegitimate son of the former Chicago bus driver now known as Spencer Tracy. His family, impoverished but proud, had legally disinherited him for selling one of Robert E. Lee's dress swords to the Smithsonian. "That sore foot's a red herring," a Madison Avenue editor told me, "the kid's on his way out."

"If you're really ill," I wrote to Truman, "I ought to know about it, and from you—if only as an office of affection."

"Office of affection—balls," he wrote back. "But thank you for your sweet letter of concern. Inasmuch as I am about to enter the death house, I could not have hoped for a prettier farewell. The reason for this journey into the shadows is as follows: My red corpuscles are destroying my white ones in a process that looks like leukemia but is not, I can assure you, nearly so dangerous or as fatal. One of the sources of this ailment is, of all things, my tonsils, and they'll be zipped out. It should all be over soon. And a happier lad I'll be, for I have had to give up even the pretense of working (something which *really* makes me ill), and medical shenanigans do tend to limit one's scope.

"Speaking of fevers (which you weren't) mine's a lulu: 102 and more for two whole *weeks*. Little T.—who, bet your boots, wastes not, wants not—has of course made copious notations on the marvelous distortions of things."

He was out of the hospital within the week, and into another phase of the recurrent depression that dogged him like a nagging cold. "You are wise, dear Malcolm," he wrote, "to stay out of this city. It is no place for you, and it is unquestionably no place for me; I just can't assume the sneering facade that might help me to survive this huge snake pit; everything you say here is instantly repeated; I mean, everything you haven't said. Who are my friends and who aren't? Nothing is ever nothing; something is never something. Everything comes out quite differently from what it so innocently *is*. Kafka said it all. He would have loved New York.

"Write to me—and for the particular day of September 30, send me a greeting with forget-me-nots—or, *should* you be passing that showroom on Seventh Avenue—a little Duesenberg runabout, preferably with white-walled tires, for my birthday, that is. I'll be twenty-two."

He'd been that age for five days when, to signal his "resurrection," I agreed to meet him at a midtown bar called Tony's Trouville. The only person there, he sat with his back against a striped wall, legs dangling, for all the world like a child dressed up who'd been told to be good and sit still.

"I tried to reach you, to call it off," he said. "I'm in the dumps."

"What's wrong?"

"The old story. I can't live where I live, can't be where I want to be. Other people go home. I have to wait for an engraved invitation from Northampton."

The Picture of Little T.C. in a Prospect . . . / 15

" 'Fish got to swim, birds got to fly,' you mean? 'Can't help . . .' "

"Okay," he said, "be smart . . . but that's how I am."

Mary Lou Aswell gave us dinner that night and we went on to visit Ankey on Patchin Place and finally dropped in on a party at Maya Deren's on Morton Street. Nobody could change his mood or break his sullen silence. Since I was flying to Boston from La Guardia, we shared a taxi that dropped him off at his apartment.

"Don't give up on me," he said as the doorman stood by. "I mean, don't give me up."

"Why do you think I might?"

"It's what I always think," he said. "And I've always been right."

"I'm moving to Brooklyn," he said on the phone a week later, "two rooms in a brownstone. This may be good-bye forever."

Back in New York, I was having lunch with Ankey one day when she said: "Let's cross the river and track Truman down. I have this compulsion to make sure he's for real."

The late afternoon in Brooklyn was dark. Strangers helped us find the address in a neighborhood undisturbed since the nineteenth century. Stopping at a house much like every other, we went up a musty staircase and found Truman in a room overwhelmed by wallpaper. He gave us ferocious hugs, sat us down to bourbon and Ritz crackers out of the box.

It was the first time I'd seen him and Ankey alone. Same height, they had the same flamingo-and-ivory complexion, the same butterscotch hair cut in bangs, equally dwarflike proportions and doll-like heads. The tennis shoes they wore were each gone in the left toe.

At once they entered into a cabal of their own. "When I was *your* age," said Ankey, whose age was exactly his, "I could recite all of the bridge by heart. That's a riddle."

"*His* Brooklyn wasn't this . . . his was Brooklyn Heights," Truman told her. "How do you keep the moons in your cuticles so white and clear?"

Left out, I cased his digs: a sepia print of the Colosseum above a disemboweled Singer; an antimacassar on a Morris chair; Andalusian draperies with tassels; ghostly cabbage roses on a threadbare carpet.

The only things in sight conceivably his were a record player, a black-and-gold ashtray from the Rainbow Room, books (among them Newton Arvin's *Whitman*), a portable Olivetti in its case, a photograph of himself, and the Webster's Unabridged against which it was propped.

"Don't you get to feeling sort of buried over here, Truman?" I asked.

"Of course," he said, "that's why I'm here. No-man's-land. Ask a cabdriver to take you somewhere, he has to look at a map. It's not just Brooklyn they're lost in, they're lost in 1946. This cruddy hotel where I get dinner . . . for the people who live there, everything turns on what radio program, how many scoops of ice cream, who had a maid and maybe a Persian-lamb coat with mink cuffs in 1922. My landlady thinks the Jews are poisoning the water system. Her brother still writes to Father Coughlin. The subway's literally abysmal, but it's like crossing the border and you can make the trip both ways any day in the week."

"I went to Staten Island once," said Ankey. "It was like Australia."

Brooklyn had provided Truman with a place to work, and with problems unforeseen. Less than two months into his self-imposed exile, loneliness and a recognition of how "the ordinary demands of daily living can devour a person body and soul" had brought him to despair. "How can I ever clear away these mountains of obstructions," he wrote, "and get on with what I have to do? Histrionic as it must sound, I wonder whether I shall indeed survive the winter; everything I do turns against me. It is simply harrowing now for me to be alone; there is so little I can do for myself. And there is no one to turn to, really no one. All of my friends are of course wonderful and, I know, would do most anything asked of them. Unfortunately, this does not bring relief or alter the circumstance."

With the relief of weekends in Northampton and frequent return visits to his parents' roof, he did indeed survive the winter. But one problem that had at first seemed an annoyance had developed into a persistent worry: How was he going to join his professional life with his emotional life? What *modus vivendi* was possible for the gregarious young artist and the cloistered scholar? As much a bird out of habitat in Northampton as Newton Arvin was in Manhattan, Truman was nevertheless the one more free to come and go, and so he did. But from what I detected in phone talks with him, his campus visits were always briefer than he wished, and Newton's sojourns in New York had a way of being cut short by real, or convenient, demands for his early return to academe.

I'd not seen Truman for months when, one evening early in February, I saw Arvin. The point of this occasion was Newton's contribution to an article on the nature of the postwar college generation that I'd been commissioned to do, but the substance of the interview was, inevitably, Truman.

At the depot, as my train from Boston pulled in, Newton was wearing neat ankle-high boots, a close-fitting gray overcoat, a felt hat protected by a plastic covering. Through high-piled banks of snow we walked up the hill to Harar's for a quick dinner and then went on to his place, an attic apartment in a big frame house. Spare, tidy, and anonymous, it had the uninhabited and slightly forlorn air of a furniture show-window at night.

"Truman's found a solution," he said as he placed his boots outside the entrance, "perhaps a necessary one. . . . Those rooms in Brooklyn. *He* thinks he's escaping confinement. *I* think he's gone back to Alabama and his tree house. You've seen the place, you gather my meaning . . . back to all the shabby little icons of gentility he pretends to despise, to the kind of people he used to know . . . lives obsessed by trivia and simplified by bigotry."

Bringing me ice cubes in a glass, he handed me a pint bottle of Scotch. "But there's a difference, of course," he continued. "That big world he used to sight through the branches is no longer a dream. For the price of a subway fare he can enter it and leave it. He needs both, I suppose—Turgenev and Flaubert to intrigue the artist part of his nature on Thursday night, El Morocco and café society to let him play the boulevardier on Saturday. An odd balance, you might say. But as long as he lives, I think he'll try to maintain it."

Over his shoulder, matted and framed, Cartier-Bresson's photograph of Truman in New Orleans made its ambiguous invitation.

"You know that he's been up here with me several times." He

motioned toward a window where a streetlamp shone through high branches outlined with snow. "Who knows? Perhaps this is still another tree house. I can't tell whether he's happy here or not. But he comes back . . . he comes back."

In New York to keep a dinner date with Truman a week later, I spent the afternoon at the Museum of Modern Art's double show: Henry Moore and Cartier-Bresson. Looking first at the sculptures, I found myself unexpectedly moved by the way in which Moore, indulging himself in the grotesque, invoked the serene. The photographs, by contrast, seemed to me seductive and larcenous, shaming the eyes they attracted. Both exhilarated and disturbed by the experience, I went uptown to Truman's and found him alone, listening to a murky recording of early jazz.

"What," he asked, "is a Hartford Wit?"

"You doing a crossword puzzle?"

"I just want to *know*," he said.

I told him.

"Well," he said, "at least that makes a little sense. These young men keep turning up at Newton's with dissertations—is that what I mean, dissertations?—in the glove compartments of their Volkswagens. One of them came up from Yale with this five-hundred-page manuscript on the Hartford Wits. Just the idea baffles me. I think about him. You and I are having dinner at Schrafft's."

"Why Schrafft's?"

"Because," he said with a sort of emphatic demureness, "I have reason to remain incognito."

My task, when I'd said good-bye to Truman that evening, was to pick up a painting given to me by Theodoros Stamos as a reward for having supplied titles for the works in his recent show. When I got to his studio, Stamos was wrapping it, a process that took so long that, when I'd lugged the painting to Grand Central, I found I'd missed my last train. When the painting wouldn't fit into any of the twenty-five-cent lockers, I took it back to Truman's for the night.

Asleep in his guest bed, I was soon awake.

"Malcolm," Truman was saying, "what exactly do academic people mean by a sense of evil? Newton says Hawthorne had it and Melville had it, and he thinks I do. Does it mean believing, really believing, in something like the devil? Or does it just mean that you can see that there's something terribly wrong with God and the universe and say so? Do *you* think I have a sense of evil?"

"Djuna Barnes speaks of 'the mad strip of the inappropriate that runs through creation.' "

"That," he said, "I can understand."

In the course of his collaboration with Henri Cartier-Bresson on the New Orleans story, Truman had spoken of me to the eminent photographer and had later arranged for us to meet. In the seven months since that event, Cartier-Bresson and I had become friends and were about to become working partners on a transcontinental trip for which we had obtained a publisher's commission. Happy to tell Truman about this development, I found him as, just back from another visit to Northampton, he waited for me at the Algonquin.

"The happiest weekend ever," he said, and took from his wallet a snapshot of Newton: a smiling middle-aged man whose gold rims now seemed to glint with a touch of the roué.

"I think I'm developing a little taste for the life you academics lead," said Truman. "We went to dinner with the president of the college and some of the faculty one evening—a completely civilized occasion, I thought, and we had lunches with some types—*you* know, pipes that won't stay lit, ribbon ties, suede patches on J. Press elbows? One of them was working on Bronson Alcott, another on someone called Joaquin Miller. They must have wondered what *this* one was doing there. But they were absolutely sweet to me. Newton wants to ask you something. You'll say I put him up to it, but I didn't."

"What does he want to ask?"

"It's this: We're thinking of Nantucket for the summer, but Newton has this conviction that I'd be overwhelming to live with. Even when I'm being a perfect mouse, reading in a corner of the room somewhere, he says I'm overwhelming. He'll be on his Melville, with luck I'll write *finis* to 'Voices.' Would you consider sharing a house with us there?"

"To save Newton Arvin from being swamped by the likes of you?"

He sat back and gave me a scrutinizing, possibly angry, look. "We're trying," he said, "to be realistic."

On the road with Cartier-Bresson, I would not see Truman again for nearly five months, months during which his life and letters, I was not a little surprised to hear, had come into harmony. "I am as happy as I ever thought I could be," he wrote from Nantucket in late July. "This comes from a desk at which I can hear, if not see, the arriving surf (how's that for taming an intransitive verb?) and when you are reading this I'll have crossed the last 't' of my book—which I'm anxious for you to read *in toto*. O, dear, what a long slow struggle. But it's done—and so am I, to a turn, I mean—ever so golden, and all over, too; for there are heavenly stretches of sand here where one can go trunkless.

"Speaking of things to see, have you turned your John the Baptist gaze on my unutterably awful photo in the recent *Vogue?* Never again, I swear. What a travesty!

"Boston: Newton took me there last week, my first visit ever, and I loved it—for such diverse experiences as dinner with F. O. Matthiessen and a marvelously tacky show at the Old Howard (I'm an old burleycue buff, you'll remember). Matthiessen I did not especially take to; only someone like Proust could tell me why—so I will have to wait until someone like that comes along. Harry Levin I *did* like— even though I felt I must be the sort of person who tunes him tight as a drum.

"Now that I'm really, *really* writing *finis* to my book, I'm not so much relieved, as you might think, as angry. The strain to finish it in time for what the publishers consider D day has been intolerable and I'm convinced in my heart that it is a failure. Jesus. It strikes me (but what does it matter now?) that I've been forced into a sort of competition with myself and that's not fair. O dear, so *what*."

With doubts he had kept to himself, Truman had promoted my acquaintance with Cartier-Bresson and encouraged my collaboration with him. When the collaboration and the relationship came into trouble, it was Truman who, by accident, confirmed the deceit that undermined and ended both. This was not the first instance in which

Truman's analytical clarity about the way people operated had impressed me. But it was the one in which, for the first time, I felt that my vaguely avuncular role in his life had undergone a change amounting almost to a reversal. The idea that Truman might come to be my Dutch uncle was outrageous. Yet, for many years to come, this would be increasingly the case.

Meanwhile, I tried to maintain, if no longer to protect, the aura of éminence grise with which he had endowed me and to pretend to a degree of wisdom I could not in my heart claim. My journal entries at this time tell me only that I frequently saw Truman, or talked with him by phone. Most of these are bare notations stating when and where, but some of them—like the evening we spent with my old friend Bowden Broadwater and his bride, Mary McCarthy—are attempts to capture an occasion in some detail:

10.6.47 New York. Dinner with T. Afterward, dawdling along Fifty-seventh Street, we are about to pass the Broadwaters' entryway when I suggest we pay a call.

"Would Mary McCarthy like me?" he says. "She frightens me."

"She's not as scary as people make out," I tell him, "of course she'll like you."

"I have the impression she hates everybody."

"She hates Stalinists and bad style. You don't fit."

I locate the nameplate and bell button, lift my index finger. "Well?"

"Oh—why not," he says. "She can't *eat* me."

Our timing is bad. Mary is clearing plates of artichoke debris to make room for the steak, sizzling on a grill, which she is about to serve to their guests—Delmore Schwartz and Wayne Andrews. I apologize, suggest we find another occasion. Mary insists we stay.

Supplied with Scotch and soda, T. and I sit on the edge of the meal and remain for the evening. In the course of it, Delmore, who knows I've spent the late summer at Yaddo, backs me into a corner.

"Caligula Lowell still wandering the woods buck naked," he says, "passing out over Vergil and Kentucky bourbon?"

"Not with Roethke around," I tell him. "They keep close tabs on one another."

"I got the picture from Isaac Rosenfeld," he says. "Which one of them's headed for the funny farm first?"

"Come off it, they're as sane as you are."

"Poor guys," says Delmore.

Truman is seated between Mary and Bowden and, I expect, caught in the sort of Nick and Nora crossfire they tend to indulge in when they have an audience, perhaps even when they don't. I keep an eye out for a sign from him that we should be moving on.

Delmore comes back at me: "I hear you've been seeing a lot of my ex-wife."

Not lately, I tell him, adding that I was about to ask him where she is.

"Simple," he says, "find out where Lowell is."

"I *know* where Lowell is."

The look he gives me is flat-eyed. "Haven't I told you what you want to know?"

There's a chime of laughter from across the room. Truman, accepting another drink, wriggles back into his chair. The lamb has lain down with the lioness. We stay on. . . .

But not, as I learned a few days later, in the midst of that peaceable kingdom I had supposed.

"It's funny about McCarthy and Bowden," wrote Truman, "but I keep thinking about that evening. They are obviously people you like, but are you oblivious to the fact that they have no more in common with you than cats with a canary? They stand for all of the things in this world I most dislike. If only they'd cut the comedy and allow themselves a modicum of honesty. How can such brainy individuals continue to be so self-deceived, so eager to ride herd on everyone who's dared to do anything that doesn't meet with their

The Picture of Little T.C. in a Prospect . . . / 23

exquisite approval? I am afraid they are members of that ever-increasing tribe—the cold-hearted ones. Exclude feelings and emotions as they do and you just have to die a little inside yourself, every day. Mary, of course, has certain demonstrated talents, unhealthy though they may be. . . ."

We met next at his place in New York. "Brooklyn," he said, "I'm through with it . . . a little episode that became a bad joke. I've spent all day recovering."

"From what?—moving?"

"Nothing *quite* so plebeian. A hangover, torn ligaments. I was out until three A.M. with Mister John Gielgud. He taught me how to do the rumba," he said, and handed me a bundle of page proofs. "Read them as if you'd never heard of me. Then cross your heart, hope to die, and say what you think."

Other Voices, Other Rooms, I discovered, was a dream I could interpret. Everything Truman had told me was there—in translation, in disguise, yet unmistakably. Not expecting so strict a roman à clef, I could guess identities, reconstruct metaphors, match motive and clue as though the novel were a detective story the outcome of which I already knew.

When I took the proofs back to him one night, I found only his parents. "Truman's out to a show," said his father, "come on in, glad to see you." Accepting the proofs, he put them aside, leaving me uneasily aware that I'd never before been in his parents' company when Truman wasn't present.

"You know that friend of Truman's," asked his father, "the professor?"

"Newton Arvin."

"Fine man," he said, "like you, good for the boy. His mother here thinks the same way, she knows what I mean."

He turned to his wife. "Right, Nina?"

Smiling privately, she seemed to be on the edge of sleep.

"You come, glad to see you," he said. "Come any time, glad to see you. We get some funny customers, I tell you. Know what I mean?"

Not quite sure that I did, I said, "I do."

"This book he's been carrying around for how many years now. Suppose it don't add up? How's he going to pay the rent, feed the kitty?"

The book, I told him, would "add up," that there was no cause for worry.

"You think *so?* Nina, you hear?"

But he spoke only to a door still swinging from his wife's passage as, empty glass in hand, she returned to the kitchen.

"I got that problem, too," he said. "How about a cigar?"

On the first of December, Truman on the phone. "Three guesses," he said. "I've got an invitation, an assignment. It involves travel."

"Atlantic City? Niagara Falls? Two weeks at Mammoth Cave, all expenses paid?"

"Very funny," he said, "you could be a comedian. But you're right about one thing—carte blanche. I'm off to Hollywood, to do a story any way I want. I may not come back."

I spent the Christmas holidays in Bermuda and, my journal tells me, extended my stay until "1.9.48."

The flying boat (you sit face to face in a compartment, as on a European train) splashes down in Baltimore. I take the first train north and phone Truman when I get to Penn Station.

"Where've you been?" he says. "Why weren't you here to welcome me back? Can you come over . . . this minute?"

I find him in a haze of cigarette smoke, a litter of butts, newspapers, cups dark with coffee dregs. In black pants, nubbly sweater, Capezios, he's pallid and thin.

"The place probably looks like some kind of hideout," he says.

"What's the matter?"

"I don't know." He wipes his right eye with the palm of his hand. "Everything."

"What's everything?"

"I can't sleep. One endless hangover, days, weeks."

The Picture of Little T.C. in a Prospect . . . / 25

"Since you got back?"

"Before . . . even in Hollywood. I've been living on cereal and instant coffee."

"Joe and Nina?"

"They're in Cuba." He reaches down and from the side of the couch produces a fifth of Old Grand-dad. "You like some of this?"

"Not now."

"Do you realize that my book's coming out in ten days?" he says. "From what I've been told, the reviews are going to turn my stomach."

He pours a drink into a cup. His hand, dark with nicotine, is trembling.

"Know something, Truman? You're coming home with me."

"Don't be silly. I can't even make my way to Lexington Avenue." He sips his drink, stares at the floor.

"How far *is* Weston?" he says.

I pack a bag I find in a bedroom closet, bundle him into an overcoat. Out on the sidewalk, he stands shivering like a puppy in a blanket. The doorman's whistle brings a cab.

My car's where I left it, in a lot near the Westport railroad station, banked with snow. Truman helps me scrape the windshield and rear window. Into Westport like a float in an ice carnival, we stop for a blue-plate special at the greasy spoon on main street. Leaving him there over coffee, I make a quick trip to a grocery store.

The road out of town is a frosty tunnel. My uphill driveway has been obliterated by drifts and smoothed over. We abandon the car and drag luggage and paper bags as we stump, knee-deep, up to the house. There we have to dig with our hands to make a space big enough for the storm door to swing open. Stamping ourselves dry, we begin to thaw out in the warmth of a log fire, Courvoisier, Bessie Smith on the turntable. On a couch by the fireplace, Truman lies flat as a mummy and is soon asleep. I put a blanket over him and leave him there.

1.10.48   New-fallen snow on snow. We're more snow-bound than ever. Truman, glazed, sits on a kitchen stool watching me squeeze orange juice and fry eggs.

To get him out of Hollywood, I start him talking about it—a ploy that works. By noon, when the mutters and rumblings of the furnace have punctuated a reel of reminiscence in which Charlie and Oona, Kate and Bette and Joan have all come in for close-ups and fade-outs, he seems almost himself again.

Outside, a hushed grayness, another heavy sky waiting to spill. We open cartons and cans, stare from the windows, speak when we feel like speaking.

"What if everyone hates the book?" he says. "Those thugs that wait for people like me—that pack of wolves around the *Partisan*. What if they decide to gang up? What defense do you have against reviews anyway?"

Poets, I remind him, are lucky even to *get* reviewed.

"But," he says, "what if someone sets out to demolish you? I have it on impeccable authority there's one review so vicious the editors have refused to print it."

"Who told you that?"

"A kind friend, ho ho. But I believe him."

We play gin rummy; feed carrots to a pony that turns up at the back door; take turns reading S. J. Perelman aloud; listen to Wanda Landowska; make a salmon soufflé. The radio says snow is general over southern New England; small craft warnings are up from Eastport to Block Island.

1.11.48   A car with chains makes it halfway up the drive: Barney C. with eggs and the Sunday papers. No reviews of *Other Voices,* but big splashy full-page advertisements: This Is Truman Capote in huge type under a photograph of T. reclining in his waistcoat. Sloe-eyed, looking out from beneath his baby bangs with a sort of insouciant challenge, he has one hand prettily "disposed," as in some plaster piece of kitsch sculpture. I tear out the page, thumbtack it to the edge of the mantel.

The Picture of Little T.C. in a Prospect . . . / 27

"Why did you do that?" he asks.

"I want to think, speculate—on what I'd be apt to say if I'd never laid eyes on you."

He stares. I stare.

"Well?"

"I don't know. Do you *want* to look like the last pressed flower in *The Yellow Book?*"

"What's that?" he says.

1.12.48   The glittering crust surrounding the house looks solid but isn't. On our way to the car, I sink to my knees, Truman to his waist, and his suitcase tumbles open. At the foot of the hill, he stops to look back. "Good-bye, little house," he calls into the stillness, "don't forget me, little house."

By the time we've dug the car out, the sun is high. We drive through snowshine and long blue shadows to the depot. Waiting for his train to pull out, I spot him framed in a frosty window and lift my hand. He makes fish mouths through the pane, saying something that makes him smile.

Back at the house, I park in the road, reach the door by stepping in the tracks we've just made. The fire has gone out. The page torn from the *Herald-Tribune* hangs from the mantelpiece.

"Precisely what I predicted," he said on the phone next day. "The knives are flashing."

"What knives?"

"The *Times,* Sunday after next. They're going to slice me paper thin."

"What about the *Trib?*"

"A rave. But what good is that? Who reads the *Herald-Tribune* anymore?"

"*Time?*"

"I hear it's snotty."

"Well, at least it's coverage. . . ."

"*Coverage!* I've had more of that than the Virgin Mary."

Coverage, indeed. Two weeks later, when I got to Missouri to begin a term as poet-in-residence at Stephens College, an item in the *St. Louis Post-Dispatch* suggested that news of Truman's debut had matched that of the President's decline:

To the Editors,
   Your newspaper seems to be full of two things these days—Truman Capote and Truman kaput.

                                        Art Reiss, Leesburg, Mo.

Truman went to Haiti while I was in Missouri, but not before we'd made plans for dinner when we'd both be back in New York at the end of February. On the appointed date, thunderstorms over Ohio forced my plane to make an emergency landing in Dayton and it was well after nine when, hurrying into the lobby of the Algonquin, I found him autographing a copy of his book for a tall young man wearing a Wallace for President button.
   "How's the Bible Belt?" he said.
   "How was Haiti?" I asked as we were shown to the table he'd reserved.
   "Almost died," he said. "Some kind of jungle fever so baffling it scared the doctors. And I don't mean the witch doctors. I couldn't tell if the drums and chants I heard were up in the hills somewhere or in my head. I'd ask the nurses but they'd never say because they never understood what I was talking about. Then I convinced myself they weren't nurses at all, simply some quiet girls who'd been told to stay with me until I'd closed my eyes for the last time. Then I gave up and went into these long jags of weeping. . . .
   "Wolcott Gibbs," he said, as he waved a hand across the room. "I got to know him when I was a sort of glorified office boy at *The New Yorker*. Used to be a sourpuss . . . now it turns out he's crazy about my book. Look, would you drop me off on your way? I have an appointment—on Gramercy Park. . . .
   "As I was saying, I learned something—all those tears and sobs weren't just for me. I mean, I think I understood for the first time in

my life that I wasn't nearly as interested in saving my *skin* as in saving what I *know,* stories I've got to tell. The thought that I'd never have the chance to tell them was worse than the idea of death itself. Oh . . . maybe everyone has stories to tell. What I mean is, I have something to say that hasn't been said, simply because no one else knows what I know in the *way* I know it."

A waiter, conspicuously hovering, reminded us that it was after midnight.

"Would you believe me if I told you I'd had a letter from Ernest Hemingway?"

"Why shouldn't I?"

"Because it's not the kind of letter you'd think."

"Well, what kind is it?"

"A denunciation, a diatribe, out of the blue. I can't figure out if he was plastered at the time or if he'd momentarily gone off his head, can't understand why he wrote it at all."

"What's his point?"

"If there *is* a point, it's a warning to keep off his turf. Cuckoo as that sounds, it's the only explanation. A lot of people are put off by the publicity the book's been getting, but at least they know there's a *book.* Hemingway goes straight for *me.*"

"You sure it's not a hoax?"

"From Finca Vigia, San Francisco de Paula? Who else would go to the trouble?"

The waiter put down our check. "My treat," said Truman, "I'd pay a lot more to a psychiatrist."

I retrieved my suitcase and we got into a cab.

"Who," I asked, "is on Gramercy Park?"

"A new friend."

"?"

"You'd call him John, everyone else calls him Julie. He's here on location, making a picture. It sounds god-awful: *Skipper Next to God.*"

"Are you talking about John Garfield?"

"I'm as surprised as you are," he said. "After all, he's still Mister Tough Guy to most of the American population."

Our taxi pulled up before a tall house.

"I've got keys," said Truman. "God knows how long I'll have to wait. But at least there's a good record collection."

Our next meeting was coincidental. Invited by our mutual friend the editor Leo Lerman to one of his Sunday night "at homes," I entered a room where five hundred people, or perhaps no more than a hundred, obscured the walls, the furniture, the wine supply, and one another. Shuffling into the multitude, I was stopped by a shout: "Malcolm!"

The crowd I'd joined parted before me like the Red Sea, to make a passageway across the length of the room. At the end of it stood a figure in velvet pants, dancing pumps, a turtleneck sweater over which, on a chain of silver, dangled a medallion as big as a saucer: Truman. Sprinting toward me, he gave me an ascending series of hugs of such vigor I felt as though I were being climbed.

"Like my outfit?" he said. "Julie was supposed to be here."

Flustered and off-base, I edged toward the wine table and was interrupted by Aline Bernstein, tugging at my sleeve. In her other hand she held a glass of something that looked like Scotch.

"Where did you get that?" I asked.

One finger at her lips, she said, "Come."

We inched into a bedroom. Fishing in the pocket of a coat on one of the beds, she produced a pint bottle of Haig & Haig.

"Doctor's orders," she said. "I'm on a diet—steak and this. Find a cup and help yourself."

A large-boned man with snowy hair poked his head in.

"Carlo!" said Aline, and gave him a kiss. "You two know each other?"

"You're the man who wrote 'Little Elegy for Gertrude Stein,'" said Carl Van Vechten as we shook hands. "I'm the man who scissored it out of *Harper's* and sent it to Alice Toklas."

"I'd wondered," I told him. "In her letter about it she said only that she had it from a friend, someone she didn't name."

"I must say you got a warm greeting from Truman," he said. His grin contained a hint of benediction. "So you're the famous professor from Smith?"

The Picture of Little T.C. in a Prospect . . . / 31

"John's at Vassar," said Aline. "We ride the local to Poughkeepsie together."

"Excuse *me,*" said Van Vechten.

Between planes at La Guardia a month later, I phoned Truman at his apartment.

"I'm alone," he said, "could you stay over for a night?"

Canceling my plane, I found him in his working clothes: corduroys, white shirt, an open vest; and he was wearing horn-rimmed glasses.

"Why the specs?"

"I like to play with them," he said. "The awful truth is I need them. Sit down, I'll tell you some sad stories. A martini?"

"You know any certified paranoids?" he called from the kitchen.

"One certified," I called back, "half a dozen who haven't achieved clinical status."

Handing me a glass, he said, "I'm beginning to feel funny about a lot of things and I'm not sure of the symptoms."

"Be philosophical, like Delmore Schwartz. 'Just because I'm paranoid,' he says, 'doesn't mean everyone isn't against me.' "

"Be serious," said Truman. "I have to get out of this city, permanently. I used to be sure of a few things. Now I'm not. Why these personal attacks? I don't just mean Hemingway, I mean all these dealers in innuendo, as if I were spreading germs. Why don't they look at my *book,* say what they think about that . . . instead of digging their claws into me?"

"You're being naïve," I told him. "Haven't you encouraged that kind of reaction, even asked for it?"

"How have I asked for it?"

"That jacket photograph, to start with. . . ."

"It's sold a lot of copies, hasn't it? Been printed in every paper from here to Salt Lake City, hasn't it? I mean something else, and I'm not the only one."

He handed me a clipping out of a recent issue of *Horizon*—an excerpt from an editorial by its editor, Cyril Connolly. " 'Get Capote,' " it read. "At this minute the words are resounding on many a 60th floor and 'get him' of course means make him and break him, smother him with laurels and then vent on him the obscure hatred which is inherent in the notion of another's superiority."

Next morning, rummaging for breakfast, I shut the refrigerator and turned to find Truman in his bathrobe at the kitchen table.

"Last night," I asked, "were you being totally honest? Or were you fishing for something?"

He looked up, eyes wide. "Honest about what?"

"Your big show of anguish, why there's so much more gossip about you than serious attention to your book. *You* read the columns. Who's to separate that kind of chaff from the truth?"

"Some of that chaff *is* the truth," he said. "What kind of truth do *you* mean?"

"The simple fact that you work harder and longer than anyone else in the game."

"So?"

"To stringers on a butterfly chase, that's a pretty dreary piece of information. But why keep it out of sight if you're only going to suffer the consequences you say you do?"

"Don't you fret," he said. "This kid knows how to skin his own cat."

He dropped a slice of bread into the toaster. "I'm making a declaration of independence, I'm going to Paris."

"Why Paris?"

"My book's *succès fou* there, they tell me, why shouldn't *I* be?"

The teakettle shrieked.

"Actually," he said, "I hate to go, because of Newton."

"Then why do it?"

"All I can say is, there are certain limits to what one can endure."

I drove to California and spent the summer in Berkeley, lecturing to classes so crowded and sprawling they seemed like political rallies. While there, I got letters from Paris—not from Truman but from other friends whose reports confirmed Truman's notion that he was the victim of some intangible conspiracy of malediction. Its nature, as far as I could see, was gratuitous, and its claims could sometimes be ascribed to envy. Still, the consistent disparagement of Truman by people I had believed normally charitable began to trouble me as, thrust and parry, I found myself uneasily engaged in the defense of a friend who needed none.

Both of us were back in New York by September when, one evening, we were sitting at a window table in the rooftop bar of the Beekman Towers Hotel.

"Gide gave me this ring," said Truman and held out his hand. "It's sapphire. Cocteau made me a costume, fresh laurel leaves and a mousseline toga—and took me to a party. One day I went to see Colette, tea for two, in a boudoir that smelled of sachet and cat pee. Cocteau said she'd never heard of me, but when he told her I looked ten years old and had a mind as wicked as Egypt, she got interested. The old darling, she looks like a doll saved from a fire."

Across the river the lights of Brooklyn's modest skyline had begun to come on. "I once thought of living right here in this hotel," he said. "But it never occurred to me it's where you can see all of Brooklyn and all the middle of Manhattan at once."

"Capote territory, you mean?"

His eyes lingered on the water between. "Home is home, just a little worse than it ever was. Two days back, and it's as though I'd never left. I've got to find my own place."

In no time he'd found one—an "efficiency" of two rooms and a sort of playpen kitchen furnished in what appeared to be stuff hauled in from a theatrical warehouse: gilt chairs, painted shutters, mirrors scrolled with Venetian flourishes, velvet in draped swatches, harem pillows, a blackamoor holding a torch.

"It's all mine," he said, "picked by hand. I saw Garbo coming out of this junk shop on Third Avenue, so I went in. What are you doing for dinner?"

A quick meal at the Oyster Bar in Grand Central, I told him, because I had a ticket for A *Streetcar Named Desire*.

"Come with me," he said, "I've got a dinner date with old Streetcar himself—you'll see his new character: pepper-and-salt tweeds, a brand-new voice. Can you imagine an *Oxford drawl*? . . . A long black cigarette holder to finish off the *tout ensemble*."

Unwilling to waste my ticket, I decided to forego the playwright for the play.

I had meanwhile myself moved to new quarters, a house I'd rented in Westport. From there, once a week, I'd go to New York to sit on the septuagenarian board of a publishing house which expected me to come up with ideas that might free it from almost exclusive fiscal dependence on the continuing popularity of *Black Beauty, Treasure Island,* and the plays of George Bernard Shaw. Since I soon found that the ideas I presented sank without ripples into the impenetrable lethargy of that boardroom only to resurface on the lists of other publishers, my place there was as redundant as my prospects were bleak. Depressed after one of these sessions, I called on Truman. Generous in his new affluence, he took me to lunch at The Colony.

As we were being escorted to our table, I caught sight of the playwright John Van Druten, waving in our direction rather like a baby saying bye-bye. Truman, pretending not to notice, made no return gesture.

In a minute Van Druten was at our table, bending in a courtly bow. "Truman, young man," he said. "I've missed the sight of you this long while."

"That . . . must . . . be," said Truman, underlining the banality of things, "because I've been *away!*"

"And where is away?"

"Paris."

"And how did you find Paris?"

"To tell the God's truth, cold and gloomy."

"And you're back now, for the winter?"

"I really can't say."

"I hope I'll have a chance to see more of you. Will you ring me? Actually, I've been lunching here almost every day."

"That's nice," said Truman, and lifted his frozen daiquiri.

"It's been good to see you, my boy." Holding his napkin, Van Druten went back to his table.

I watched until he was seated, then turned to Truman. "Rudeness is no prerogative," I said, "even for a kid celebrity."

The Picture of Little T.C. in a Prospect . . . / 35

"I've had quite enough of Mister V.D., thank you."

The space between us yawned.

Screening his face with a menu card, he said: "I suggest we change the subject. What are you going to have?"

The coquilles St. Jacques I ordered cooled. It was three o'clock before—in a gloom punctuated by gambits not taken up—we left the restaurant. Since the afternoon was summery and we had nothing in particular to do, we started for Central Park and strolled around the pond that catches the shadow of the Plaza.

"This is one of the places where I used to play hookey," he said. "Every day when it wasn't raining."

"*Every* day?"

"Well, every other day. I just could not sit in a schoolroom. Days I had to, I'd anesthetize myself, put myself in a coma, and dream up paperweight cities and towns where everything happened the way I wanted it to. Mostly, I just didn't go. . . . I'd go to the library, that private one, it's called the New York Society Library. That's where I met Willa Cather. Would you believe we became good friends? She used to be there with that girl friend of hers. . . . They're still living together somewhere near me, on Park Avenue. No. I think she died last year."

"Willa Cather did."

"Anyway, when it wasn't that, it was the Roxy or the Radio City Music Hall, two stage shows and the movie. Remember Evelyn and Her Magic Violin? Borrah Minevitch and His Harmonica Rascals? Ted Lewis . . . is *ev*erybody *ha*ppy?"

One day early in December, I answered my office phone. "I'm holed up," said Truman. "Bring some eats. I've got something to tell you."

I rang his bell at noon.

"You're lucky to find me," he said.

"How so?"

"Marlon Brando."

"What's he got to do with anything?"

"Well, duckling, drag up a chair—but don't lean back, it's break-able." Handing me a drink, he lit a cigarette. "Mister Stanley Kowalski came by yesterday in this *gear,*" he said, and made a sweep of his hand, knees to forehead. "Before you can say Robinson Crusoe—"

"Jack Robinson."

"Before you can say Jack Robinson, I'm on the seat of this jukebox Harley-Davidson zipping in and out of traffic down to the Battery, me hanging on to that beer barrel like some pickup bobby-soxer. Scared? Out of my chicken wits, a complete conviction I'd never see the light of another day. I can't tell whether it was on purpose or not—careening way over, zooming to dead stops, then just standing still and revving up or whatever they call it. There's something pretty cuckoo about that one, let me tell you. Anyway, I was limp, not to mention frozen in the extremities, when we got back here. Whereupon Mr. K. stretches out—there, on that couch. Without so much as an aye, no, kiss my foot, simply displays the length of him in all that leather drag, stares at the ceiling as if I didn't exist, goes to sleep . . . to *sleep,* mind you . . . for three solid hours."

"What did you do?"

"What *could* I do? I looked the situation over, tried to figure out what it meant, shrugged my shoulders, and sat down on that." He pointed to a golden rocking chair. "Sat there like Whistler's Mother and read Edith Wharton's *Custom of the Country.* Maybe they're all cuckoo. Monty Clift—another one not dealing from a full deck. Won't go outside the door, not even to eat. Sits all day in his underwear and tootles on a trumpet. Well, enough of nutsy actors. What you got in that bag?"

I spread out my smorgasbord. He brought plates and silver from the miniature kitchen. "That's not the thing I have to tell you," he said. "I'm giving a party, a big one."

"So what else is new?"

"Wait and I'll *tell* you." He got up to freshen his glass. "I've met someone."

"So?"

"So the way to make it happen again, without *imposing* myself, is to give a rather large party at the Park Avenue place, invite him and his spouse . . . yes, there's that to consider, eight years of it, and don't make a face . . . and anyway, I decided this would be the most graceful way to work it."

The Picture of Little T.C. in a Prospect . . . / 37

"Couldn't you think of something less elaborate?"

"Never you mind. If things proceed, *as* planned, let me assure you it will be worth *every* effort."

It was late when, on the designated Sunday evening, I got to the party. In the elevator with me were a man in a trench coat and a woman in mink. She I recognized—Joan McCracken, the dancer known as "the little girl who falls down" in *Oklahoma!* He I did not. His hair was red, face craggy, eyes sea-green. A sullenness about him hinted at tension under control. He might have been thirty, fifty. No matter, I knew he was the excuse for the party.

The door to the Capote apartment was open. We left our coats with a maid and became part of a crowd spilling over into hallways and the kitchen, from which Truman emerged at once. "Know something? I didn't have to do this after all," he said. "Everything's settled. When there's a chance, I'll point him out."

That did not happen. Coming late, as I thought, I had come early. Or had I merely joined one evening's segment of some timeless gathering of the clan? Beatrice Lillie was there, Tallulah Bankhead expected. Bennett Cerf was telling funny stories to Libby Holman, Josh White lecturing Stella Adler. As Wystan Auden, his feet in carpet slippers, was about to depart without a coat, the marquis of Milford-Haven was checking his. The party had the air of a rehearsal call for a play that would never be performed. Following Auden's lead, I soon headed for the elevator and encountered him on the sidewalk. "I told Truman I'd come for half an hour," he said. "The point of occasions of this sort evades me, unless one knows everyone . . . then I still don't see."

A cab drew up and disgorged a young woman, a young man, and a man who looked like Johann Sebastian Bach. Auden climbed in and drove off.

"Speed!" said the young woman. "We promised to call mother at midnight."

"I'd rather do that from Lenny's," said Speed.

Followed at a petty pace by the man who looked like Bach, they disappeared into the lobby.

When the doorman's whistle produced another cab, I went home.

* * *

At a tea party on the following day, the host was Leo Lerman, the guest of honor Evelyn Waugh. The other guests were mostly writers delighted for a chance to meet the novelist whose work had provided many of them with models, and all of us with the fading but still useful phraseology of Trocadero chic. From the start, the afternoon was a fiasco approaching the sick-making. Ensconced in the center of the room, Mr. Waugh had no intention of engaging in conversation; he was there to give audience. Introduced to four or five people in succession, he waved each of them aside before they could open their mouths. In minutes there was a zone of interdiction about his chair no one dared to cross twice.

Smarting from my own abrupt dismissal, I found Truman at my side. "Did *you* get the treatment?" he asked. "That mushroomy paw dropping yours before you've had a chance to shake it? Little eyes fixed on the ceiling when you try to talk?"

We watched as, one by one, others were presented and summarily rebuffed. "Who does that little pig think he is?" said someone behind us. "He's supposed to be worried about the decline of manners."

A shuffling in the crowd, by then so big as to overwhelm the man in the middle, produced an opening. Through it came Jean Stafford. "They're setting up a relief bar," she announced in her Daisy Buchanan voice. "Major cases should line up at once."

"Major cases of what?" I asked.

"Outrage," she said.

Truman and I were among those who began to trade in their cups of Earl Grey for tumblers of Old Grand-dad. "The other night," he said, "were you able to pick him out?"

"Red hair?"

He nodded. "Come the first day you can," he said. "We'll talk."

I got to Truman's at noon and put cold cuts, French bread, Port Salut, and cherry pie on the coffee table; he put Fats Waller on the turntable.

"I've made up my mind," he said. "I mean, *we've* made up *our* minds. Ever think you'd hear me say that? We're pulling up stakes and heading for Europe."

"For the winter?"

The Picture of Little T.C. in a Prospect . . . / 39

"For good—let's say, 'indefinitely.' "

"Give up this apartment?"

He nodded. "Jack will keep his . . . just in case something might force us to come back."

"*Ain't misbehavin'*," sang Waller, "*I'm saving my love for you.*"

"I'm taking that with me," said Truman, "Fats and Lee Wylie. Then Flaubert, Virginia Woolf, Chekhov . . . maybe some Faulkner. Do you think Faulkner might seem different overseas? When I'm reading him, I feel threatened by something in the back of my head that won't declare itself, something maybe too close to home. Listen, you ought to get to know Jack . . . black Philadelphia Irish with the temper to go with it. Why not now? He has no phone but I know he's there."

Our taxi dropped us in the middle of a block of tenements where trains of the Third Avenue elevated made thunderstorms overhead. In a schoolyard paved with concrete, some kids were playing stickball in the sooty remnants of a recent snowstorm. Jack's name was on the mailbox in an entryway shared by a Chinese laundry. The bell did not work. When we'd climbed three flights of a clammy stairwell that had tin walls painted apple green, like those in Victorian waiting rooms, Truman rapped on a scarred green door. Jack opened it.

He was my man in the elevator, all right, but without the sullen demeanor I remembered. He gave Truman a hug and shook my hand. Waiting to be shown into the flat, I realized all at once that we *were* in it: one room with a bunk bed, a sagging settee, a table and chairs in an ell that served as a kitchen. There was a gray stoneware sink, a brass spigot, a claw-footed bathtub across the top of which was a board covered with checkered oilcloth. Outside, on the dripping fire escape, were five red geraniums in a row. There was no bathroom, but a W.C. in the hall, which—as I learned in a few minutes—had no window and was unheated. To flush the toilet, you had to reach for a wooden handle and pull the chain. Yet the flat itself had a miniature coziness about it entirely inviting—hand-painted flourishes of leaves, abstract stars on the bunk and chairs, a shipshape Scandinavian cleanliness.

When Jack produced drinks, we sat around the table as though we were about to play cards. "I've told Malcolm about our idea of Europe. . . . I didn't tell him you thought Ischia," said Truman, and turned to me. "What do you know about Ischia?"

"It's in the Mezzogiorno. It's volcanic. It's mentioned in Gibbon."

"What *I* want," said Truman, "is a place with sun. Period. Then something pretty to look at when I raise my heavy head from the typewriter. People . . . I couldn't care less. People I can do without."

Over the rim of his whisky glass, Jack's eyes met mine.

"I want quiet," continued Truman, "beautiful quiet and a nice little post office with outsize postage stamps and a donkey with a straw hat and flowers in his ears I can ride into the village and . . ."

Truman was in good hands, I thought. Once more he'd found the right person at the right time. Mary Lou Aswell had already spoken for all of us. "Don't be deceived by that look of helplessness," she had told a reporter. "Little T. has an uncanny way of choosing just those people who understand him, and will help him. It's in his stars, or his destiny, or his health line, or whatever you want to call it, that he travel in the right direction . . . his instinct leads him to the people who are on his side."

Alone, she might have added; he travels alone, except that there's always someone with him.

As Truman became absorbed in his new life, I turned my attention to a long-contemplated project now supported by a publisher's advance—a critical biography of Gertrude Stein. Editorial conferences still brought me to New York every Wednesday, when we'd meet for jazz and gossip, but it was not until he and Jack were about to sail away that I realized I was concerned about him in ways I'd not yet had a chance to express. On February 21, 1949, my journal reports:

A farewell visit. In the course of it I tell Truman I've begun to follow him in the columns of the tabloids the way other people follow comic strips.

"Well . . ." he says. "I ain't no Li'l Abner . . . but I sure get around Dogpatch."

"Other people get around, nobody knows about it. How come it's always you?"

The Picture of Little T.C. in a Prospect . . . / 41

He smiles a pussycat smile.

"Half the stories are planted, I'm told. Twenty-five dollars an item. Is that true?"

"Of course it's true. If I can spread a little of the national wealth around, why not? Twenty-five dollars is a lot of money to pick up for just a phone call."

"But won't there come a day when that item called Truman Capote will turn into a public commodity? Won't the figure begin to take on a life of its own—separate from the person?"

"So what? *I* know who I am."

"That's what Gertrude Stein thought. Then when she became famous, she wasn't so sure. 'I am I because my little dog knows me,' she told herself, but it didn't do. 'That doesn't prove anything about me,' she said, 'it only proves something about the dog.' Truman, you don't even have a dog."

"When I get one, I'll ask him. Will that make you feel better? What you have to understand is, I don't so much want a reputation as I want a career. If a reputation can help me get it, what's wrong with a reputation? Have you got your car here?"

I did.

"Would you drop me at Jack's? We can say bon voyage on the way."

We drive through slush, park in front of the Chinese laundry, which, as usual, is closed. "What you were saying about Gertrude Stein . . ." says Truman. "Who except pedants ever knew about her until she made herself famous? It wasn't the work that did it. . . . Can you honestly say you know anyone who's read *Tender Buttons* through? The thing that made her famous was the *story* of the work and all that went *with* it. It may be a sad commentary, one you academics have trouble accepting, but people are people."

Rain beats hard on the roof of the car. The noise of an elevated train comes on like a cyclone, leaves a widening stillness. "This is it," he says. "Don't fret about me, just don't for*get* me."

Before he's reached the tenement door, I call out.

"Truman!"

He turns.

"Get a dog!"

His return from Europe in December, as it turned out, would be made under my auspices and at my expense. Meanwhile, with no word from him for months, I wrote in the hope of learning that his choice of Ischia had proved to be happy.

"Yes, yes," he wrote back, "I'm not only happy but in a condition in which I have rarely found myself—a state of contentment. It's an enchanting island, Ischia, and we've had the great luck to find a whole floor to ourselves in a *pensione* that looks far down to the edge of the sea. You would love it, and I cannot understand why you do not pack up at once and *descend*. We plan to stay at least until mid-summer. We both read a great deal and I'm glad to report that I'm working rather a tremendous lot. The swimming is superb: water clear as kittens' eyes, and great volcanic rocks that serve as diving boards.

"Bands of amusing people come drifting in and out, but it's se-rene, *very* serene, for the most of it. Jack is splendid: a face like saddle leather and, among other things I've discovered, he can handle a boat. This past weekend we sailed clear around the island."

This letter was followed the next day by another.

"This ain't, in your case, *déjà vu,*" wrote Truman, "but a postscript to say and ask what I didn't yesterday.

"Yes, Wystan, he is very much here. I know you admire him and sometimes I do, too—on the *page*. But in person and day to day he's not the easiest pill to swallow: He ought to be running a school, perhaps a military academy—all these meticulous rules about what to do and precisely how to do it. Truth to tell, I'm weary of him and have watched him closely enough to say flatly: he's a dictatorial bas-tard.

"If I sound cranky, it's only in this instance. The days are beautiful—full summer before summer has even begun—except that now and then there are a rough two or three days with foam over the rocks and the natives sitting like crows. It's the sirocco, and when it comes there's really nothing else to do but take it, which in all these centuries they have *not* learned to do.

"I, on the other hand, keep my nose to the grindstone mornings, then turn to other occupations, *comme ça:* Princess Margaret is coming to the island today and everyone keeps calling up at me because I've been lining up baskets of nosegays and marguerites to toss from the balcony. *Quel camp.* Also, I'm in the most critical stage of baking a devil's food cake, and that demands my unswerving attention. Therefore you must excuse the brevity of this note. Write to me. Mail time is my day's excitement.

"P.S. Have you heard anything about my book? It is so very strange—nobody mentions it, not even, in his letter to me, my editor. I have a feeling that it has evaporated or, indeed, was never printed at all. Do you know anything about this boy William Goyen? His story in the March *Horizon,* while a very bad story indeed, is certainly well written."

Fully engaged on my biography of Gertrude Stein, I accepted another invitation to Yaddo, where, on June 15, I made this entry in my journal:

Arrived here late morning, I learn I've been given Truman's old tower room. When I climb the dark stairs, the harp on the back of the door merely whines. Someone has removed the leaden balls.

I take my typewriter out of its case, place it on the ivory-white desk. A whoosh of wind comes soughing through the surrounding pines; a mourning dove whimpers outside the door to the terrace; a shaft of light hits the choir stall. Framed in the huge main window, green hills roll toward the old battlefields. A scratching, apparently made with a diamond ring across the bottom of the pane, makes a declaration of love dated August 22, 1897. Sitting in the crazy bishop's chair, I listen to other voices in other rooms.

Truman and Jack were now in North Africa, a fact of which I was not aware until I got a letter late in June. "A curious place," wrote Truman, "there's every kind of activity, most of it raffish, to say the very least, and all manner of humankind—outré, or decadent, elegant or abandoned to hashish or sex, or both of these at once. A little on the scary side, too, and you have to get accustomed to noises the likes of which you've never heard, faces of a character you've never seen, *or* imagined—and hashish fumes and the smell of *thé arabe*. For all that, there's a charm that gets to you.

"Janie and Paul Bowles live in this hotel, which means we have company, even too much of it. Gore Vidal has been here—*has,* I'm overjoyed to say, and is not likely to return. When I think *I'm* paranoid, I listen to him and feel better at once. Did I have a chance to tell you what happened just before we left New York? Hold your hat.

"It's Sunday morning, me nicely *déshabillé* over coffee. The doorbell rings. Who pushes in, hopped-up and crazy-eyed, but G.V. 'Truman,' he says, 'they're out to get us!' and starts off on this totally incomprehensible routine about 'them' and how we have to 'stand pat' and 'close ranks,' etc. 'What in the hell are you talking about,' says I, 'I think you've come to the wrong door. If you don't mind, I'd like to close it.' Can you imagine?

"Cecil Beaton is here, staying in a house owned by the Guinnesses. Wouldn't you know that we two iron-winged butterflies would find ourselves in the same hollyhock? If not for him, I'd move on, although I *do* like these sugar-soft beaches, toward one of which I'm about to repair, to the accompaniment of flutes."

I had by this time accepted an invitation by the governing board of New York's Young Men's and Young Women's Hebrew Association to become director of activities in that part of their educational program known as the Poetry Center. In the course of putting together a season of programs that would include readings by such figures as Dylan Thomas, Robert Frost, e. e. cummings, Stephen Spender, Allen Tate, and Mark Van Doren, it occurred to me that Truman, who, as far as I knew, had never made a public appearance as a writer, might allow me to add his name to our already illustrious roster.

The Picture of Little T.C. in a Prospect . . . / 45

He was at once receptive, except as to the matter of the fee I'd been empowered to offer him. I had to make a plea to the financial overseers of the Poetry Center for a higher amount that would also include the cost of transatlantic passage. When this was granted, Truman and I agreed on the date of December 8.

"Paris is dark, cold and, oddly, silent," he wrote, "and progress on my book has been maddeningly slow. Maybe I'm just tired of sparking up the foreign scene. Now I'm dealing with a bad case of grippe, but do not think it will interfere with plans to get to the Poetry Center on the 8th. In any case, I am about to alleviate my symptoms by having Thanksgiving dinner at Maxim's.

"Air France (Air Chance, they call it here) should put me into Idlewild on the morning of the 5th, about eleven. Will I see you there? Second thought: It's an arduous trip through the jungles of Queens, so I will honestly not expect you.

"To prove I've taken your advice, I'll have with me a dog—a Pekingese puppy with a story: he was given to Janie Bowles by a friend of Cecil's and then when J. couldn't take him to England—the dog, that is—because of the British quarantine, she gave him to me. His name is Muffin and he looks like one—incredibly clever and funny.

"Delighted to hear you have your own *pied-à-terre*. Just 'off' Sutton Place? How *far* off?"

On the bright windy morning of December 5, I watched from the observation deck at Idlewild as the Constellation bearing Truman, Paris via Gander, touched down and taxied up. When the ramp was settled into place and the door wrenched open, out he stepped, bareheaded, with a little dog squashed in his left arm. When I waved, he picked me out and waved back, then lifted the dog's paw and waved it in my direction before he disappeared into the customs shed.

Half an hour later we were en route to Manhattan, but not as the crow flies. "I can't face up to going home," said Truman, "not yet, anyway. Let's have lunch."

Turning off the parkway, I headed for the Forest Hills Inn. There, Muffin ignored the hamburger prepared for him and sat patiently as we ordered martinis.

"I made a vow I wouldn't come back before *Summer Crossing* was finished," said Truman. "Here I am. The trouble was Paris, it's absolute hell taking care of two dogs and two parrots and trying to do anything else."

"Parrots?"

"We brought them from Morocco. All that in one hotel room, a menagerie." Muffin looked up and licked his tongue. "Absolute hell. . . ."

I inquired about Jack.

"He'll be coming over on the *Queen Mary*," he said, "next Thursday from Cherbourg . . . with the other dog, and twenty-four pieces of luggage . . . all our worldly possessions."

"You think you're ready? . . . to come home?"

He surveyed the restaurant, as though he might find the answer there.

"I'm not sure," he said. "I have to find out."

Late that afternoon I delivered him to Park Avenue, and two nights later met him at a party, where he introduced me to his old friend Phoebe Pierce. Perhaps twenty-two or -three, she had water-blue eyes, skin like a peace rose, and wore earrings with little diamonds that swung as she spoke. "I wish they were mine," she said, "but they're only borrowed, for the occasion."

"Phoebe's a thief," said Truman. "She was arrested for grand larceny when she was fifteen years old."

As Truman had long ago told me, she was not otherwise arrested: Their high school love affair was the beginning of a friendship that had remained warm.

"Truman, I must run," she said as the clock struck midnight. "I've got a date with this dreamboat cadet from Brazil who's staying at the Plaza with his old lady. His name is Manuelo, I'm going to bring him to your reading."

Moments later, waving from the doorway in a mink coat far too big for her, she blew Truman a kiss.

"That's borrowed, too," said Truman. "Look, I don't want to go home tonight. Would it be all right if I stayed with you?"

"What's the matter?"

"I don't know," he said. "Sometimes, even when everything's all right, I get frightened."

When I got up next morning, I found a note on the kitchen table: "I'll need *escort*. Call for me at seven."

When I did, he was in bed, "too sick to move."

"*Sick* sick?" I asked. "Or anxiety sick?"

"Both."

He stared at the ceiling as though he were in a trance, then shut his eyes.

"Should we call it off?"

"Give me a brandy," he said, "to stave off the shakes."

Maneuvering himself to the edge of the bed, he accepted the slug I poured and downed it in one gulp. "Look in that closet, you'll find my suit, black velvet with a dull gold lining."

Our taxi pulled up alongside one of the sawhorse barriers holding back the crowd that overflowed the lobby and spilled onto Lexington Avenue. Poetry Center ushers had to help us get by the flashing bulbs of photographers and the monitoring eyes of a special detail of policemen. Ignoring the Green Room's many mirrors, Truman began a restless tour of the premises.

His trepidation was contagious. While I could see that his young admirers, many of them with haircuts that imitated his, were out in force, I couldn't help wondering: How would the sober Poetry Center audience receive this childlike packet of a man with his fauntleroy velvet, his dancing pumps, his baby seal's voice, his tendency to illustrate his points with little arabesques of emphasis?

At zero hour I took the stage alone and began an introduction which I heard myself making as though I were listening to a recording in another room. When, at last, the record and the echo in my own echo chamber stopped, Truman walked on, climbed a high stool in the glow of pink spotlights, adjusted his big horn-rimmed glasses (titters from the back rows), lifted a copy of *A Tree of Night,* and began.

Backstage, as the sound engineer kept fiddling with his dials to make sure that the extraordinary voice would come out as low and loud as possible, the hands of the wall clock shifted audibly. Otherwise, it was just Truman's words and profound silence. Turning a page, he looked straight into the semidarkness, from which, like the report of cracking ice, came an involuntary shout of laughter, quickly stifled. This was followed by a ripple of applause, then by a roar like an explosion. Everyone was laughing, everyone was "breaking up," including Truman himself. Shifting on his perch, he spoke an aside, adjusted his glasses, and had to wait for wave on wave of renewed laughter to subside.

Whatever turn it was he had taken, it led to a wide-open road that ended in a blast of applause, cries of "Bravo!" "Encore!" Bowing low, blowing kisses with both hands, he returned again and again and, with a hop and a skip, left for good only when the stage manager had started the house lights blinking.

Truman stayed in Manhattan just long enough to know that he was *not* ready to come home. Meeting at parties by accident, we would meet for dinners by design, usually at the Algonquin. There one evening early in February he spoke of plans for returning to Europe, once again to stay "indefinitely." But no departure date had been set, and there were more immediate things on his mind. "I'm giving a *rather* special little dinner party tomorrow," he said. "You're not invited."

"I may break into tears," I said. "Who's coming?"

"Charlie and Oona, Garbo and Cecil, ZaSu Pitts and Phoebe."

"Where are you giving it?"

"*Chez* Jack."

"What are you all going to sit on?"

"Don't," he said, "be bourgeois."

While our old rapport appeared to be constant, our paths had sharply diverged: his toward doors that now opened to him everywhere, mine toward attendance upon Dylan Thomas, who, having come to America at my invitation, had at once involved me in a friendship that had about it, as an observer would one day astutely point out, "the character of an hallucination." Out of touch with Truman for many months, I caught up with him only in time to say bon voyage on the night before he and Jack were to board a freighter for Italy. This occasion, hurried and crowded, was less than satisfactory for me and, as I learned by a letter early in May, for him as well.

The Picture of Little T.C. in a Prospect . . . / 49

"You were more than dear to come that very last night," he wrote from Taormina, "and I have had twinges of remorse about the way things turned out, because I would have liked to have seen you alone.

"The crossing was extraordinary: twenty-one days, and our shipmates were an odd lot of gloomy Turks who began all of their remarks with 'We Turks' (think this or that): Consequently, I'm rather happily relieved to be here on the high solid earth of Taormina; it is beyond saying beautiful, a springtime I can only describe as unearthly. You would adore it; and we've come into possession of the most charming villa* just a twenty-minute stroll from the center. There's a wildly tangled garden, two bedrooms, two terraces, an enormous salon, kitchen, bathroom, and a hawk's-eye view of the blue mountains of the Italian peninsula, snow, sea. Fifty dollars a month. Can you believe it?

"André Gide has a place not far from here. Such a lonely figure in his velvet pants, Shakespearian cape, and maestro's fedora. He haunts the barbershop having his face lathered by boys of ten and twelve; and there's a scandal abroad in the piazza, not because he arranges to take these boys home with him, but because he seldom sends them back with more than two hundred lire (20¢). Otherwise, the whole place is blessedly free of literary folk or, come to think of it, folk of any kind. You must come and stay. Meanwhile, write me, because we Turks miss you."

Preoccupied with Dylan Thomas, trying to keep his affairs straight, those on his lecture circuit and those in particular hotel rooms and boudoirs of Manhattan and Brooklyn, I had little time for personal correspondence, as Truman was quick to remind me. "Why don't I hear from you?" he wrote. "The one and only reason I send letters is to make sure I *get* letters. Please understand that I want this on a paying basis."

"Cecil has been here and gone—a sojourn not memorable for him, I suspect, because he doesn't care for the beach and when we don't go there the only diversions are shopping in the market or sitting down to aperitifs and people-watching in the piazza. Worse than

---

*Fontana Vecchia, where D. H. Lawrence lived in the early twenties.

that, since we are stay-at-homes who can't cook much more than a three-minute egg, we depend upon a girl we've hired for the august office of mistress of the *cucina*. But we've discovered that she can't cook, either (although I must say her attempts to cover up the fact are ingenious, and now and then edible), and since we can't bear to fire anyone so spirited—and with so profound a belief in the powers of *malocchio*—we're back where we started.

"Anyway, I think Taormina would suit you every bit as much as it does me: Etna with its cone of snow in the hard-blue distance, a room with a view down to the sea, and across a hazy or sometimes glittering stretch of water to Calabria, a shop where you can buy English newspapers; even a bar where they know how to make an American martini. So, pack up your Olivetti—along with a few cans of Danish ham and Armour's corned beef (Italian meat is abominable) and come as soon as you can."

When I could come, he was in Venice, toward which I made my way after a summer on Cape Ann, a visit with Dylan and his latest American girl (a close friend of Truman's) in London, another to Paris for a series of interviews with Alice B. Toklas. When I arrived in the late afternoon, the clerk at the Hotel Manin Pilsen handed me a note: "*Ciao!* Have *secured* a room—such as it may turn out to be. Am living across the Canal. Wld have been at the *stazione* to meet you except that Nina was departing at the same moment, from the airport. Will be down to get you (in a taxi, honey) at 6:30. T."

Off San Marco, overlooking a basin where inactive gondolas were lined up four and five abreast, the hotel was antiseptically clean, Teutonic, and graceless. My room was dark until I opened shutters onto a sound-box air shaft over a laundry where women were singing several melodies at once.

A brisk knock on the door. Truman bounced in. "Well, old buddy, welcome to Venezia," he said. "Have you ever seen anything more hopelessly beautiful? Wait, just wait. It's the most enchanting thing on earth, and maybe the saddest. You are going to lose your Chinese mind." He gave his growly laugh, stretched out flat on one of the beds. "Nina exhausts me," he said. "Are all mothers exhausting? Emotionally?"

Soon joined by Jack, we wove through shuffling crowds in byways to Harry's Bar, only to find ourselves stymied in its miniature muddle with no place to stand or sit. But not for long. At a word from Truman, a waiter lifted a table over the heads of other diners and set it up in a matter of seconds. "They know me here," said Truman. "Isn't that nice?"

A tall man with an ur-British bearing swiveled around from his place at the bar and, nodding toward Truman, lifted his glass. Truman did the same. "You know who that is?" he said. "*No*body knows who that is. It's Henry Green."

Dinner over, we stopped in the piazza for *espresso* at Florian's, strolled to the *piazzetta,* and stepped into a gondola that took us across the mouth of the Grand Canal to the Giudecca. The plash of its oars was so soft we might have been riding Charon's ferry.

The flat they'd rented was situated on a long waterside promenade. Its rooms were big, bedight with Italianate stuff, shiny fabrics and fringes as kitschy and comfortable as Mama Leone's parlor. They had a new dog, a Kerry blue named Kelly, which had a habit of streaking about the place as though possessed.

"What's the latest word on our Sarah and Dylan Thomas?" asked Truman. "Did her dash to London turn out the way she'd planned it?"

Perhaps, I told him.

"What does *that* mean?"

"Dylan says he's in love with her. In the next breath he says he's in love with his wife, and always has been."

The lighted upper deck of a freighter headed for the marina slid by the windows.

"I think I met him once," said Truman, "in a sort of arty-shabby club in London. Mousey hair and yellow teeth? All I can say is, I wish her well. Did you see my little Alice B. Toklas in Paris? Did you meet any of those classy dikes around Natalie What's-her-name Barney? In the temple of love or whatever she calls it?"

"Alice likes you," I reported. "She thinks you're smart, that you've got a head on your shoulders."

"She's really a dear," he says, "if only she'd shave off that Fu Manchu moustache."

It was midnight when he and Jack walked me to the Zitelle vaporetto stop, where Kelly, darting between us, went skidding off the seawall and landed upright in a passing gondola. Shrieks, rumblings, sounds of scraping. As the gondolier picked up the dog and handed him over by the scruff, Jack attempted to apologize, to no avail. Along with a group of Venetians, we stood waiting for the vaporetto. The gondola came by once again.

"*Cretino!*" yelled the gondolier. "*Il cane stupido si butto in acqua,*" called out one of his passengers. "*Americani imbecilli!*"

The long evening is over [reads a journal entry for September 22, 1950], the violins of San Marco silent. A big moon rides over the campanile, lighting the stacked tables and chairs at Florian's, sending de Chirico shadows down the length of the colonnade. Snatches of song from the narrow *passaggetti* and bridges leading from the piazza tell that the candle-lit nightclubs have put up their shutters.

We dawdle toward the gondola landing beneath the pillar of Saint Theodore and his crocodile and are about to say good night when Kelly goes racing toward the Bridge of Sighs, stands barking on the white steps, comes tearing back in a sort of moon-crazy frolic. Jack tries to coax him into his leash. "Let him run," says Truman. "I've just decided: I don't want to cross that water once more today. Malcolm's going to put us up."

The night clerk is not at his desk. With Kelly on short tether, we go up by the stairs and settle in.

Moonlight, a sense of absurdity, the mosaic dazzle of Venice . . . something keeps me awake and adrift. Oppressed by lack of focus, loss of scale, unable to take in or account for what I've seen, I can but envy Truman's gift for instant appropriation. Other people come to see Venice. He all but suggests that Venice has been waiting to see him, and makes the notion seem natural. For the first time since I've known him he's without complaint and in the clear. His new novel is taking final shape; a book of his occasional writings is just off the press; another whole year in Italy is, he says, "a prospect of bliss." He seems to float

The Picture of Little T.C. in a Prospect . . . / 53

in an aura of affection given and received. Instead of acting on compulsions to flaunt himself, he simply *is* himself. Yet, and yet . . . the distinction between his exhibition-ism and his self-expression is thin. To "maintain reserve" would be as alien to Truman as a call to emulate the spiritual disciplines of Plotinus. If he feels like dancing to a rumba beat all by himself across the pavements of San Marco, he does—rewarded by applause from the tables at Quadri and cries of "Bravo!" from the loungers under the flagpoles. If he feels like tying a Hermès scarf to his belt loop or a Bulgari bangle to his wrist, no whisper of decorum deters him. He works as much as he plays. Hours at the typewriter are matched by hours at the cabanas of the Excelsior and long lunchtimes at Harry's, kissing people he knows and being kissed by people he doesn't know. His ambitions are as closely calculated as his pleasures are care-less. And if he isn't ready to go home by midnight, he doesn't go home. . . .

6:00 A.M. [reads my next day's journal entry], laughter from the laundry below, a pounding on the door, sends Kelly into a frenzy of watchdog importance. I can't make out what's being said in the hall, but it's rude, angry, and embellished with touches of Serenissima vulgate. Truman, attempting to muffle the dog, shouts back in kitchen Italian. The door remains bolted; we go back to sleep.

By nine, shaved and showered, we're ready to face the desk. When Truman produces a few thousand lire, ostensibly to pay for a copy of yesterday's *Il Gazzettino,* the air is cleared. We're dismissed with a long smile and a low bow.

We separate for the day, meet again at All' Angelo. There, our dinner companions are Donald Windham, the novelist, and Bessie Breuer, the novelist, who, without prologue, tells us she has been 'taking care of dear Ingrid ever since she broke up with Roberto.' This piece of information provides no lead anyone follows and we are soon off to La Fenice and the American Ballet's version of *Romeo and Juliet*.

Midnight. Our gondola nuzzles up to the mossy steps of the Palazzo Venier dei Leoni. Peggy Guggenheim is waiting in the front garden next to her Marino Marini bronze of a youth astride a little horse. (The boy's removable and well-polished erection, as on all "occasions," is firmly in place.) Since she has never met more than two or three of her guests, including Truman, Miss Guggenheim greets us with as much curiosity as warmth and waves us on to join others already milling about rooms hung with Kandinskys and Kokoschkas, Mondrians and Max Ernsts.

This occasion seems, at first, not so much a party as a midnight pilgrimage to hallowed premises—especially since our hostess keeps turning up in this room or that, surveying mute little groups with a worried smile, as though their presence were something for which she cannot entirely account. When supper is laid out on a long buffet, things begin to come together as, plates in hand, everyone retires to the library where the paintings are less tyrannizing and there are places to perch, shelves to put things on. When the dancers have reduced the buffet to crumbs, there's a lull in which the distant pizzicati of Vivaldi on the record player make the stillness only more oppressive.

"Malcolm!" The voice is Truman's, from across the room, where, on a white leather couch, he seems to be sitting in Miss Guggenheim's lap. "Pick out something to dance to!"

Taking charge, he calls on John Kriza to help Miss G. clear the room. Joining her and her crew, I push and shove until there's an adequate space of marble, then flip through her record collection, Palestrina to Duke Ellington, and select "Take the 'A' Train." The dancers begin to jitterbug; the palazzo becomes a high school gymnasium on prom night. In a sedate two-step Truman and Miss Guggenheim weave in and out.

As our gondola back to San Marco slides by the frosted

domes of the Salute, she remains on the steps of the landing to wave us out of sight.

"Poor dear," says Truman. "She's frightened of almost everything. I rather liked her. Didn't you?"

On the day I was to leave, Truman brought a copy of *Local Color* to lunch and inscribed it for me. "My prettiest book," he said, "inside and out. Maybe because I get the most kick out of describing things without having to pretend I've made them up, not things so much, as atmosphere. Read first the piece about my train ride in Spain . . . the butterflies."

We walked to my hotel, where, as I finished packing, he sat on the edge of the bed.

"When will you be coming home, Truman?"

"Not for years," he said. "Whatever for?"

Back in Taormina for the winter, he did not write until late in January, when I had moved from a house in Westport to an apartment in Cambridge, Massachusetts. "I'm just back from a wintry week in Venice," he said, "so beautiful, a little snow falling on the Grand Canal, San Marco vast and empty, a great burst of warmth when you enter Harry's Bar. I should be sending a gaudy post card of Venice-by-night, but a letter is best, for I have things to mention. It is almost full spring here in Sicily; the slopes of the village awash with almond blossom, days when we can even have lunch on the terrace with the sea below sparkling like mica.

"You'll be pleased to hear that I'm well toward the end of my book, perhaps even closer. If I am very patient and can keep to routine, I should write the last page by early summer. I don't mean that, since I've always got the last page written before the first one. What I mean is, the last page in the *process*.

"Is it too late for little me to be a part of the Poetry Center's next season? I'd like so much to. Should there be a chance, let me know. I have the most stunning new suit (olive velvet, of a kind that *glows*) and I *must* have some place to show it off."

Glad to be able to add his name to the events of the upcoming season, I wrote to tell him so, only to learn he'd changed his mind.

Photo by R. Thorne McKenna

"Well, dear heart," he wrote. "I am not coming home after all. I have given into popular demand—namely, that I do not ever again set foot on American soil. The decision is no hardship, because I never *did* want to come back and now I'm happy to know I don't have to.

"About June, I'm delighted to think that you will be here—meaning Italy and either of two possibilities: If we're not in residence in Taormina we will be in some all-by-itself *piccolo palazzo* in Venice. In either case, promise that you will come."

A chance to stay at Yaddo again made me defer plans for Europe until late summer, when, instead of visiting Truman in Italy, I meant to spend some time with Dylan in Wales.

"*Drear* one," wrote Truman, "you *are* a creature of habit—and pretty tiresome habits they are. Yaddo, Y-a-a-d-d-o through time and tide. Haven't you had enough of carbuncular poets, limp ladies scrawling biographies of obscure composers, hairy novelists from the stockyards? I think you are in mortal danger: You will end up as one of those graveyard ghosts who float from one writers' colony to another and only materialize in some bottom-of-the-page obituary.

"All the same I can't wait to see your sweet lollipop face. Which is to say you must come to Venice before July 25th."

On that date I was in London, lunching with my new friend Edith Sitwell and, at midnight, boarding a Third Class sleeper for Wales and Dylan Thomas. Truman and I would not meet again until October, when, once more, he was by himself in Brooklyn—not in the neighborhood he'd known, but in an old Brooklyn Heights residence a friend of his had converted into apartment units. Ostensibly, this move was undertaken to provide him with working space not available in Jack's cookie-jar flat, and with a base of operations for those sorties into Manhattan night life for which Jack had little inclination. But he was often at Jack's. As we dined there *à trois* one evening, I learned that Truman had set his sights on Broadway and thought he could accomplish this goal with a dramatic version of the novel he had published earlier that year, *The Grass Harp*.

Until the mid-March opening of the play in Boston, everyone held his hand but no one could warm it. When the rough course was run, a single performance stood out: his own. Dressed in Sicilian velvet, he gave a reading of the script to a hard-boiled band of angels in someone's Fifth Avenue apartment, and got his backing on the spot. Staying with it through every rehearsal, he began to regard the man directing it as diabolical and fought with him to save its soul. He rewrote it, got Cecil Beaton to dress it, went to Boston with it, back to New York with it, and as far as I could tell, came out of the experience not one whit wiser than he was at the moment of its conception.

The career of *The Grass Harp* was a paradigm and, to someone of Truman's gifts, should have been a warning: Inflated, tricked out, and played for laughs, a gentle lyric conceived in the checkered shade of a remembered childhood was too frail a thing to survive the impositions of show biz razzmatazz. Such were my thoughts on the night when, three blocks from the Colonial Theater where the play had just expired, I sat in the mortuary silence of the Ritz Bar with Truman and some of his stoic friends: Jack, Cecil Beaton, William Goyen, Jane Bowles, and a woman crusader against alcoholism named Marty Mann. When I turned to wave a last good-night to Truman as he sat in the pink glow of that Louis Quatorze setting, I would not have believed it would be another year and a half before I'd see him again or that, when I did, he'd be adrift in a rowboat in the Tyrrhenian Sea.

Since his name now turned up in the papers as frequently as the Duke of Windsor's, I did not have to depend on him to know where he was or what he was doing. *How* he was, I had to interpret from the remarks of friends, most of whom seemed eager to remove the scales from my eyes. "I'm just back from Rome," wrote one of these, "where by chance I saw Truman C. one evening on the via Veneto. He sat there, enormously fat, cuddling a scrunchy dog, looking and talking like some defrocked monsignor from Des Moines, and generally acting as though everyone was fascinated by everything he was doing, which they weren't. The picture, I can assure you, was not pretty. How have you put up with such megalomania all these years? If there were an annual award for the Monster American, he'd win this year's, hands down."

The Picture of Little T.C. in a Prospect . . . / 59

"A bolt from the blue!" wrote Truman in answer to a note I'd sent in care of his publishers. "Actually, I've meant to write you for months (and months) but we have been so *movementé*, to understate, that it hardly ever seemed the right moment. However, we have settled in Portofino for the summer—and I am catching my breath. You would love Portofino, or do you know it? I am finishing a play, and a story, but how I ever reach the point of finishing *any*thing is beyond me.

"But we don't know your news and you don't know ours; and I want to—know your news, I mean. I've had a curious winter in Rome and in London—part of it spent making a movie with John Huston—the whole thing was kind of fun and the picture, *Beat the Devil,* is at least the camp of all time. Other than that have been working on the above-mentioned.

"Is there any chance you will be coming to Italy this summer? Malcolm, why haven't you written us?"

To redress, I wrote at once and received in reply a letter from Portofino on stationery filched from Claridge's. "I was touched, relieved, and worried by your sweet note today," he wrote. "Worried because of what you say about your health. I hope (so much) that you are feeling better now, and that there will be no delay in your trip. Because by all means you must come to stay with us in Portofino. It is very charming; the swimming is wonderful—we will be here until September 3rd. Please let us know, with some degree of accuracy, when to expect you."

I named the date, sailed for Spain to experience for myself what it was in Granada that marked a turning point in the writing career of Gertrude Stein, and took the *Andrea Doria* on to Genoa and a taxi to Portofino, where I found, as my journal tells me,

> no Truman, because he's not returned from a masked ball in Venice.
>
> "You get the picture," says Jack. "He's following a conga line in the Palazzo Labia, I'm boiling an egg and slicing a salami under that 10-watt bulb. He's shuttling between the Gritti and the Excelsior in the Contessa Volpi's Chris-Craft, I'm taking the dogs to piss on every

pillar and post from here to the bus stop. '*Il uomo degli cani,*' they call me, Christ knows what else."

As the dogs, alert for their supper, watch his every movement, the *padrona* comes by with a handful of letters, all of them for Truman. Late sun puts reflections from the marina on the ceiling.

"Well," says Jack, "let me feed these creatures. Looks like we're on our own. How about a Manhattan? I've got the record to go with it."

"*And tell me what street, compares with Mott Street, in July,*" sings Lee Wylie. I make drinks. The mood of things begins to change.

"You miss New York, Jack?"

"Every other day. Maybe only the idea of it."

"What about Truman?"

"I don't think," he says. "If he does—whenever he does—it's his father and Nina. He's more tied in with that than he ought to be, but it's a fact. Truman needs some kind of family. Too bad that's the only one he's got."

"*I'll take Manhattan, the Bronx and Staten . . . Island, too. It's lovely going through the zoo,*" sings Miss Wylie.

"Let's go down to the hotel," says Jack. "It's their night for *zuppa di pesce.* If we get a table outside, we can see Truman when he comes."

But our evening passes without him. Jack's gloom is Sibelian. We part early.

Ready for bed, I turn out the light, go to the window. Truman's description of the place is apt; I could be peering through a backdrop for *Cavalleria Rusticana.* Among the few souls still abroad in the piazza is Jack, leading the dogs.

8.31.53 Out early, I order an *espresso,* listen to Sunday bells, watch shopkeepers putting out racks of beach gear, Roman stripes, gimcrack ceramics. At the flat Jack's in shorts and a straw hat, mixing something in a bowl. We'll make a little *giro,* he says, around the headland to San Fruttuoso, a pebble beach where we won't be swamped by trippers down from Genoa. We load picnic supplies into a motorboat.

As we skid across the bay, the dogs stand at the prow like figureheads. Slowing down off San Fruttuoso, we can see that the Genoese have got there first. The beach is crowded with families under impromptu tents of poles and blankets, or gathered on the shady side of beached fishing boats. It's impossible to lie or sit on the hot melon-size stones for more than a minute. Portable radios squawk and screech, beach balls whizz overhead. The effluvia of blood sausage and purple onion tincture the Sabbath air. We make the best of it for an hour, then agree we've had it.

But the outboard motor won't turn over. Jack yanks until his arms are limp. Dogs yap, children shout advice, whole families, masticating in unison, watch us with sorrowing indifference. There's a shed at the end of the beach housing fishing craft and outboards. Jack tries to find help there. No luck. He comes back to say they're sending for a mechanic who lives halfway up the slope.

Since this man may not come for hours, Jack suggests I find a seat on the *motoscafo* about to make the run to Portofino. I'm reluctant, but he insists. Truman can't bear to come back to an empty house, he says, someone ought to be there.

I'm in the prow, studying the blue mountains beyond Rapallo when I spot a lone figure in a drifting rowboat: Truman. As the *motoscafo* cuts a swath through the still water, I wave my arms and shout over the spray. He waves back, motions toward the shore, begins to row. Disembarked, I wait at the landing.

"Where *were* you?" He pulls up the oars. "Where is everybody? There was no sign of life, anywhere." He tethers his boat to the quay, steps out, gives me a damp hug.

When we've gone halfway across the piazza, I become aware of someone bearing down on us. Slightly bent, this figure is wearing espadrilles, crisply pressed British officers' shorts, a white shirt.

"Truman! What luck to find you off the bat!"

"*Hel*-lo, Noel. Someone told me you'd be coming."

As I'm wondering what's behind the distinctly cool edge to Truman's greeting, we find chairs on a *caffè* terrace and order Cinzanos.

"I'm with Rex and Lilli," says Coward. "The house is rather *up*." He points to the slope opposite the Hotel Splendido. "This is my first stroll out. I hadn't imagined the place so small, but dear me it is entrancing."

His survey takes in the facades of boutiques and the sailing craft tied up at the seawall.

"Look—nannies in their Liberty blouses and plimsolls." He indicates two middle-aged gentlemen in canvas chairs on the afterdeck of a yawl. "East Grinstead, my dear, East Grinstead. What led you to this astonishing place, Truman?"

"Some people in Rome," says T. "They had the flat two summers ago."

"You came, sight unseen?"

"They had photographs."

"Nothing would do it justice, I suppose—the relations of things are so intimate and unexpected."

Coward looks over his shoulder: Half a dozen other people are out in the midday sun—a long-haired girl squinting into a Michelin guide; one fiftyish Italian in a beige silk suit; another in blue jeans and a shirt printed with a nautical symbol under letters spelling St.-Tropez; three Scandinavians, the tallest of whom could be Leif Ericson. "Well!" he says. "This *is* the place. But I dare not linger." He drains his aperitif. "The Harrisons are termagants about dining hours and there's still that fearful climb, in the jeep. Truman, my cherub, when can we meet?"

"Can you come to dinner? I live up there."

Coward raises his eyes to the flowerpots lined up on the

window ledges of Casa Capote. "I'd adore to, darling, but I'm promised to the Luces' and one simply doesn't say no to Madam Ambassador."

"When did *they* get here?"

"This morning, I believe. They're on a yacht." He points toward the marina. "The enormous one, with the limousine cradled on deck, wouldn't you know. Perhaps I could come by be*fore* dinner? About seven?"

He comes at seven, accompanied by a lady friend whose banalities, delivered nonstop and with an air of intellectual audacity, drive us to the windows, gasping for air.

"Look"—Coward is leaning, as I am, on a windowsill—"that sensational black one. It belongs to Arturo Lopez."

We watch the sleek craft head for open water.

". . . of course, when *that* happened," continues the voice behind us, "I knew it was time to call a halt. I don't mind being *used,* I can tell you, that's all part of the game, isn't it? But I do mind being exploited and that's the difference between the way we do things in D.C. and the way they do things here. . . ."

We keep to the windows, like people in a burning building.

"Noel," the voice says, finally, "we must bid these charming people good-bye. The launch will be waiting."

She wraps a filmy scarf about her neck. Half a dozen bracelets shimmy to the wrist of the hand she holds out to me. "I've so much enjoyed talking with you," she says.

By the time she has gone like a diminishing echo, we are plopped in chairs, shoes off. "I can't face it," says Truman. "That woman has undone me."

"Can't face what?" says Jack.

"I can't face pounding out one more quivering slab of *vitello.* Let's splurge, let's dine as God meant us to."

The restaurant he chooses is a hanging garden above the marina, open to the night air, which suddenly contains a rumor of autumn. When I see him shiver, I take off my jacket and put it over his shoulders. He starts to fish in the pockets.

"Hands off," I tell him. But he's already extracted the postcards I've written.

"Postcards are open letters," he says. "I want to know what you're saying about me."

"What if I've said nothing about you?"

"I wouldn't believe it."

"Believe what you want to believe," I tell him, and concentrate on the *Piatti di Giorno* as if it were a late canto of Ezra Pound's.

Midnight. Sodium light on the pastel facades makes them all of one pockmarked color. Jack has turned in. Truman and I are having a nightcap at a *caffè* when Coward approaches from the waterside, alone.

The Picture of Little T.C. in a Prospect . . . / 65

"That woman—heaven preserve us," he says. "I had no idea what I was about to inflict upon you. May I sit down?"

"What was your dinner like?" asks Truman.

"Torture, at first, exquisite and Chinese. Then Madam Clare began to speak . . . over her, under her, and straight through her. The rest of us took courage. But Clare, I'm afraid, tends rather to mind her tongue in front of Henry. I thought it touching, actually. One doesn't somehow think of her as a wife, anyone's."

This is the end of his report. What he really wants to talk about is writing, Truman's. "You know, I *adore* what you've done," he says, "that extraordinary way you have of putting a fantastic edge on perfectly ordinary things. How do you do it? In the course of a working day, for example, when in your mind you're not seeing anything unusual at all. Do you plan for it? Does it simply *come?*"

Truman gives him an impassive glance. "If it's there *to* come, I suppose. I don't go chasing it with a net. I don't add it to anything. I mean, I don't *add* it as you'd add an ingredient to soup. What else do you want me to say?"

"Nothing you don't care to say, my dear. But in spite of the widespread impression that there's nothing to support the notion, you and I know there's something called the professional secret. And the reason it re*mains* secret is because no one believes it, even when, as you and I might expect, it's spelled out for fair. All I'm asking is, what's yours?"

Truman takes a sip, looks toward the water, from which comes an undercurrent of several kinds of music.

"Well . . . *if,*" he says, "*if* I have this way . . ."

We wait for the pronouncement.

"Whatever it is, it's not worth talking about."

Coward turns to me. "*You* know what I mean. It's not an unforgivable thing to ask, now, is it?"

"Truman knows exactly what you're saying," I tell him, "but he wants to let on he doesn't."

(Under his breath, Truman sings, *"Hair is curly, teeth are pearly. You're some ugly chile."*)

"The thing he's afraid of," I continued, "and God knows why, is what he's got most of: animal intelligence, about the way people think, what they exist for, how they scheme to keep themselves alive. So far, those things don't show much in his books. Most people don't suspect they're even there, like some secret he's willing to be found out in but won't himself do anything to assert. He's afraid of it because he doesn't want to be responsible for it. He wants to walk a tightrope, spin glass."

(*"Is it Granada I see,"* sings Truman, *"or only Asbury Park?"*)

"There's a question: How can you continue to be the Venetian glass nephew if it should get about that your real gift is horse sense?"

Bored, or pretending to be, Truman goes on humming

to himself. Our conversation, as Coward recognizes, has nowhere to go.

Later, walking back, I tell Truman he's been rude, that Coward had said nothing to warrant such abrupt dismissal.

"Ho . . . hummmm," he says. "The sad old dear, why should I tell *him* anything?"

9.1.53   Less crotchety, I hope, Truman leaves his typewriter midmorning and suggests we go for a swim. Half a mile out into the waters of the Tyrrhenian, he cuts the motor. Legs and arms dangling, we drift and talk—about money, his money, because he's come to the point, he says, when he won't have any.

"Didn't that movie with John Huston bring you a pretty penny?"

"A small fortune," he says, "and it's gone. My father convinced me he needed it. He was, as they say, sliding into bankruptcy. God knows what else, Nina the way she is."

"All of it?"

"Every last dollar."

"Wasn't that being generous to a fault?"

"Maybe. Oh, what the hell. I'm not out for stars. When do you get a chance to do a good deed that *is* a good deed? He's a proud man. I had it, he knew I had it. He's been good to me, a far sight better than my real father ever was."

The surrounding mountains are clear and grainy, like stones under a magnifying glass. I feel I'm afloat in the center of a brimming cup.

Truman asks, perhaps dutifully, about Dylan. I tell him I'm on my way to Wales with one purpose—to dissuade him from making another American tour.

"I'd hope so," he says. "More than one person has told me you carry him around on a lettuce leaf. Haven't you found out what those grubbing English writers are like?"

"Dylan's a Welshman."

The Picture of Little T.C. in a Prospect . . . / 69

"No difference. They go from the nipple to the bottle without changing diapers. Why spend half your life taking care of someone whose mind is on nothing but a pint of beer and a piece of tail? Why should you join a poor man's pub crawl to the grave?"

"Dylan's not poor. He makes more money than I do, a lot more."

"All the more reason to quit playing wet nurse to an overgrown baby who'll destroy every last thing he can get his hands on, including himself."

I don't *have* to, I tell him. In this case, I've wanted to. But no more.

"I'll believe that a month from now."

A speedboat careens across our prow and leaves us rocking.

"You know what your trouble is, Malcolm?"

"Besides ulcers, poverty, stupidity?"

"I'm dead serious. The sad and undeniable thing about you is: you'd rather be a martyr than a success."

Back on even keel, we drift with currents in the changing view.

"I've got a chance to turn 'House of Flowers' into a musical," he says. "The hard part is, once you start working, once I start working, on something that can't ever be my own, I lose touch with the part that *is* my own, like bad money driving out good."

"Why do you do it, then?"

"Opportunities come along," he says. "There's a lot of that bad money involved, or the promise of it. Why not? Doesn't your Dylan Thomas spend time on lots more things than poetry? Documentaries? BBC programs? Didn't I even read that he has a play?"

Through sailing craft at anchor, we reach the seawall, cross to an outdoor place for lunch. Coward, the most elegant of white hunters in buckled khaki shorts and silk fly-button shirt, comes by. We pull up a chair. Truman tells him I'm en route to Wales.

"Wales!" he says. "There's precious little sun in Wales. Come to Jamaica, do what I do. The minute I get to my dear Blue Harbour, I put a shroud over the typewriter and anything else that suggests work and mesmerize myself—for five full days I bake like a lizard in the sand. It's an initiation, a conversion. Then I ignore the sun and get on with it. Oh, except for what you might call a little cosmetic refreshment, say half an hour after breakfast. In fact, my house is for sale. You can buy it this minute. For a bolt-hole, it's perfect."

Truman turns to me. "There's your chance," he says.

"You mean, 'Daylight come and me wanna go home'?"

"Isn't it heaven, Port Maria?" says Coward. "Those green bluffs dropping to the water? I'm told your angelic countrymen are willing to pay a smashing price merely because it's my home. I can't find it in my heart to deny them."

Catching sight of the Harrisons outside a shop, he rises. "Bless me," he says, "I must be off. I told Rex and Lilli I'd be home before they were. So it must be—*arrivederci*."

Soon it's time for my own departure. Truman drives me to the station in Santa Margherita in the midget convertible he keeps in a garage nearby. "Poor Noel," he says, "he wants to be historical and he knows how ephemeral his sort of thing is. I wish you'd have found a chance to mention his 'contribution to the theater' or something high-sounding like that. I tend to take him for granted. He feels it."

My train for Paris slides in.

"When you coming home, Truman?"

"Not until I absolutely have to, maybe tomorrow."

From the compartment window I see him as he was seven years ago: a chunky kid in T-shirt and shorts, alone in a crowd, glasses pushed up to his forehead, waving good-bye.

"Was delighted, and startled," he wrote three weeks later, "to have your letter this morning: It seems as though you were here only a weekend ago—now you are back in Boston or Connecticut or New York: wherever it is you *do* live. Perhaps it's only that time is so peculiar here—it's beautiful now, the piazza deserted and the sea like 'shook foil.' I have been working very well (for a change). . . .

"The dogs are full of fleas—we've spent all morning bathing them in some odd South African ointment. We still have no carnet for the car—heaven knows how we'll leave here, or when. Not until the middle of October, in any event.

"I hope you had a good time at Château Frontenac; you *do* go to the damnedest places—I wonder if anyone has ever had, over a protracted period, a more extraordinary love life: possibly Marilyn Monroe.

"Had a fine offer last week from Carol Reed to do the film script for *A High Wind in Jamaica*. Does it make you happy to learn that I turned it down?

"It was wonderful seeing you, having you here—I always love you very much. Write me."

They would be soon leaving Portofino. "I think for St. Moritz," wrote Truman, "(from sea to snow). I have finished *House of Flowers* and am waiting to hear about the composer, etc. You will be rather amazed when you hear who it is—someone I know you love, but would not associate with me. A very good choice, I think—though it may seem odd at first. I won't tell you, because I'm not sure about it.

"The weather here is wonderful—Jack still goes swimming, but I've given it up. Am sharpening my ice skates instead."

Truman's skepticism about my efforts with Dylan Thomas was well-founded, his prophecy fulfilled. When Dylan came to New York in October, he concealed from anyone who might have helped him the fact that he was seriously ill, and died just as physicians in England had told him he would. Truman had no knowledge of this when, in November, he wrote from Switzerland that he was "snowbound in the Alps—it is true—the earliest snowstorm in Swiss history and *we* have to get bogged down in it." Learning of Dylan's death when he got to Paris, he wrote me a consoling note at once, unaware that, as he acknowledged my bereavement, he was about to experience a bereavement of his own.

To come to grips, perhaps to peace, with the fact of Dylan's death, I got away as soon as I could and spent weeks alone on an island in the Bahamas. Back in New York by early January, I went to the Drake Hotel to keep a luncheon appointment with Carson McCullers.

"Bad news," she said, "Nina Capote has killed herself. Truman's come flying back from Paris."

I went to a phone in the lobby; his line was busy. When I'd left the table to call several times more without success, Carson suggested I come with her, to Gypsy Rose Lee's, where she was a house guest, and phone Truman from there. Leaning heavily on her cane, she followed me out to the street. I had to all but lift her bodily into a taxi.

"Is it 153 East 63rd Street," she said aloud, "or 351?"

The driver, swiveling, gave us a hard, flat glance and drove to 153.

"I think this is it," said Carson. "I seem to remember the door."

Inside, as bursts of typewriter noises resounded from the floor above, she settled herself at a table in an alcove that had walls painted, and boldly signed, by Vertès. Nodding at the ceiling, she said: "Gypsy, another novel. She'll be down when the kid gets home from school. If you go into the kitchen and open the end cabinet, you'll find my private supply of J. W. Dant. There's a wall phone you can use. Tell Truman to call when he'd like to talk."

Truman's voice was weary. He'd be staying at the apartment with his father; he was concerned about me. Some of the stories he'd heard about Dylan's death were "truly morbid." I told him not to believe them, that the truth was bad enough. He said he'd phone when the situation at home was clear.

I took Carson her drink. "What did he say?" she asked. "Did he sound sad or did he sound relieved?"

"Sad."

"Did you mention me?"

"No."

"Just as well," she said. "He's mad at me. He accuses me of making trouble and then leaving it. He just can't stand the idea that I knew Newton long before he did."

The Picture of Little T.C. in a Prospect . . . | 73

* * *

Two weeks later he phoned me at my office. He was having some people in that night, he said, after the late show at a nightclub called the Latin Quarter. I must come.

"But," he said, "first you have to guess who the party's *for.*"

"Garbo?"

"Not her kind of thing."

"Isak Dinesen? Billie Holiday?"

"Not even close. Christine, she's an absolute dear."

"Christine who?"

"Jorgenson. Actually, she's sort of heartbreaking, but spunky, too. You'll understand when you see her. Call for me here around eleven."

The program that evening at the Poetry Center was a joint reading by Richard Wilbur and Richard Eberhart. As soon as the doors were open, I could see that their presence in New York had attracted so many old friends of theirs and mine that the occasion took on the feeling of a class reunion. At a reception afterward, I forgot about Truman until midnight, when I phoned to tell him I wouldn't be coming to his party.

"Why *not?*" he said. "What's so scintillating where *you* are?"

Poets, I told him, old friends.

"Malcolm, my pet"—the acid in his voice would melt wire— "that's cornball stuff. You goin' be one li'l cornball *all* your life?"

"Probably."

"All I have to say is this: You *be* there, hear?" The phone clicked.

When I got to the Latin Quarter about one, the maître d' took me to a big round table where three people were already seated—Donald Windham, a woman I recognized as the comedienne Alice Pearce, a man I didn't know. Truman came in with Judith Anderson, Jane and Paul Bowles, and Oliver Smith. The overture to the late show precluded conversation.

Miss Jorgenson, as thin as a coatrack on which someone had hung an evening gown, came out singing "Getting to Know You" in a half-croaking voice and moved through an upsy-daisy patty-cake-man choreography on high heels that seemed about to collapse. This was followed by other numbers chosen, apparently, to suit an androgynous register. Bizarre and pathetic, the performance was finally inof- fensive, almost winning in its bravery against odds.

In a babushka and a camel's hair wraparound coat, sniffling into a balled-up handkerchief, Miss Jorgenson joined our table. She'd caught this awful cold, she said. Perhaps we could tell by her voice? Nevertheless, she told us, the management was thinking of extending her engagement if, that is, she would agree to a cut in salary.

A hand loaded with rings reached across to hers and covered it firmly.

"My dear," said Judith Anderson. "An artist never, *never* agrees to a reduction in salary. It is undignified, it is unnecessary. I speak as one who has every reason to know." With an air of unchallenged rectitude, she surveyed the room and lifted her crème de menthe. Miss Jorgenson stared.

Libby Holman and Montgomery Clift were on the way, Truman told us. When they got here, we'd all go on to his place.

"Gosh," said Miss Jorgenson, "I'm plumb sorry as anything, but I can't go anywhere tonight." She fished a second damp handkerchief out of a pocket. "The only place for this little girl is bed."

Called to the phone, Truman came back to say that the others had given up. Suddenly bored by his sniffling star and the petering out of everything else, he called for the check.

"She's even sadder than I thought," he said, as we settled into a taxi. "Six months, she'll be playing carnivals."

Asleep in Truman's guest bed, I was awakened by the sounds of something being munched on. The night-table clock said 3:06. All the lights were on. Truman was sitting up, newspapers all about him, poking fragments of peanut brittle into his mouth as he perused the gossip column of the *Daily Mirror*.

"Want to see an item," he said, "about yours truly?"

I put a pillow over my head.

"Mail it to me."

As Truman began to assume the role of mascot to café society, we began to drift further apart. Since the friends we shared were few, and the people he was coming to know belonged to that channel of

New York life where art, high fashion, and big money flow together, our common ground was shrinking. On winter mornings when, waking late, he'd be scanning the papers to see what Cholly Knickerbocker or Leonard Lyons had to say about him, I'd be scanning lecture notes on Emily Dickinson or Herman Melville in the halls of the University of Connecticut nearly two hundred miles away. When we did meet, the occasion was apt to be one at which, like a country cousin or, as he once put it, "family," I'd be dutifully asked to come along.

One of these, costing me a night's sleep, nevertheless afforded me a glimpse into that world where he would soon be permanently sealed.

Like his first reading at the Poetry Center, Truman's second was sold out in advance, to no one's surprise, least of all his. But somehow this did not bolster his confidence or inure him to the intense stage fright that always seemed at odds with his temperament. When I reached the Green Room, his eyes were as frightened as a lost dog's, his hands sweaty cold.

"You're seeing the last of me," he said.

"How so?"

"I'm going back to Paris. Jack's still in the hotel there, with the dogs. He's had it, he says, and I can't blame him. Listen, there's a party afterwards you have to come to."

"Tonight?"

"It's Harold Arlen's birthday."

"I have a class to teach at eight in the morning, five hours from here."

His eyes narrowed. "I happen to know," he said, "that teaching school in the sticks has not prevented you from enjoying certain other entertainments I could mention."

After the reading, another virtuoso performance that began in a low key and ended in clamor, Truman went ahead while I stayed in my office for an hour of paper work. Then, the only thing on my mind was what I was going to say about Herman Melville to my eight o'clock class, most of whom were already asleep in their dormitory beds. It was midnight when I got to Harold Arlen's. A bushy-haired man showed me where to put my coat—on a bed on which lay the playwright William Inge, sound asleep. "Bill's resting, if you know what I mean," said the bushy-haired man. "I'm a stranger here myself—George Kaufman."

As we shook hands, Truman appeared. "Anyone you'd like to meet right off?"

I told him I'd like a drink and he showed me where to get it. When I could look around, I first noticed Jack's ex-wife sprawled against a mound of pillows and looking rather like one of the "French dolls" the girls of 1925 kept on their beds. Thin and bony—she would die of cancer within the year—she smiled a detached smile and lit a black cigarette with a gold tip. Standing at the end of the sofa was Marlene Dietrich, encircled by the arms of Montgomery Clift. Mutually transfixed, they appeared to exchange monosyllables now and then but, for the most part, simply stood there, staring into one another's eyes. Dietrich was wearing something less like fabric than molten silver. Clift's suit was too big for him; he seemed to have shrunk in it. Very slowly and deliberately, they would kiss, holding one another like praying mantises.

A second drink and I knew I'd missed my last train. Giddy in the prospect of a night without sleep, I moved toward Janet Flanner—the only person there, excepting Truman, with whom I'd previously exchanged as much as a word. But at that moment Harold Arlen sat down at the piano and the room froze. He had a new song for us, he announced, a song for "Judy's" next picture. In a voice that scratched at every phrase, he began his ballad of the man that got away. In the echoed bravos and long applause that followed, I found Truman at my side.

"Having a good time?" he asked.

"There *is* someone I'd like to talk with," I said. "Janet Flanner."

"*Suivez-moi.*"

But we did not make it through the crowd. Abe Burrows had replaced Arlen at the piano and *his* show had begun. "What you all want to hear?" he called, and sent a ripple across the keyboard. "What you all want Abie to play?"

Dietrich's voice rang out. "The Holland song, Abe, play the Holland song!" To a general murmur of approval, Burrows ran his chubby fingers over the keys once more. "*Why don't the boys,*" he sang, and made googly eyes around the room, *"why don't the boys take their fingers out of the dikes and go"*—a dirty chuckle here—*"and go, and go on home to their girls."*

Dietrich led the applause, urging him into a sequence of his own show tunes, to which, from the moment, no one paid the least attention.

Three thirty. In the diminished company, Truman sat on the floor, his head against Harold Arlen's knee. The rest of us, a circle of stockinged feet on a coffee table, sipped brandy and waited for someone to say something. Framed in a doorway leading to a library, Dietrich and Clift, stiff and upright as dolls in a box, prolonged their catatonic clinch.

Daylight found me dozing through lower Connecticut on the milk train. By seven thirty, bending to my notes at the counter of a campus diner, I bit into a powdered doughnut and marked a footnote: "The incest motive in *Pierre*, for example, might certainly have come to Melville from Webster or Ford, but it is still more reminiscent of the sentimental, the Gothic, or in general the romantic school."

The Grass Harp, its career brief, its succès d'estime modest, nevertheless had provided Truman with an entry into the theater. He hoped now to make a more solid place there with his musical comedy version of "House of Flowers," a short story based on his experiences in Haiti. This production was scheduled for the end of the year, most of which Truman would spend abroad and out of range. Except for what I read in the papers and news magazines, I had no word of him, a circumstance that promised to become permanent. Old friends like me were being replaced by show business acquaintances who, in turn, would soon themselves be displaced as Truman's affections turned to individuals in the international society of the conspicuously rich.

I followed this ascension, if that's what it was, as news services reported it, trying to spot the telling facts embedded in the hype of columnists' fancies. One day's report would have him ensconced like a baby Voltaire in the ateliers of the Ile-de-France; another would have him pillowed on the afterdeck of a Greek shipping tycoon's yacht at anchor off Skyros; still another would have him weekending in this or that great house, jollying up the gentry with his wit and wisdom, playing *charades en travesti,* and otherwise being "seen with."

Crediting no more than half of these reports, I still wondered what had so swiftly deflected Truman's obsession with working space and working hours, an obsession that had governed him through all the years of our acquaintance. Knowing where he was, I could not tell where he was going; and so took comfort in the fact that he had never in his life embarked without a well-calculated destination. Yet what was the purpose of this extended cruise among the Isles of the Blest? His milieu of playwrights, designers, editors, and movie producers had no doubt been a source of professional advantage and of measurable reward. What would he get from the notoriously rich that he wouldn't have to pay for?

Midsummer, he was back in New York and I was bound for Italy and England. On the day before I sailed, we met in the early August hush of the Plaza's Oak Room. Approaching his table, I could feel the weight of his disapproval.

"What's your problem?" I asked.

"Have you never been told, my dear Malcolm, that one never, never wears a bow tie with a button-down collar?"

"I only break the rules I know," I told him. "That's one of them."

Chin in hand, he leaned on the table in a caricature of weariness. "Something wrong?"

"I can't work," he said. "I haven't worked in months, except for the effort of tearing up a novel I'd almost completed. With my two bare hands."

He snapped his swizzle stick in two, then in four. His drink was untouched. "I hope you haven't made plans for dinner," he said. "If I go home, I'm trapped."

After a meal at The Colony, we went on to The Blue Angel. In both places he took the attentions of people who came to our table with an unruffled air of noblesse oblige. Someone told him his movie was "mad, *mad* fun." Someone reported what C.C. said to Boo-boo in the ladies' room at Bergdorf—"actually, she'd had this fainting spell at Ohrbach's and rushed uptown, in case it was serious."

The Picture of Little T.C. in a Prospect . . . / 79

These chirpings were counterpoint. On Truman's mind was a burden of doubt and gloomy self-assessment. Six years into a public career as a novelist, he had begun to lose ground to newer and more robust talents, and to find himself beyond the pale of even those critics who, charitably ignoring the circus tactics of promotion, had once read him soberly and reviewed him favorably. Between the man of letters and the man about town, the balance had gone badly out of whack; the boy of shining promise had been overtaken by the boulevardier. Truman understood this, I learned, a little better than I did. Yet his contempt for the world of "serious" literature and its judges remained lively, and his aversion to that kind of academic squalor where the lares and penates are the *TLS* and the diaper pail, the *OED* and the candle in the Chianti jug was pronounced. But this had not prevented him from reading either those "gray people," as he called them, and their "drab quarterlies," or the collections of literary criticism in which it was essential that, one way or the other, he figure.

Was it already the fact that Truman as a public commodity had caused Truman as a writer to be closed out? Respectful of even the most dronelike of my colleagues, I knew they still made distinctions between aspiration and ambition, genius and talent, achievement and exhibitionism. Within a decade such distinctions would be seriously blurred. But in August 1954 Truman's aesthetic pretensions were fast losing credibility, and he knew it. The portrait of the artist as a precocious Little Lord Fauntleroy had been intriguing, amusing, and acceptable; the portrait of the artist as a lapdog in the salons of Sutton Place and the XVIe Arrondissement was not.

As we were about to leave the nightclub, he took from his pocket a white envelope and handed it across the table. "My little bon voyage present," he said. "Post it the minute you get to Venice." The envelope was addressed:

Miss Katharine Hepburn
Palazzo Poppadopoli
1365 San Polo
Venezia

"You'll love her," he said. "She's staying there with Constance Collier while she makes a movie, about this old maid schoolteacher who goes to Venice and gets laid by Rossano Brazzi. My note says they should ask you to lunch or something, and that's what they'll do."

House of Flowers opened at the end of December, went tottering into the new year, and collapsed. Beautiful and vapid, it had too much star-studded weight to carry, too much scenery, by Oliver Messel, to justify, too much business to do in the confines of a creaking veranda in Port-au-Prince. Deserted in midcareer by its original director Peter Brook and by its choreographer George Balanchine, it arrived on Broadway as "an extended vaudeville act," as Truman said later, "for Miss Pearl Bailey."

Truman was not aware that I had attended the opening night, when, three nights later, I waited for him in the Green Room. Arriving promptly at seven (he had insisted on a rehearsal), he proceeded to take charge of lights, amplifiers, curtains, acoustics. To make sure that just the particularly flattering nuance of pink light would strike his face, just the right shadows, he asked me to assume his place on stage while he studied the effects from different parts of the empty auditorium.

"Pretend you're reading from my book," he called down from the last row. "I want to see how close I can hold it . . . without using my glasses . . . and still show my face."

I followed his directions.

"In your *left* hand," he called. "I want my right one free for gestures."

Impatient with these diddling adjustments, I spoke low enough, or so I thought, to be heard only by stagehands. "Truman, baby," I said, sotto voce, "this ain't *Camille.*"

"Who *said* it wasn't?" Truman called out. "Let me see what happens if you put the mike a little to the left."

Just before curtain time Harold Arlen came backstage, where, from the wings, we listened to Truman's reading and watched his performance. "I love that young man," said Arlen. "One of the most enchanting souls I've ever encountered. He's very fond of you. What's going to become of him?"

The Picture of Little T.C. in a Prospect . . . / 81

A roar of laughter interrupted us. Truman, waiting for quiet, glanced our way.

"Why do you ask?"

"I'm not certain he can take care of all that talent. Are you?"

"I used to be. Now I'm not. . . ."

"But you believe in him."

"In some ways, more than he believes in himself."

My presence at this third reading of Truman's was unofficial—a response to his request that I be "on hand" and that I introduce him. Dylan's death had taken the heart out of any thought of satisfaction I might still obtain from my work at the Poetry Center and I had handed in my resignation months before. No longer a weekly commuter to New York, I now gave my attention to teaching and to writing down memories of Dylan's career in America. By late spring of 1955 it was apparent to my publisher, if not yet to me, that I had the makings of a book. After delivering the manuscript late in July, I went to Europe on a seven-week trip that began and ended in Naples. There I boarded a ship carrying cargo and ninety passengers on a fifteen-day crossing to Hoboken. Leghorn was our first port of call. Next day we docked in Genoa, where, we were told, the ship would remain in port for eighteen hours. Already familiar with Genoa, whose charms I tended to equate with Buffalo's, I quit the ship, took a taxi to the *stazione,* a train to Santa Margherita, a bus to Portofino. The piazza was gray and deserted; unswept leaves lay matted in the gutters of the colonnade; the boutiques were boarded up; a white dog on the seawall slept on his paws. Truman was right. The wind on the marina did give the effect of "shook foil." Sitting down on one of the few chairs left outside "our" *caffè,* I ordered a negrone. Looking up, I could see that the windows of Casa Capote were closed, the geraniums on the sills left to wither.

Saddened by the crepuscular sense of everything, I watched the skittering leaves, studied the lifeless buildings, then opened the copy of *Time* I'd brought from the ship. Turning pages without reading them, I sensed that something had caught my eye. Flipping back, I saw what it was: Truman, smiling his big baby's smile, dancing in the arms of Marilyn Monroe. Unprepared for the little bolt of rage that ran through me, I stared at the marina for one long moment, then took a postcard from my pocket and, with a pen that crackled, sent my friend a message. Its burden was simple, designed to scathe: Was *this* the best hope of American letters? I asked. Was *this* the Portrait of the Artist as a Young Man? "Joyce's motto was, Silence, exile, and cunning," I said. "What's *yours?*" and signed it, "Reader of *Time*."

Almost tipped from my chair by a rush of wind, I took shelter in an arcade under scribbles of lightning, buckets of rain. Waiting for the squall to blow itself out, I put my postcard in a box and, for emphasis, clicked the lid. A few minutes later the sun came out like a door opened. Already nibbled by regret, I crossed a pavement steaming gold and climbed into a bus for Genoa and the long voyage home.

A moment of outrage had tricked me into the ranks of Truman's detractors. With time to suffer so hard a fall from grace, I began to dwell on my apostasy, probe my motives, and to find them without charity or honor. If friendship had indeed given me prerogatives of judgment, I should have exercised these long ago, or shut up. Truman was responsible to himself, not to my expectations. The ties that bound us had become a bit thin, but there was still no reason to further raddle them with sarcasm which, I had to recognize, was as much a plea for attention as it was an act of judgment.

His response came in October, when he wrote: "Despite the (to me) startlingly unjust contents of your Portofino card, I hopefully assume it was intended as some sort of good-friend, stern-critic comment. If it was meant otherwise, and your words were weighed, then frankly, dear heart, I don't know what the hell you are talking about. You have, and will always have, a most particular place in my affections. If I have disappointed you as an artist (as you suggest), that is one thing; but certainly as a person, as a friend, I have done nothing to deserve your misguided candor. If memory serves, this is the second time you have rounded on me; on the previous occasion I correctly deciphered the clumsy hand of a malevolent informer. But I am not a detective by profession, and so shall have to leave the clues to this latest attack untraced. However, rest in the knowledge that you are on the popular side; my stock in all quarters is very low, and if the number of folk I have apparently offended were laid end to end they would girdle the globe.

"I've had a quiet, working summer. Moreover, I lost thirty pounds: Am just a svelte bag of golden bones. We're going back to the city next week.

"Please reconsider, and write your perhaps unworthy, but still loving, very loving—T."

This was more than I deserved; and when my memoir of the last years of Dylan Thomas was published in November, his message was among the first to arrive: "I THINK YOUR BOOK IS WONDERFUL. LOVE TRUMAN." The telegram itself was an index: Friendship had been reduced to its offices.

Nearly ten years had passed since Truman, to the music of harp strings, had stepped into my life, and now I would not see him for three more. Geography was partly responsible for this, but the larger factor was his apparent fascination with a stratum of society whose well-heeled and happy few found him sufficiently astonishing, amusing, and ornamental to take him, as time would bitterly tell, in.

Missing Truman, I could only applaud the success which his failures in the theater did not impede, and observe with some degree of concern his membership, honorary though it might be, in a segment of the population so rarefied as to render him sacrosanct. Still at a point in my life where I did not know that dear friends went away, I had yet to learn that proximity is nine tenths of friendship, absence the swamp where all the gratuitous bearers of resentment blithely cluster and breed. Without "my" Truman, I began unconsciously to accept the image that belonged to anybody. The fact that I had long since predicted the ultimate disparity of man and mask was of no account and little comfort. Out of touch with one, I was alternatively entertained and appalled by the public parade of the other and, like Harold Arlen, asked myself, What will become of him?

Meanwhile we existed for one another by tokens and missed connections: a postcard, written at a window in Leningrad overlooking the Neva on New Year's Eve; a snapshot of him and a bulldog ("my own *force de frappe*") from Switzerland; a note from Rome. One summer day in London, writing to him in Spain from a room on the second floor of the Connaught Hotel, I did not know that he was at the same moment writing to me in Boston from a room on the third floor of the Connaught Hotel. Through hit and miss, one thing about him remained constant: his generosity in sharing his friends with his friends. In this, as in his gritty devotion to his work, he operated unobtrusively and pulled strings—making sure that I would meet one of "my best Russian pals" at 1 Pirogovska Street, Odessa; that, when I went to Ireland, I would have a letter of introduction to John ("craggy and funny and wildly intelligent") Huston; that I would call on Adlai Stevenson, "a dear; he brought me a teddy bear all the way from Alaska."

One August day aboard the little S.S. *Hermes* docked in Piraeus, I was having a prelunch drink with the English novelist Rose Macaulay when Diana Cooper came into the lounge where we were sitting. Lady Diana was costumed in a closely pleated white skirt, a naval blazer with insignia on its breast pocket, and a cap so heavy with "scrambled eggs" it might have belonged to an admiral. "Rose! Look!" she said as, like a little girl, she spun around to show how her skirt flared out. But Miss Macaulay, peering into a handbook on Mycenaean wall paintings, missed the performance, which, in the circumstance, I was left to applaud. At six that evening, after we had all gone our separate ways in Athens, I was handed a note to the effect that Lady Diana Cooper and Lady Juliet Duff would be pleased were I to join them for dinner. Puzzled—I'd been seeing them on land and sea for ten days—I met them, as they had proposed, in the lounge and learned what the sudden formality was about. "We had tea with Cecil Beaton at the Gran Bretagne," said Lady Diana. "Cecil had a note from Truman Capote, *sternly* instructing him to see that we looked you up. We kept our mouths shut and said we would."

"My son Michael adores him," said Lady Juliet. "Is he really so much the tyrant?"

Responding to a postcard from the Villa Meltemi, Paros, Greece, I told Truman I'd be coming to Europe as soon as I had finished my work with the Ford Foundation, an assignment involving the choice of writers to whom the foundation was about to grant large sums of money. His return letter promised an end to a long breach: He would be giving a reading at the Poetry Center in December, another in Cambridge, for *The Harvard Advocate.*

"Did I tell you," he wrote, "that I have a short novel (*Breakfast at Tiffany's*) coming out in October? Very curious to have your reaction.

"Delighted about your sinecure-sounding Ford Foundation chores. Maybe you can manage to pour some of the gravy on my barren plate. Lord knows no one needs *aid* more than me. We will be here until September 1st. Would love to see you on Paros, but perhaps we will connect in Venice. . . . Anyway, I'm glad to have you back in my life, for you've been sorely missed. Because you know I love you a great good deal. . . ."

To be back in Truman's life, I would soon learn, was simply to be on call; to witness, if not to swell, his progress; to attend far more than to participate. When the editors of the *Advocate* asked me to introduce the reading he was to give in December, I told them he needed no introduction, that my presence on the platform would be supernumerary, and reported as much to Truman.

"On the whole," he wrote from Willow Street, Brooklyn, "I rather wish you would introduce me: it quietens an audience and focuses their attention—last year, at Chicago, they decided not to have an introduction, and I suppose it was 'effective,' but it took me ten minutes to get the audience in a listening mood. However, do what you think best." What I thought best was irrelevant.

At the window of his Boston hotel room, I watched dark figures crossing the bird-tracked snow of Copley Square and waited for Truman to emerge from the shower the noise of which, unalleviated by song, had now been drumming for five minutes. Half an hour earlier I had myself crossed the square in a mood of trepidation balanced by curiosity. But this was all dispersed at a glance; three years ago might have been yesterday. I could see that Truman had gained some weight, lost some hair; that he dressed with a conservatism in which I could spot no touch of sartorial heresy. But my deeper curiosity held. He was much richer, I knew, but I wondered if he were wiser. Did his strange turning toward the moneyed and powerful of this world represent merely a sunflowerlike tropism or was it a privileged observer's means of acquisition? "Little T., who—bet your boots—wastes not, wants not," had been his self-characterization twelve years ago. But that was at a time when, overtaken by an illness, he had made a writer's most of it. Could he say as much for something *he* pursued and overtook? The noise of the shower ceased.

"English," he said. The room was suddenly redolent of musk and obscure flora. "I buy it in London, a little shop in Jermyn Street."

Putting on a sort of truncated dressing gown, a black velvet *le smoking* that came barely to his waist, he went to a serving table in a corner and began dropping ice into glasses. "This thing must be seven or eight years old." He fingered a still-shiny lapel. "Remember Jack's crazy little apartment . . . that subarctic toilet in the hall? One day . . . I was by myself, in February, I think . . . I was wearing this and nothing else, *noth*ing else, not so much as a ribbon, when I went to the can, pulled the chain . . . remember? . . . and started back into the apartment only to find I'd locked myself out. The hallway was freezing, me in bare feet. What to do? I rapped on doors. Not a peep. Then I went down to that Chinese laundry . . . a sign on the door: owner sick, pick up laundry at some address on Third Avenue. The sidewalk by the schoolyard was full of wet snow, traffic splashing by, people in boots and galoshes. Know what I did? I walked the length of that block, jaybird naked except for this . . . and got to the cigar store on the corner, walked in, borrowed a dime, made my phone call, and went *back* to the place as if I were in no more hurry than someone on the way to the dentist. Scotch?"

I took the drink and bided my time. I had questions for Truman, but not now. The important thing was that the man I knew, coming easily into focus, had sent a hundred published images spinning into a world I didn't know.

We went to the *Advocate*'s cocktail party; we went to dinner at the home of his old friend Frances McFadden, where, in deepest Cambridge, we broke bread with the Robert Lowells and the Mark De Wolfe Howes and repaired to a drawing room with a multipaned window that looked out upon a whited garden. Our brandy glasses reflected the log fire toward which Truman held out his hands. "Come back to the hotel with me," he said. "I'm cold all over."

In the taxi I became aware that he was trembling. "You coming down with something?"

"It's been this way for days, fright, like something lurking."

I took off my gloves. "Here, let me rub your hands."

Like a child offering a kitten, he held them out. They were ice cold.

"That's better," he said. In the rearview mirror the driver's eyes met mine, and turned away.

Back in the hotel room he put on his smoking jacket and snuggled into the pillows of a sofa. "Make mine a double," he said, as I poured nightcaps. A television set, pictures without sound, caught my peripheral vision but seemed no part of his. "I leave it on for company," he said, "the way kids listen to music they don't hear. *Well.*" He raised his glass. "Here's to Cambridge, and its furnished souls."

"I want to know some things, Truman. Answer me if you want to, don't if you don't."

The look he fixed on me as I took the other end of the sofa was lofty with forbearance.

"You spend half your life these days—more, for all I know—with people who travel in their own sleek planes and their Silver Clouds, who keep empty villas around the Mediterranean, shooting boxes in Argyll, bank accounts in Zurich or Grand Cayman, people who own the earth from which they're insulated as completely as though they lived in time capsules. What's in it for you?"

"I had to know, to—"

"Know *what?*"

"Keep your shirt on," he said. "I simply had to know what it was like. Years and years I'd wondered: What if you woke up in the morning, so rich you were famous for it, being rich. What if you had your orange juice, read your paper, finished your coffee, all the while knowing that if there was anything to buy you could buy it, any place to go, you could go there, today. Would you make life into a game? Manipulate people like children with an ant farm? What would absolutely limitless means do to your appetites? Would you get a yen for experience per se? Sex? Food? Power? Would you buy only those things—Fabergé eggs, solid-gold putters, first folios,

Marie Antoinette's bed and chamber pot, things that other people *couldn't?* Would you try a quiet little murder or two, a little indulgence in *acte gratuit*, just to see if you could get away with it?"

"So?"

"So, I've found out what I wanted to know."

"Which is?"

"Which is that there's nothing much *to* find out. The rich are as bored with themselves as you are, as I am—children, without the imagination of children. That's the thing squelched first, imagination. It's bred out of them as carefully as manners and a taste for pheasant and truffles is bred into them. Then comes distrust—not the distrust a king might have for his courtiers, say; that's expected, the king is the king, the rules are understood . . . the kind of distrust that overtakes people who know themselves only by what other people think of them, or by what they suppose they think. *You've* seen the look. They have it by the time they're eleven years old. A man walking down the street in East Hampton, say . . . he's wearing chino shorts, a blue shirt, espadrilles. A glance, and you know he's worth ten million dollars because he's offering you ten million dollars' worth of training to disguise the fact in the very moment of advertising it. The question in his mind is, do you recognize the deception? That's what his glance your way is heavy with. When he sees that you do, he's had his high for the day. All those glitzy bashes you read about . . . benefits, charity balls . . . rituals, exorcisms to banish the curse of banality. But the thing is, those people aren't monsters. They're just as awful in their little ways as anybody else, as nice as anybody else. They may spend their lives clipping coupons and scouting tax shelters, making marriages that look like closed corporations and all that, but one way or another they build the Taj Mahal and provide for its maintenance. It's only a matter of scale, the same ambitions everyone has, with the difference in visible rewards. Once you catch the signals under the backgammon board, you've caught it all, you know it all."

"But you knew it all, ten years ago."

"Knew it, yes, the way everybody knows. But knowing by seeing, being, *having* it, there's a distinction. One hair's breadth, maybe, but that's what I'm talking about: The hair's breadth difference that will someday give me a book that will rattle teeth like the *Origin of Species*."

"You're not kidding yourself?"

"How so?"

"Kidding yourself that all you're up to is a little research on the reservation? a little fieldwork in the hogans? measuring the last of a Tricker oxford, the thickness of gold on a Coromandel screen, the angle of a Herbert Johnson pinch-front . . . the incidence of bow ties with button-down collars? Thinking that you can take it or leave it, when maybe it's already taken you? Did you ever hear of anyone rattling the pearly gates trying to get *out*? Have you ever heard of anyone close to millions of dollars not his who wasn't corrupted by the smell of them?"

"You give yourself away, pet. In the first place, those gates ain't pearly. They're iron and they work electronically. When you want out, there's a man in the gatehouse named Sidney or Crawford to *bow* you out. In the second place *and* the third place, have I ever been anywhere or done anything that didn't sooner or later turn up between covers? Hardback and paperback? If someone is willing to pay for the cab, why shouldn't I sit back and enjoy the ride? As for corruption, do you think Marcel Proust was corrupted? Sainte-Beuve? Fitzgerald? God, that word. You all use it like a branding iron."

"All who?"

"All you holy keepers of the flame—'a thin talent but an amusing one, at least before it was *corrupted* by its own pretensions'—all these great gifts that are supposed to have been *corrupted* by the demands of the marketplace or the mills of publicity. Or, as one of you put it, 'an all too human craving for sugarcoated trivia' . . . academic *merde* that shows they don't have the faintest idea the way a working writer works. *You* ought to know . . . a writer writes. When you wrote about a friend who just happened to be the hottest thing in poetry since Byron, were you *corrupted*? You had a story to tell and you told it. What's the difference?"

"We're not talking about me. There is a difference . . . some stories you *have,* the way you had the story of little Joel in *Other Voices.* Then there are stories you pur*sue.* From where I sit, and I don't mean me alone, I mean anyone who's watched you come up from Georgia. . . ."

"Alabama."

"—come up from Alabama like, like something unaccountable, like something no one could have guessed was ever *there*. . . . From where I sit, you've put all that aside as if it were some kind of mortal embarrassment. Nowadays, instead of creating, you're recording. You created Joel and all the rest of them out of what you hardly knew. They were discoveries . . . for you and for your readers. Now you *know*. There's nothing to discover because it's all there in front of you when you begin. All you can do is move your characters around like chessmen, arrange your observations like furniture in a doll's house."

"There was less imagination in *Other Voices* than you think," he said. "That was a record, too . . . a lot of facts all wrapped up in the gauze of a daydream."

"That may be so, but at least you gave the illusion of distance and the mystery of things. What's going to happen when there's no distance, no possibility of distance—when the life you live is an open book and the only people you know are public figures? How are you going to hide yourself in fame long enough to remind yourself who you are? As far as I can see, you've achieved a reputation at the cost of a career."

"My, my. We do go on. Would you like another drink? Or shall I have them send up a soapbox?"

"I'm sorry. I'll take the drink."

"The thing you can't seem to get through your pretty head is that I've never pretended to be that prose-poet you and the others tried to make me. I have this gift and these resources. With them, I do what I can. They may lead me into the shadow of the House of Usher in one book, and up a lot of creaky stairs . . . in another, they may tempt me to try my own crazy imagination of what someone like Proust sees and what someone like Walter Winchell says. Who's to order me to go on doing what I've *done*? *Other Voices* was my way of finding metaphors for what I knew but couldn't understand. In my big book, I'll do no more, no less. The only difference is that, psychologically speaking, I'm writing from the outside rather than from the inside. I don't have to *find* metaphors to illuminate my ignorance,

The Picture of Little T.C. in a Prospect . . . / 91

I have to *make* metaphors that show I can escape the limits of my own imagination, enter into the lives and imaginations of others. It's mimesis, Prof, in case you think I don't know my Auerbach, it's making a scale model of the big world that works the way I want it to work. *Other Voices* was my way of shaking myself out of the magnolias, of giving myself up in order to *be* myself. You may not like that, I daresay others won't. But don't put it down to some misuse of God-given talents or corruption of intention or failing powers. You think I'd go frog-sticking without a light?"

Next day we tested the stage at Sanders Theatre for reading space and acoustical effects. Later, when a table was rolled into his hotel room, we pulled up our chairs and, formally attired, dined like show-window dummies. "What time was it when you left here last night?"

"About two."

"That's when I went out," he said. "Why didn't you *tell* me Boston was such a lively place?"

An hour later, to a largely undergraduate audience, I spoke my introduction, then watched from the stage as, once more, he set about the task of taking an audience from skepticism to surrender. But the cost was still high. At the intermission he was shivering and seemed almost unable to speak. I rubbed his hands, then actually held him to stop his shaking and to lend him some physical warmth. His heart was beating as fast as a bird's. "I'll ask them for a bit more time," I told him.

"No," he said, "I'll be all right, once I get back out there."

And he was.

Barbados, Positano, Berlin—the places to which I lugged my portable Olivetti that year were as far-flung as Truman's. We did not meet until November when my biography of Gertrude Stein was about to be published and I was in New York for interviews arranged by my publishers to promote it. "Last week," he said when I phoned, "I became thirty-five years old. I think you ought to do something about it . . . like taking me to dinner at The Colony."

The hours we spent there were the soberest with him I could remember. Restless, self-questioning, he spoke only of what he pretended to abhor: the relationship between what the eye observes and the imagination conceives, between the fact and its resonance, between the truth of history and the truth of philosophy—the whole kit and caboodle of writers' "problems" he had all his life assigned to pedants or to talents more workaday than his own. What sparked this uncharacteristic inquiry was a conviction that he was "mired" creatively and had somehow to transcend himself. "I have this feeling that I've got to delve and explore," he said, "get out of myself and into something mysterious, do a kind of book that has no precedent."

"No precedent with you, you mean?"

"No precedent with anybody, a way of telling that would give the penumbra of fiction to something as cold as the truth."

He handed me a clipping, a news-service dispatch about the murder of a farmer named Clutter, his wife, and two children somewhere in western Kansas. "When I came across it," he said, "something in me said, 'That's it.' I think I even said it out loud. The point is, how to expand this little footnote to murder into something on the scale of Dostoevski, how to leave myself out of it, assume the omniscient view and make each smidgeon of fact reverberate . . . from blood spots on the stairs to the values of the tribe."

Later that week, en route to the airport and a plane for St. Thomas, I took a letter from my mailbox. "God, what a self-obsessed bore I must have been the other night," wrote Truman. "I still don't know what got into me. Maybe I ought to take to the hills like Jerry Salinger, or get drunk and play Prometheus like Norman, or become a public charge like Carson.

"I once knew a crow who thought she was an Airedale, and it worked, except with Airedales. But all vital signs continue to point to my being me, and taking the consequences. You were sweet to listen and I did love seeing you. While you are bathing away these weeks in the sun, please remember to send kind messages to your cold (but warm) friend."

Confident that Truman could solve any problem he could enunciate, I regarded his sober explorations of old dualities as evidence of a long-delayed brush with metaphysics. At the same time, I knew that soluble "problems" were decoys, that what he was really up against was the conundrum of his existence: He and his fictions, already equals, would soon be one.

I leave him in 1963, in two places. The second place is the setting of the story he was about to tell; the first is the setting of the story that, all told, may tell him.

10:30 P.M. Our hostess greets us at the door of an apartment high over the East River. Not quite "heiress of all the ages" but of at least a sizeable chunk of the nineteenth century (shipping and furs) she is wearing blood-red (shoes, gown, mouth) and at her side hovers the most recent of the husbands of aesthetic caliber (a conductor, a curator, a motion picture director, an author) who have helped her to shoulder the burdens of baronial patrimony.

Since Truman knows everyone assembled in her drawing room, he makes his own way while I am in turn introduced to a visiting couturier from Paris (he made the dress in which Wallis Simpson exchanged vows with the ex-king of England), a lady editor whose imprimatur was essential to the aspirations of trendsetters, two British foreign correspondents assigned to Washington, a banker noted for his collection of cubist canvases of the analytical phase, a woman whose torso is annually designated as Best Dressed, and once more, the logorrheic lady Noel Coward brought to cocktails in Portofino. By the time I can sit down, it's show-and-tell: Truman is passing around Kodachromes of his beach house in Spain, his chalet in Verbier, his dogs, his new car. "Like it?" he asks, and hands me one of an automobile in the shape of a bullet, a silver bullet. Under its half-opened astronaut's roof sits T. himself, at the wheel.

"It looks like something I saw at the World's Fair," I tell him, "the Chicago one."

"Maybe you did. . . . There aren't many others like it. That little buggy is going to take me to Kansas, starting tomorrow morning."

He turns back to the others, resuming a running commentary that is resisted, I note, only by the couturier and the banker, who seem suddenly more interested in the view. Perhaps aware of this, our hostess rises, skeletal in her swirl of bloody chiffon, and bids everyone to follow her into the new bathroom she has designed herself.

Drinks in hand, we trail through a hallway to look into a grotto on the seacoast of Bohemia: multicolored scallop shells, fans of dyed coral, anemones and angelfish, driftwood and echinoids, all the detritus of the littoral zone not quite disguising the fact that the room is a place of ablution and relief.

When we're once more in the drawing room, a slight rumble causes everyone to look up: One wall has disappeared, to reveal four tables set with pink linen and white carnations. At each of them stands a serving man in livery who helps us into our chairs, brings lobster Newburg and champagne, followed by strawberries in little silver dishes.

After supper half of the guests take leave. The rest of us repair to a paneled library, where, over demitasses and liqueurs, discussion turns on the revelations of Beverly Adland about Errol Flynn; the decline of Sid Caesar and St.-Tropez; Jacqueline Kennedy's trials with wallpaper in the White House; Sonny Whitney's plans for a condominium colony in the Algarve; the affronting vulgarity of Lady Docker's golden Rolls.

Glossy as linoleum, the picture postcard I got from Kansas a month later confirmed Truman's task without indicating the passion that had taken him to a dead box of a motel on the edge of space. In front of it stood an automobile so old it could have been the getaway car for Bonnie and Clyde. Windows reflected blurred images of what

I took to be a water tank and a cattle pen. Planted in concrete next to the motel was a road sign: Welcome to Garden City.

"Working hard on my book," said Truman, "and think it is good (so far)."

JUST LIKE JAVA

Just Like Java

N O, no, the captain's wrong," I said to my companion. "That one was taken near El Paso." I followed as she moved on to the next photograph. "We called *her* the witch of Wellfleet." "Such a sad and wretched figure," she said. "Why are you smiling?"

"Someday I'll tell you."

It was the summer of 1979. For the first time, the Venice Biennale was devoted solely to the art of photography. Touring the galleries of the main exhibition building, we'd come to the large central one housing the works of Henri Cartier-Bresson. I thought I knew all of these. But as we moved from print to print, I recognized in one new to me a distant figure, turned from the camera, who seemed intent on something in the still more distant background. "Look," I said, and brought my index finger to within an inch of the photograph. "Remind you of anyone?"

"You!" she said.

Me, I thought, and recalled a postcard from India long ago—a little *billet-doux* from Cartier-Bresson to the effect that he was thinking of me more than I would ever guess, and remembering with affection those months in the previous year when, together, we were "discovering the country and each other."

* * *

I first heard of Cartier-Bresson in the summer of 1946 when I was a resident at Yaddo. "I've just had a phone call," said Truman Capote one day at lunch. *"Harper's Bazaar* wants a piece on New Orleans. Me to write it, Cartier-Bresson to illustrate it. The *Bazaar* will pick up the tab and pay me a snazzy little fee besides."

"Who's Cartier-Bresson?"

"This photographer Carmel Snow's imported from France. Very eminent," he said, "the Museum of Modern Art's giving him a one-man show."

Later that day, while Truman was waiting for his train to New York, we went to the old Grand Union Hotel, had a drink there, and said farewell on a mile-long veranda lined with empty rocking chairs.

"I'm back," he wrote a month later, "with, let me tell you, swollen ankles and fallen arches. But my article is finished and perhaps the ordeal will after all turn out to have been worthwhile. C.-B. is going to be in Saratoga one of these days, and if he follows my considered advice will look you up."

His letter ended with a greeting I was to convey to another Yaddo resident—the sculptor Selma Burke, who, at the moment, was in no condition to accept greetings from anyone. Handed a note at breakfast—*"Au secours!* My door is unlocked, Selma"—I had found her abed, a bath towel bandaging her eyes. "Migraine," she said, "I have to stay in the dark. Read to me. There's a copy of *The Ballad of Reading Gaol* somewhere. If I start to cry, let me."

Next morning, as I was about to make another visit to her bedside, there came a knock at my door: Selma, in the company of an apple-cheeked stranger with china-blue eyes and hair close-cut as a prisoner's. Two cameras swung from his neck, a light meter and a third camera from his wrist. "My friend Cartier-Bresson," she said. "Henri needs someone to show him Saratoga. I said *you* would. I'll be back in ten minutes, in my racetrack getup."

Shy, tight-kneed as a choirboy, he sat down, refused a cigarette, fingered his cameras and meter like worry beads. "Of you I know from Truman," he said. "You call him 'little T.,' also?"

"I know of you from him."

"*Wunderkind, non?*"

At the track pennants sagged in a mild rain. "You would not mind if I walked by myself?" he asked.

As he disappeared into the crowd milling about the underside of the grandstand, Selma handed me a ten-dollar bill. "I promised my mother on her deathbed I'd never gamble," she said. "Put that on number seven."

As I was standing in line at the betting windows, Cartier came along, massaging his right arm. "A police, he grabs me here," he said, "so rough, a Cossack. No pictures. *Interdit.* I ask, 'Why?' 'No pictures,' he says only. I think what he does not say. Too many husbands with some ladies? Not with wives?"

I picked up the ticket and we started for a ramp leading to the grandstand, only to encounter Selma hurrying back. "Seven!" she called out. "Jock Whitney was right."

I handed her the lucky ticket.

"Can't touch it," she said. "Take it to the payoff window, we'll splurge."

In one of the black district's gambling-den barrooms to which Selma led us, Henri was as much at ease as she was. For more than an hour he photographed the play at pool tables and slot machines, working so unobtrusively that his subjects seemed unaware of him or, if they were, unperturbed by the intrusion of a presence so patently bland.

"Henri wants to ask you something," said Selma, "but he's embarrassed." We were sitting at a table in the dining room of the New Worden Hotel. "*Tell* him," she said, and nudged Cartier's arm.

"It is too much to demand," he said. "Elizabeth Arden . . . I am to meet her in the racing time here. We have friends . . . mutual. I must write a letter. You would write such a letter for me?"

The hotel clerk gave me a sheet of paper and an envelope. "My dear Miss Arden," I began, then followed Henri's dictation. "My friend Mme. Helena Rubinstein conveys to you her greetings—"

"*Non,*" said Henri, "*amitiés.*"

"*Amitiés,* and asks if you would be so kind as to . . ."

When he returned to New York the following day, our acquaintance had run its course, I thought, leaving me with a feeling that I'd met an individual of great personal modesty and a kind of charm I could not surely define. There was something close to seraphic about him, a tendency to self-effacement that seemed a habit of being. The extraordinary effect of it was to render him temperamentally neutral and, physically, all but anonymous. I did not expect to see him again, or to receive the letter that arrived within the week.

He was thinking of Detroit, he wrote, the city as a *"phénomène americain."* Did I consider this a good idea? If so, would I think about "meditations" to go with photographs of the city he would take? An article, maybe a small book? Intrigued by the suggestion— Detroit was my hometown—I wrote back to say as much and to accept his invitation to visit him in New York.

He lived in a borrowed walk-up in a raw brick building that stood by itself in an otherwise razed area at the Manhattan end of the Queensborough Bridge. Sea gulls wheeled and squawked around all sides of it. Traffic swirled and honked nearby. The top floor he occupied was furnished as sparsely as a convent.

He introduced me to his wife, whose name was Eli, pronounced "eely." Javanese, almond-eyed, in sari, she spoke English more fluently than he did and moved ceremonially, like a dancer which, I learned, she was. Trained by Uday Shankar, she had been with his company for years, sometimes as partner to the leading males of the troupe, sometimes as solo performer.

"New York I love," she said. "Everyone is so nice. Lincoln Kirstein, every day he allows me to do practice in his ballet school. I am so grateful. But I do not tell him I am grateful because the studio is close to Hicks on Fifth Avenue. How could I say to him, most I love the hot fudge sundaes?"

Cartier seemed restless. People had not shared his enthusiasm about Detroit. "They do not see as one would see in France," he said. "You could, John, find some publisher *sympathique?"*

Over the next month or so we somehow came to take it for granted that we would work together as a team. But the project to set us in

motion remained elusive. Detroit was put aside; then a flurry of interest in a story on the lost colonies of the Carolina banks went as quickly as it came. Meanwhile, our acquaintance developed into friendship and I was often a visitor to the flat on Fifty-eighth Street that seemed more barren every time I climbed its echoing stairs.

One of these occasions was a Javanese luncheon, elaborately prepared by Eli days in advance, for a group of their friends that included Robert Capa, the photographer noted for his battlefield pictures; Jay Leyda, the scholar involved with Far Eastern matters who was also an authority on Emily Dickinson; a short, swarthy man introduced simply as "Cagli"; and a few others whose names I didn't catch. Delighted as children getting ready to play spin the bottle, we took our places on the bare floor and made a circle around a circle of thirty-three wooden bowls in the center of which was a monumental vat of rice.

Merriment was brief. Chopsticks were difficult to handle from a cross-legged position; the sauces were either too hot, too gluey, or simply mysterious. Capa, ignoring Eli's attempts to keep conversation general, spoke only to Henri in a monologue about permission fees and news services and the cost of darkroom equipment. Silenced, the rest of us toyed listlessly with breadfruit mash, betel nuts, flakes, fins, seeds, and chips, and came to life only when Capa harnessed himself into camera straps and went rumbling down the stairs.

"Who's Cagli?" I asked Jay Leyda, sitting next to me.

"A painter, Italian."

"Would I be apt to know his work?"

"No. But Cartier thinks he's terrific. He's his pupil."

"In what?"

"You mean you don't *know*? . . . that Cartier considers photography a diversion . . . fancies himself first and foremost as a *painter?*"

With no assignment to occupy him, Henri took to wandering the streets of Manhattan and, with a special type of camera, to riding the subways from the Battery to Harlem. This camera was equipped with a device allowing the person using it to focus on a subject in one direction while actually recording an image in another. The results Cartier showed me caught people in the murky light of the subway— either oblivious to the fact that they were photographic subjects or staring, puzzled, at a man who'd found something worth taking in a setting so bleak. But the novelty of this soon wore off.

Late in October, writing on the wing from a train about to pull out toward some unnamed destination, he wondered if we could "do a sort of '*en flânant à travers N.Y.*'"—a photographic essay in which we might, each in his own way, capture a sense of the city Anno Domini 1946 that would not be a potpourri or "*vide-gousset,*" but something that would find its unity in the broad view of life and society he was convinced he and I already shared. If I couldn't at once grasp what he proposed, would I at least agree in principle that it was worth considering? "Excuse my writing," he said, "I am in a coach not a pullman."

Less sanguine about this than he, I nevertheless said I'd like to hear more of what he had in mind and dropped by to see him one afternoon in November.

"*Entrez!*" he called out. "You have met Alfred Kazin?"

They were seated at the kitchen table, guide books and maps between them. After shaking hands with Kazin, I left them to their conference. But not without a question: What was a man with so burgherish a claim on American culture as Kazin doing with a man whose social insights, if indeed he had any, were confined to such transient evidence as his camera could record? The empty living room smelled of incense. The low sun burned in a huge unframed mirror placed against a wall, a dancer's mirror, lacking only a *barre,* in which I kept myself company.

"John! Come," called Cartier, "We have now some small red nuts and aperitifs."

Over these and dinner in a nearby Chinese restaurant, I learned that Kazin had often joined Cartier in his walks about the city and that this had led to talk of a project involving photographs and commentaries. Since I could find no place for this surprising information and no way to digest it, common ground eluded us, until we called for Eli at the American Ballet Theatre School and were persuaded toward Hicks for banana splits.

Like Detroit, Manhattan was soon put on the shelf of discarded notions and, as far as I knew, so were Cartier's overtures to collaboration with Alfred Kazin. The new idea that took hold was grand, a trip we would make by car from New York to California, crossing the South and Texas going out, coming back through the middle of the country to New England. Plans in which he enlisted my help led to negotiations and, within weeks, to just the kind of contractual agreements we'd been hoping for.

"Everyone is much pleased," he said. It was the twenty-first of March and we were sitting over the remains of a *pot-au-feu* at his kitchen table. "We make now the grand tour—*les flâneurs des deux océans.*"

The publisher he'd found viewed our project as we did: a transcontinental adventure into serendipity. Cartier would be free to turn his camera on everything, anything. As cicerone and chauffeur, I would have the task of keeping a record of the subjects and scenes of his photographs and otherwise be free to observe and comment. The point of the trip would be the trip itself, its reward a book. A contract was being drawn up, our expenses would be underwritten except, said Henri, for the cost of the car in which we'd travel.

Just Like Java / 105

"This you would not mind?"

Gulls flashed about the Queensborough Bridge as I calculated cash and credit.

"Such a good car you could have for many years, no?"

"Okay," I told him, and helped myself to a cold potato.

"So. One more month and we start. In our pockets contracts."

We shook hands across the table.

"Now to celebrate," he said, "now to the Plaza."

In the Palm Court we joined his friend Muriel Draper. Her greyhound's face was powdered dead white and she was wearing a broad-brimmed black straw hat with a blood-red rose on it. "To the vernal equinox," she said, and lifted a glass of champagne, "to your great adventure, and to the downfall of that fascist beast Franco."

When Henri went to call for Eli at the ballet school, I dropped in on a party the art dealer Julian Levy was giving for Max Ernst, who, I learned, already knew of our plans. "Cartier will not believe Arizona," he said. "You will come stay in our canyon. He does not take photographs in color. That must not be."

"Without color," said Dorothea Tanning beside him (her hair was dyed a shade of blue-green close to turquoise), "Arizona is abstract, nothing."

I was about to ask Ernst how he'd come to know about our proposed trip when Miss Tanning tweaked his arm. "Max, don't look now, but I think Peggy has made her entrance."

Ernst sent a quick glance across the room. But his estranged wife, Miss Guggenheim, bulky in a coat of fur that somehow looked like a cascade of feathers, offered him only her back.

"For how long have you known Cartier-Bresson?" he asked.

"Six months or so."

"You know the term *brise-cou?*"

I shook my head.

"Look it up," he said, "before you start off."

In a midtown restaurant a few days later, Henri and I put our heads together over an outline he'd asked me to make—a prospectus spelling out in writing what had been agreed upon verbally. Lunch over, we were walking up Fifth Avenue when I discerned the figure of Martha Graham a block away and coming toward us.

"Enchantée, m'sieur," she said as I introduced them. "I'm so pleased to meet the man whose beautiful work I know."

Cartier lowered his head and stood tongue-tied, wasting his bashful smile.

As we went on, I asked, "You know who she is?"

"A dancer, no? . . . With the bare feet?"

"The great one."

"Danse moderne" in Paris I have seen," he said. "Boyfriends of Jean Cocteau, all those tight little behinds."

Next day I phoned to read him the final version of our prospectus: five hundred imaginary illustrations and a more or less blank concordance.

"Bravo!" he said. "Now we go like those babies in the woods."

On the night before we were to set out, I looked into my *Cassell's New French Dictionary.* Before *"brise-cou"* was a dot-in-a-circle indicating that the word was obsolete. It was defined as "n.m., (-) break-neck pace; (man.) rough-rider."

Some little joke of Max Ernst's, I thought, and went to bed.

Next morning, loading the car for the nearly three months we expected to be on the road, I made a last survey, picked Walker Evans's book of American photographs from a shelf and placed it face up on the backseat.

Into New York as the first light was climbing the Palisades, I pulled up at Henri's doorstep. Wearing khaki shirt and pants, combat boots, he stowed his gear: three Leicas, a camera bag, a folded tripod, a suitcase not much bigger than a bread box. Eli, in a purple sari, gave him a kiss. "Bon voyage, Ti-ti," she said. "Chon? You will drive him safely? It's a promise?"

Traffic in the Holland Tunnel kept us inching through exhaust fumes. At a point where we were stopped altogether, I asked Henri if he'd had a chance to look over the contracts we were to sign and return within a week of our departure.

No answer.

"You brought the contracts, didn't you?"

The car ahead began to creep forward.

"This decision I have made," he said. "Contracts we do not need. It is to be free, do all ways what we like."

I shifted from second into third.

"Contracts, they are for clerks, not *artistes*. When we will return, then for such matters is the time. Now we are to be bold ones, do what we see to do."

New Jersey came on in a blur of running colors.

"I am no refugee," he said. "Those publishers who bow the head and to everyone say thank you thank you you are so kind. I have no need to kiss the Stars and Stripes. This country makes welcome only those who do. America the beautiful. O say can you see. Beggars in the subway? Fat women in furs? Look!" He gestured toward the vast industrial landscape. "Possessed by guns and power, like with Krupps in the basin of the Ruhr. Capitalism, the American century, it is an arrogance."

("My dear, you don't *know?*" I can hear the silvery voice of Carmel Snow. "The Cartier-Bressons are the *tex*tile people, one of the great fortunes of the Ile-de-France.")

Trying to take in an outburst without precedent in our acquaintance, I had no chance for reflection as, image by image, he continued a tirade that reduced his experience of America to a series of agit-prop cartoons.

Late afternoon, we stopped at a roadside diner. At the end of the counter sat a young woman in a thin coat she clutched with one hand as if to hide the low-cut dress under it. If she wore makeup, it had faded; her hands were raw. Stringy-haired and gaunt, she had the look beyond despair of figures in Käthe Kollwitz's charcoal drawings. Sipping her coffee, she made an impassive survey of the men lined up along the counter, then returned to the reverie which seemed to hold her. Henri nudged my elbow. "Everything's been over her but the train," he said.

Traffic on the outskirts of Baltimore forced me to slow to fifty miles an hour, but the pace we kept was steady. "Faster!" Cartier called out. "You cannot go faster?"

"It's rush hour," I told him. "Besides, the road's patrolled."

"Stupid!" he said. "In France we go as we like—*vitesse!* one hundred kilometers, one hundred fifty. Speed limits are for peasants in the cheap Citroën. Why did you not get some car with open hood? In this I am like in a box."

Close to Baltimore, all the motels we passed showed No Vacancy signs and we finally had to resort to a "tourist home," a two-storey house full of tinted photographs of collies, curtains on which ducks in sunbonnets went single file, lampshades depicting Fragonard ladies on festooned swings.

When midnight came, I was listening to the attenuated snores of my companion in the next bed and watching reflected headlights of trucks along Route 1 slide across the ceiling. Somewhere, in the cellar of the house, or in the back of my head, I heard an iron door clank shut.

Up at dawn, I went for a walk in a neighborhood of clapboard bungalows with little lawns and front porches, and wondered what to do. Committed to Dr. Jekyll, did I also have responsibility to Mr. Hyde? Why not simply recognize the mistake, toss my bag into the trunk, start the motor, and head back?

Unaware that I would ask myself the same question every morning and every night for the next seventy-seven days, I carried my dilemma around the block and brought it back to Cartier, sitting in the porch swing, loading his cameras.

In a bright Sunday stillness that morning we "did" the white stoops of Baltimore, the first item of Americana in a collection that would include the gingerbread turrets of San Francisco's Nob Hill and the bow fronts of Boston's Louisburg Square. But our concern was less with architecture than with people. We caught them in every circumstance we could beforehand plan upon, and the thousand others chance would make available: Rotary luncheons, golf tournaments, jazz joints, oil depots, sheep ranches, shipyards, college campuses, baseball games, church picnics, farmers' markets, roadside carnivals, religious services, air shows, chambers of commerce, junior proms, historical shrines, Chicano slums, grade schools, factories, monasteries, amusement parks, graveyards, executive suites, beauty parlors, pueblos, dancing schools, funerals, zoos, corrals, barbecues, oil fields, and ice shows.

On all of these, the notes I kept were discarded long ago. With them went the commentaries I hoped would report something useful about the America I saw with my own eyes and through the eyes of a cosmopolitan foreigner with a genius for recording an ordinary event at the decisive moment when it becomes a mystery. What remains are entries in a journal I kept for myself. Some of these have bearing on what we saw; others remind me what I felt and tried to understand as the phenomenon of Henri Cartier-Bresson presented itself to me day by day, mile by mile.

4.21.47   Washington. Breakfast with gigantic Charles Olson and his tiny wife Connie in the sculptor's studio they've rented—then on to do monuments in a cold rain, the flag on the Capitol drooping. C.-B. is particularly taken with the city's geometrical patterns: long lines of glazed automobiles, crisscrossing sidewalks, streets forming vistas that end in mist. Government buildings in the emptiness suggest a world's fair that's over but not yet dismantled. "Much as I have expected," says C.-B., "when the power is absolute it makes a mausoleum."

Early evening, we say good-bye to the Olsons, cross the Potomac, and get to Fredericksburg in time to attend a dance for middle-aged blacks in the Odd Fellows Hall. Admission 25¢.

4.23.47   Roanoke. Fourteen and fifteen hours long, our working days are charged with expectation, governed by chance. At the wheel, I assume freedom of decision in any matter involving itinerary. On foot, I sometimes precede Cartier, at times follow. At no time, he lets me know, am I in the right place.

His eye is polyhedral, like a fly's. Focusing on one thing, he quivers in the imminence of ten others. Satisfaction with one shot is ephemeral; those ten others have meanwhile got away. When there's nothing in view, he's mute, unapproachable, hummingbird tense. By noon, most days, he's already taken hundreds of shots; hundreds more by sundown, and our working evening begins.

I scout people in action, keep alert for signs and scenes that mean more than they say. When nothing of interest occurs for fifteen minutes, the lacuna bristles with unspoken accusation. When I take the lead, I'm told to get out of the way. When I hover a few paces behind, I'm told to keep my distance. (Cartier to a New York reporter: "Photographers need less film and more patience. Taking pictures constantly is the sign of the amateur. . . . I cannot bear to rush when I am working. I must go alone, wait— then wait some more.")

4.24.47 Nashville 6:00 A.M. Awaking, I'm transfixed: The eye of a Leica is staring into mine.
A click. I blink.
"Bon jour," says Henri.
("Space for him," says one of his critics, "is where he can manage to anticipate or triangulate a spot from which he can press his shutter; time, for him, is the chosen instant in a continuum of preparatory moments when he can finally press.")

4.28.47 Memphis. At a dime-store lunch counter, a young man in overalls falls to the floor. Arms and legs flailing, his eyeballs white, he drools puffy matter from the corners of his mouth, subsides into a catatonic clench.
Cartier grabs his camera, dances about to catch him from all angles, and is interrupted only when a doctor and a nurse come hurrying in. As he returns to the counter to finish his breakfast of ham, eggs, grits and honey, cinnamon rolls, and coffee, I wait outside. (Cartier to an interviewer: "It requires close attention and studying to make pictures. When I see a thing that is ugly or pitiful, sometimes I can photograph and other times I am not able to hold my camera. I will not take this picture of a person in distress. It would be like interfering at a sickbed. You must honor all persons. You must be compassionate and forget you have in your hand this instrument that can record such misery.")

"This instrument" was both agent and sign of a vast duplicity. At some point long ago, it seemed to me, the available world had for Cartier become a world of "subjects" dispossessed of claims to the dignity of selfhood. As I began to succumb to the same dehumanizing process, I saw how easy it is to impose on the innocent and unsuspecting, deceive them with sympathetic words, and rob them with smiles. Since we appeared to be no more than harmless tourists or passersby, we were invited into the fetid cabins of poor-white sharecroppers, tolerated in black ghettos that sprawled on the edges of towns like exhausted chicken-runs, given tea in the funereal sitting rooms of antebellum mansions. The desolation and hopelessness of the lives we touched was heartbreaking. Listening to stories of desertion and death, we encouraged those who told them to show us their pathetic mementoes and, untouched, left them standing in doorways appealing for one more minute of the attention our presence had granted and our cameras confirmed. Self-loathing that might have followed these episodes was an indulgence we could not, professionally, afford. There were contact prints to count, cameras to reload, something on the horizon to overtake.

As a sort of ancillary project we might fulfil in the course of the trip, we had accepted a commission by *Harper's Bazaar* to do a story in which we would, each in his own way, "catch" creative people in the settings where they lived and worked.

One of these was William Faulkner. In the morning we spent with him, he showed us through his house and told us its history, posed for pictures in its jungle-shiny garden, and unaware that "poses" were anathema to Cartier, lingered just long enough to allow himself to be caught *un*posed. This accomplished, I could tell by Henri's dangling Leica (our private signal in "polite" situations) that he was as ready to move on as I, hungry by then for conversation or any other form of human contact, was prepared to stay. As we rambled along the edges of a giant magnolia tree, I was about to say our time was up when, lifting his camera, Henri signaled me to continue conversation while he maneuvered for a shot of Faulkner against the white portico of the house. Grasping for a topic, I asked Faulkner about his reactions to the extraordinary interest French critics seemed to take in his

© Henri Cartier-Bresson

work. He smiled an inward sort of smile for a moment and raised his head with a jerk. "Those fellows over there," he said, "I'd say they treat me pretty well."

Cartier spoke up. "In Paris, M'sieur Faulkner is to a Frenchman as Babe Ruth is to a man in America."

By the time we got back to the house, his Leica was dangling once more. Thanking Faulkner for his time, I apologized for interrupting him so early.

"Why, bless you," he said. "I'm always glad for a chance to leave off, just to talk for a spell."

We had barely left the driveway and its crudely painted sign— letters dripping gore like an ad for a horror movie: No Visitors Allowed—when Cartier asked: "To you he is great, Faulkner? Him you regard above Hemingway?"

"To me, great is the word only for Henry James."

"This I do not see. In England once I have read Henry James. So many words . . . *poétique, vermiculaire, compliqué.* Nothing happens. Pages I read, hundreds. Nothing. All persons speak like Sainte-Beuve, l'Académie Française. I say to myself, what is going on? This you would call great?"

"*Ev*erything happens in James," I said, the pedagogue in me sprinting. "Talk's his way of action, you must listen. Hundreds of pages, say, you have this man and this woman, lovers who have not loved. By page four hundred one, possibilities should be exhausted, all passion spent, but no, they come to the moment of their first kiss. You understand the whole story in this moment. A kiss—a streak of lightning that illuminates the whole landscape of the book, shows all meanings in one instant."

"This I will consider," he said.

We returned to our tourist court, its plastic tulips in white tubs, its flamingoes standing on one leg.

Robert Flaherty, then filming the *Louisiana Story* on location not far from the town of Abbeville, provided respite which Cartier must have needed as much as I. A serious man himself, Flaherty had a way of banishing the seriousness of everyone around him—including that of Cartier. Looking rather like an emotionally successful King Lear,

his white hair in a stringy aureole, his cheeks ruddy, his pants sagging, he'd lift a shot glass of Jameson's Irish, shout, "Down with the Protestants!" drink up, and expect everyone to do the same. Cartier took this with good grace, put his cameras aside as the film crew filled the house with its own shop-talk, and showed his dispossession only in a tendency to fall asleep when things were most lively.

In our days with Flaherty we joined the crew at boardinghouse-style meals, spent evenings watching the day's rushes, went scudding through the bayous in a powerful Chris-Craft, and late one night,

Just Like Java / 115

drank the whisky his wife poured into paper cups as we leaned against the stanchions of an offshore oil rig and watched him direct the final scene of his picture.

As a pirogue carrying a frightened little boy drifted into darkness—the last take of a scene repeated five times—the camera crew stood silent. In the chittering clamor of insect noises, no one made a move until Flaherty, lifting a megaphone, called out, "Come on back, J.C. . . . We can all go to bed now, J.C." and floodlights wiped out the scene.

Cartier was asleep, his head propped against the base of a stanchion, his paper cup empty. When I nudged him, he sat bolt upright and reached into the space around him.

"Où est-il, my camera!"

"You didn't bring it," I told him. *"Ce n'est pas ici."*

Texas went on forever and we saw only one another. Stepping up our working day from fifteen to eighteen hours, we stopped in flaming sunsets to eat from trays that girls in sateen skirts and knee-high boots clamped to the doors of the car, then fell, exhausted, onto beds in rooms that had long ago become the same room—on its walls the same clown faces, the same Van Gogh sunflower, the same sad Indian at the end of the trail.

Too tired to sleep, too weary to eat as we moved westward, I could feel the flesh dropping from my bones. But this was all part of the job, I told myself, and went on gritting my teeth, vomiting in the rest rooms of gas stations and on the shoulder strips of highways, clocking the nights on ceilings that crawled with reflections, my own and those from passing headlights. What I could not get used to was total isolation in the company of a man whose sense of humor was nil, or beyond me, and whose rigidity of mind obviated argument and enjoined silence.

I had known other humanitarians indifferent to people, Marxists who could not tolerate the smudge of the masses, well-married men whose wives alone escaped their rampant misogyny. But I had never for long been close to anyone whose experience was unleavened by perceptions of absurdity and a need to share them. When, on the clothesline of some desolate little overnight cabin, Cartier's scanty "slip masculin" and my ample shorts swung together in the breeze like the emblems of misalliance they were, who'd dare to say?

Notes I made at lunch counters or any other place with a surface to write on were becoming blunt and brief. Identifications of time, place, and thing for Cartier's eventual use I took as routine; but once-expansive observations of my own were reduced to staccato notations, efforts at analysis to weary et ceteras. As my "official" record became thinner and more difficult to decipher, entries in my journal became longer and more detailed. Unconsciously, I had begun to produce sound tracks to go with Cartier's photographs, particularly those of people.

5.14.47   Taos, New Mexico. No Tourists Welcome. Invited in advance, we ignore this sign on Mabel Dodge Luhan's driveway and stop in front of a big square house of stained wood paneled with glass. When I pull the bell-rope, there's a distant tinkling and the slap-slap of sandals on tile. The door is opened by a young man in a white dressing gown worn carelessly enough to show that he's wearing nothing else.

"Mrs. Luhan will be down directly," he says, and shows us into an airy room with sunlit openings onto terraces and a courtyard. "So many people come to Taos to see what's left of poor Mr. Lawrence. You'll be seeing Frieda and Brett?"

This afternoon, I tell him.

"Don't fall for the stories you're apt to hear. That tiresome little fracas about the ashes is ancient history now."

My face is blank.

"*Law*rence's ashes," he says. "Mabel and Brett were accused of plotting to steal them when all they had in mind was to scare some sense into Frieda. She had this habit of leaving them in strange places the way other people are always losing their umbrellas. If you'd care to poke about, do. I must run."

Doves flutter up from the rim of a fountain. One of them

lights on the back of a chair, one on a candelabrum, another on a book-filled armoire.

Completely in white, save for a pale pink headband, Mabel Dodge Luhan comes in, extends a hand to each of us, wafts a dove from a chair, sits down. "Is the light sufficient?" she asks Cartier. She is heavily powdered, rouged, mascaraed. "Could you do me with a dove?"

She reaches into a painted cigarette box which holds kernels of corn and begins to make clucking sounds. The birds do not oblige.

Unaware that Cartier's camera has already clicked twenty times, she addresses me as though he were not present. "I suppose that man knows what he wants," she says. "I've seen his book. The portrait of Matisse made me think of my own doves. Should I speak French?"

Obviously restless, Henri has got to the far end of the room.

"M'sieur? Est-ce que possible à prendre la photo près de la fontaine? Toutes les places, sauf le jardin. Je n'aime pas le soleil, le soleil ne m'aime pas."

"This light is very good," says Henri. "I need no more." With exaggerated professionalism he lifts a camera to his right eye, closes his left eye, clicks. "Good! Thank you, madam."

"It's all over? My goodness." She pats both sides of her headband, stares through her *maquillage.* "I'm not sure I'm even presentable."

"I am being so bored," says Henri as we start off. An enormous station wagon is coming up the driveway. At the wheel is a handsome figure of an Indian whose thick black braids rest symmetrically on the brilliant zigzag blanket he's wearing across his shoulders. I slow down; Henri stares.

"That's her husband," I tell him. "His name is Tony."

The residence of the Honorable Dorothy Brett is a small adobe by the side of the road. In its entrance patio are paintings on easels of Navajo ceremonials, along with tubes of paint, brushes in pots, spattered rags, and an unfriendly dog. His bark holds us at bay without, apparently, signaling our arrival. Brett eventually appears in the doorway and greets us with a bright, fish-eyed stare as she points to the tooled-leather box in her left hand. "Deaf as a post!" she shouts. "Can't hear a thing without my ears, you'll have to talk [she raps on the box] into my ears!"

Her hair is frizzled and silvery. She is wearing workmen's pants, a brocaded vest, and bracelets that circle both arms to the elbows. "You think you want me like this?" She reaches out, as if to indicate the whole room. "Say so if you don't."

The walls are covered with unframed canvases—whirling abstractions in primary colors, Indians astride pinto ponies, squadrons of fighter planes in formation. The eclectic exhibition is not, as it seems, the product of a high school art class, but all hers. "Wouldn't guess I'd studied years on end at the Slade, would you? Thick as thieves with all that lot—Carrington, Mark What's-his-name . . . Gertler! Ottoline . . . Garsington, don't cha know, lived there more than I lived on the Embankment. What's left of that's right here." She points to a mantel where, among bric-a-brac, is a tile with a phoenix in flames next to a photograph of Lawrence by Edward Weston.

Every time Cartier picks up his camera, her stare freezes on her face. "I simply adore these gadgets," she tells him. "Bought one for myself, quite like yours. It has a name. Let me think . . . I have no mind anymore. Can't remember the name of the deuced thing. Took some pictures but the idiots who sold it me had fixed the range at infinity. Infinity! Everything came out absolute farce. Does Frieda know you're coming? That's her." She gestures toward the open door. "A stone's throw, you might say."

Affixed to Frieda Lawrence's doorpost is a cluster of multicolored ears of corn and, on the wall beside it, a row of small ceramic tiles, each stamped with a phoenix in flames. A stocky man with a heavy Italian accent leads us into a room hung with paintings by Lawrence: nude, green-eyed figures with meat-red lips involved in oddly joyless concourse and, in some instances, intercourse. There's a cage of lovebirds and a scatter of books, among them *Finnegans Wake* and *The Journal of Albion Moonlight*. A table supports an album of *Annie Get Your Gun* and a glazed plate with a phoenix on it.

Frieda Lawrence—Catherine the Great in hair ribbons, Mary Janes, bobby sox, puffing a cigarette; a voice booming, rasping, Germanic. "Zit down, zit down," she says. "You have met Angelino, my Angie? You have seen hiss paintings? You shall zee sculptures, alzo. Thees ribbons, ach! [she pulls at her yellow-gray hair] other people haff ribbons, zey stay poot. Mine are flying around alwayss." She is wearing a full-skirted peasant dress. Her face is rough and red. "Ve vill start wiz ze birds—you will take ziss?" Cartier focuses his camera as she goes toward the half-dozen birds chirping and hopping about. "Tweet-tweet-tweet," she says. "Ze birdies will talk wiz mamma? Ze birdies will have zere picture took?" The birds cower, suddenly silent. "Zey are not in ze moot," she says. "So now we go in sunlight. Angie, give me plees a cigarette." Henri works fast. "Angie . . ." She points to her friend. "You must take of Angie pictures in hiss studio." She leads us outdoors, makes a sweep of her hand. "Look!" she says. "Iss beautiful! Lorenzo said, of all places, you know what? of all places, he said, Taos takes the cake! Now he iss in hiss chapel, up zere in mountains." She indicates a distant rise. "And I am here . . . through ze long vinter I am here, because I luff zis place also. Young men like you . . ." She turns to me. "Zey do here great sings. In Santa Fe iss cocktail parties, zey do nozzing. Here . . . ah! . . . iss beauty, iss true democracy. Ziss morning only . . . a taxi driver iss buried in hiss grave. Everyone goes, everyone iss hiss friend." She lights a cigarette. "You go to

California? You will see poet Jeffers? To him, say from Frieda luff. His face, it is one angel's face you will photograph."

In Angie's studio, Henri takes many shots, or pretends to, lingering longest before a ceramic head of Lawrence. Frieda claps her hands. "He iss fine artist, Angie . . . you sink so?" We nod. It is time to go.

For me the chance to see in one day the three dominant women in the later life of D. H. Lawrence was too good to waste. Henri did not resist it, but he was more interested in exploring Taos pueblo, ranch life, and anything else that indicated we had finally come into the great West. As with many other Europeans, the West remained for him a romantic idea surviving time and change intact, and unlikely to suffer erosion. One Saturday afternoon in a dusty Texas town we'd come out of a diner to find cowhands in twos and threes hurrying down the street. Fascinated, Henri forgot even the camera on his wrist as these men were joined by others in high-heeled boots and high-domed hats intent on getting to the same place. Back in the car, we followed to the point where they'd disappeared around a corner and found them standing in line for a matinee double feature: Gene Autry and Randolph Scott.

"Saturday afternoon at the RKO corral," I said. "Isn't that a picture for us?"

It was not.

In Sedona, Arizona, where Max Ernst and Dorothea Tanning put us up in their half-finished house at the bottom of a canyon, Cartier seemed genuinely at ease for the first time in a month—because he was among friends of his own, perhaps, in a circumstance where his camera was redundant. Transformed, he spoke and listened, exercised his shy charm when that seemed called for, and put it aside when it was not. Taken off guard, I found myself staring at him as though he were someone it might be pleasant to know.

Since talk at dinner was mainly dialogue between him and Ernst about acquaintances who survived the war, or did not, Miss Tanning suggested that she and I take our coffee in an adjoining room.

Just Like Java / 121

"New York," she said, "we say we gave it up because it was getting dirtier every day, or more uncomfortable, or that we were frightened by the crime rate. Actually, we were bored. In the beginning there were all those marvelous dispossessed Europeans still steeped in Bauhaus and the Barcelona Pavilion and the Tatlin monument and all the other great things. . . . Peggy's gallery, everyone seemed to go there before they went anywhere else. Then, not so much. Too many of the refugees began to revert to their bad old selves. Rich and selfish, they could never understand this country. They spoiled it for those of us who did. I get homesick. Max, never. For him, a new day is the first day."

She poured a second demitasse. "Look behind you."

I turned to the painting at my back.

"It's mine," she said. "I call it 'Very Happy Picture.' Recognize the subject?"

"Grand Central?"

"You might think, how can anyone be homesick for Grand Central Station. I am."

As I was preparing for bed in a room that smelled of fresh-cut wood, Ernst looked in.

"Did you look it up," he asked, "that word I gave you, *brise-cou*?"

Uncertain as to whether he expected me to smile, roll my eyes, or shake my head, I tried a smile which apparently said more than I meant it to say.

"I thought so," he said, "but you'll survive."

5.17.47   Kingman, Arizona. We stop on a one-sided Main Street of wooden facades parallel with railroad tracks, above which stands a water tank still touched by afternoon sun while everything below is dark. Looking for a meal, we walk by shut stores and come to a doorway shivering with neon: GOOD EATS. A close-packed row of jalopies and pickup trucks at the curb suggests the place is well patronized. Down a flight of stairs, we enter a room rancid with bacon grease and dead cigarettes, trembling with the beat of piano, drum, bass fiddle. The six or seven tables are empty. Along the bar are: a young Indian slumped asleep, his beer untouched, a shot glass next to his ear; cowhands in black hats, checkered shirts, boots stitched with scroll-work; a white man in a Stetson talking to a black man who's leaning on a broom.

The band concludes its set; the bass fiddle lights a ciga-rette. Drum and piano stare into space. The bartender, one arm across the top of his cash register, works a crossword puzzle. Purple when we entered, the room changes slowly to viridescent green. A thrum from the bass vamps the trio into "Mexicali Rose."

"At last!" says Cartier, ecstasy in his voice, "the *real* America!"

Two days later, in Los Angeles, Jean Renoir stood on the veranda of a big battleship-gray house and called out: "Henri! *Comment ça va?*" Stocky, with a broad soft face and lively eyes, he wore a flannel shirt rolled to the elbows; instead of a legendary director of films, he could have been a peasant.

"Valentino was living in this house," he told us as we went in. "Now my neighbor is Clifford Odets. *Le temps, c'est le changer, n'est-ce pas?*" Since he chose to speak to Cartier in French, I had to hang on as they recalled the people and events of their common war work—Henri's with a French government film unit, Renoir's with the American Office of War Information.

We must stay to lunch, said Renoir, but first he'd like to show us "old" Hollywood. I drove where he told me to through a dilapidated area of turrets and cupolas, arches fringed with wooden balls, con-servatories domed with broken glass, exhausted gardens survived only by naked palm trees.

"One has seen such houses," said Cartier, "in Charlot."

"*Oui,*" said Renoir. "*L'espèce de maison grande où le petit homme fait la charade de comte ou de duc . . . la nostalgie de la sénescence. Non?*"

Returned to the house, we were joined by Renoir's wife Dido and by his father's model, Gabrielle Renard, a very old woman with wispy gray hair tied with a black ribbon. In a many-windowed sun-room we sat down at a table on which had been placed a red-and-white checkered cloth, a cheese board, and slim unlabeled bottles of red wine. Lilacs crowded the windowpanes. Lunch was light envelope of omelet enclosing a green salad, served with crusty bread still warm.

"*Moi . . .*" said Renoir. "*J'ai supposé que j'arrive ici . . . a fait le sens de la manière continentale. Mais non. Les maîtres de* Universal Studios *avez d'autres idées; je fais le 'musical' pour la vedette,* Mees *Deanna Durbin.*" He stared, bug-eyed, at Cartier, shrugged his shoulders, and poured himself a glass of wine. "Tut, tut," he said to the wineglass, "Mees *Deanna Durbin.*"

Reading my thoughts, he asked if I'd like to see the paintings. I left the table and wandered, finding Renoirs in every room, along stairwells, piled on bedroom floors, crowded even into bathrooms. Gabrielle Renard's blue eyes, red hair, and white skin freaked with blue were the subject of a dozen of them.

When I rejoined the table, Mme. Renoir smiled and pointed toward the backyard. "*La même Gabrielle,*" she said, "*là.*" The old woman was sitting in a wooden chair, a tub of water at her feet. She had just washed her hair. Gray streaks of it clung to her cheeks. Her eyes were closed.

The challenge of Hollywood, for me at least, was "Hollywood," how to avoid the clichés of the bizarre and disparate in describing what I observed and what I from time to time pointed out as subjects Cartier might take. But when things I found amusing left him stonefaced, or when he puzzled over some anomaly I'd already labored too long to explain (the Page Boy Maternity Shop, on Wilshire Boulevard, for instance), I lost interest. Reversals of intention were taking place—on his part, a shift from reportage and regional coverage to isolated instances of the odd or abnormal; on my part, from the grandly devised ends of our project to its means, foremost of which was the means to keep going.

Our arrival in Los Angeles, to stay for ten days with a woman friend of mine, had been in itself exhilarating, and our visit with the Renoirs served to reintroduce me to civilization. But euphoria had its term and its price. Next morning, I could not get out of bed. When I did, my legs would not support me. The physician called in by my friend prescribed codeine, a heating pad, and complete rest. During the next four days Cartier was picked up and delivered by acquaintances of his, most of whom, I learned from his bedside reports, were French citizens involved with motion pictures or the French consulate, or the French cultural foundation supported by Charles Boyer.

"Photography is not so much a technique," Cartier had often said, "as it is an attitude." The assumption being that his own attitude transcended amateurish gadgetry and the temptation of strange emulsions. Now that I knew something about this attitude, I began to review my feelings about Walker Evans, Paul Strand, William Notman and others in the art whom I most admired. Was there such a thing as "personality" in photography, a signature and style as instantly apparent as those of twenty poets I could name? If so, was it sometimes achieved by accident in the mindless industry by which, scientists have told us, a baboon at a typewriter would eventually turn out *Hamlet*?

In the days I spent in bed my hostess brought me books—among them the volume of Cartier-Bresson photographs published by the Museum of Modern Art. Looking at these with new eyes, I came to old conclusions: "Stolen" or accidental or, in their invasions, sometimes inducing shame in the observer, they were uniformly superb. Studied closely, they revealed the kind of subliminal design scholars liked to show by reducing great paintings to geometry. Depicting actuality, they touched mystery. In their presentations of the human they were often so subtly funny and so wise as to bring to mind Hogarth and Daumier. Was Cartier keeping something from me? Was it possible that he existed on some plane of perception at once so keen, farseeing, and compassionate as to elude the vulgarity of my apprehension?

On the fifth day of my incarceration, already upright for most of the previous twenty-four hours, I was ready to go again. Heading for the RKO-Pathé studios, we were moving at sixty miles an hour on a freeway when he spotted something I could not see. "Stop!" he yelled.

"Not now," I told him, and kept rolling with the lanes doing sixty on both sides of us.

"Stop! I say, stop!"

My habit of acquiescence had become absolute. Brakes screeched; we shuddered to a halt.

Dead still, our shoulders hunched as if to ward off blows, we endured a cascade of shrieks, honks, and curses, as cars careened to the left and right. Henri said nothing; I said nothing. The first scramble of traffic we had caused was already being repeated by another.

Off the freeway minutes later I stopped the car, lurched out, and vomited in a gutter. "I take a walk," said Henri. "I am no use." In half an hour we started over again, to a projection room showing of his war film, *Le Retour,* for an invited audience composed of the Renoirs, Man Ray, Charles Boyer and his wife, and a few others.

Afterward we went to Man Ray's place on Vine Street near Hollywood Boulevard, an apartment in a four-storey building entered through a courtyard of palm trees and hibiscuses. It was a period piece: adobe walls, molasses-colored baseboards, photographs in tooled-silver frames, mission furniture, a Spanish shawl draped over a baby grand.

Man Ray—short, compact, with jet black eyes—had the hunching stance of an actor playing a gangster and the accent of a Chicago bookie. "You guys know sumpin'?" He backed Henri and me into a corner where peacock feathers sprouted from an umbrella stand. "Every pitcher I take I take upside down. You get your subject, see . . . like you think you want, okay? That pitcher's still just somebody's mug. The thing is, what's left when you see it upside down? What's gonna separate Man Ray's shot of Cousin Clara's puss from one taken by Uncle Jake? *I* tell you what . . . what's left over. Nuttin' left over, nuttin' *there*. Upside down, the big difference . . . I tell ya."

On the way out I turned to Cartier. "You believe all that?"

"Why not?" he said. "Man Ray in his mind is most a painter."

"No one believes me when I say I like it here," said Aldous Huxley one afternoon, "but I do." After we'd met him in the sort of barracks where he and other writers under contract were confined, he had suggested we stroll about the studio lot. "My house is six thousand feet over the desert. Actually, what it overlooks is half Switzerland, half

North Africa, mountain forests and sagebrush, with a view of blessed emptiness that satisfies the soul. As I tell my friends, unlike Dr. Johnson I prefer climate to conversation."

Henri's camera, swiveling away from a bespectacled cowboy engrossed in a copy of *The New Yorker,* recorded his fleeting smile.

"But the people here are extraordinary. I don't mean my own friends, though it's been a comfort to find Chaplin and Gerald Heard and Chris Isherwood within reach. I mean the people in things like microbiology and marine research, the nuclear physicists trying to humanize the terror that terrorizes humans, scholars who never *saw* the Bodleian turning up new materials on Bacon and Kyd. . . ."

We stopped to watch a procession of Model T Fords, all of which had been carefully sprayed with ersatz dust.

"If this country could only understand what it has. . . ."

Resistant to Lilliputian attempts like ours to pinpoint its character, Los Angeles documented itself. (Of the thousands of shots Cartier took there, only one, as far as I know, was ever used for a documentary purpose, that of a strikingly handsome young couple seated at an outdoor counter in the Farmers Market and caught by his camera in a passionate embrace, their eyes closed. A year later this photograph somehow found its way from Cartier's files to the office of a national magazine where, used to illustrate an article on teen-age delinquency and sexual promiscuity, it became exhibit A in a lawsuit pursued by the young couple. Their contention was that they were not delinquents and, to prove it, they put in evidence a marriage license dated three years earlier.) On our last day in the city, each uncomfortably aware that we had not scratched the surface of a phenomenon that had overwhelmed us, we turned from random coverage in order to add to our gallery of portraits:

5.27.47   The room Stravinsky uses as a studio has the point-device economy and efficient elegance of a ship's bridge. One sheet of music, a masterpiece of calligraphy from his own hand, has been placed above the keyboard of a Steinway. On a bone-white wall hangs one framed drawing: a head of Beethoven as a young man. Under its massive, self-possessed stare Stravinsky's movements seem light as an acrobat's. Without being asked to, he places himself in half a dozen likely photographic settings.

"This you must see," he says, and whisks from his desk a newspaper clipping, an account of the arrest by government agents, for tax evasion, of one Dr. Petrouchka. "It comes in the post," he says. "No name, nothing. This country has everything!"

We join Mme. Stravinsky, whose name is Vera, for coffee in a drawing room dominated by a cage of white birds. Considerably larger in girth and stature than her husband, whom she calls Eager, she pours from a silver coffeepot and presides in the manner of someone honoring a familiar ritual. "Our neighbor, Oona Chaplin, has found this terrific *boulanger*," she says, and holds out a plate of powdered digits. As she and Cartier begin to reminisce in French, Stravinsky taps my knee.

"Come," he says, "we shall visit the garden." We step onto a terrace above which is another terrace with trellises and an orange tree. "On days I wonder who I am," he says, "I climb to see the ocean. One look, then I climb down. You have seen the Pacific?"

"Never."

"Then *you* must climb."

I scramble up to the second terrace. "Now," he calls, "you are strong? You lift yourself to the branch, you look away from the sun, you see, like a floor maybe, one piece of blue."

"I see!"

"Bravo!"

When it's time to leave, he walks me to the car while Henri and Mme. Stravinsky follow behind. "You must not be so much the journalist," he says. "A journalist must hurry and do much, he must always *use* things. The poet, he has only to *be*, and to wait. Patience. You have lived with this man Cartier-Bresson, I know already you have much patience."

Just Like Java / 129

After a farewell lunch with Jean and Dido Renoir, we drive to Santa Monica and find Katherine Anne Porter in a pastel bungalow on a street lined with pastel bungalows which meet, like railroad tracks, in infinity. Immaculate in white except for high-heeled black patent leather shoes, she leads us to a backyard lawn clipped close as a carpet and sits in a rattan chair with a cobra hood through which sunlight filters onto her powdered face. "California," she says, "I've had thirty-four weeks of it. I keep count like a prisoner . . . two hundred and thirty-eight days and no end in sight."

"Why do you stay?"

"Angel, I'm under contract, which is to say I'm like a fox with his leg in a trap, even though the people who've hired me seem barely to know of my existence. But they do send checks . . . and if I'm to believe my old Dr. Sawbones, it's the right place for me. He sees my salvation in a change of chemistry, literally, as if it's simply a matter of draining the crankcase and starting over."

She turns her eyes on Henri as, down on one knee, he squints into his camera. "M'sieur Cartier-Bresson! Would it distress you to know that I live in dread of photographers and find them totally dispensable?"

"No, madam," says Cartier. "It is the way I feel myself."

Finding little of interest but scenery as we drove north, Cartier put color film in his camera for the first time. Dubious about the value of color, he was nevertheless prepared to make "private experiments" and proceeded in this with great care, but also with an air of engaging in something illicit. Instead of a hundred shots made on the run, our morning's work was sometimes only two or three: a silver-winged plane on the edge of a wheat field; the bell tower of a Spanish monastery; a barnside covered with fading posters, as if color were something he meant to reserve for things inanimate. His dalliance with the medium made for a comparatively leisurely pace of travel, but it was a relief to be able to focus once again on people:

5.28.47   Big Sur. Henry Miller's house on Partington Ridge is small, flat-roofed, pink-washed. The Pacific hangs in the front yard as bland and featureless as a drop cloth. *"Tropic of Cancer* paid for it," he says. "French money's as good as any other kind." His eyes, almond-shaped, give his face a resemblance to that of a Buddhist monk. In shirt sleeves, flimsy black pants, he leads us to lookout points, all of which have the same blank and overwhelming view. "I'm going broke," he says, "just paying for what you see. But any trouble's worth it. Those years in Paris, I got freedom . . . the big thing I wanted then. Here, I got something better . . . peace of mind."

Inside the house, he picks jelly glasses from a mound of unwashed dishes, rinses them under the tap. "I spent fourteen months doing what you're doing—*The Air-Conditioned Nightmare.* What I published doesn't come to one tenth of what I collected. Let's have some Scotch . . . I think it's Scotch." He produces Old Thompson, sets it on the table, asks us to help ourselves. "I been reading a piece about me." He points to a magazine splayed open on the seat of a chair. "You know this big-shot professor Fowlie?"

Very well, I tell him.

"'Zat so! Catholic, ain't he? Real old-fashioned R. C. Christer?"

A door opens behind me. A heavy-set man comes reeling in, muttering. After him comes a young woman, quite sober, carrying an infant. "My baby—ain't she beautiful?" says Miller. "Her name is Valentine." The young woman is his wife.

As he attempts to introduce us, the man (a writer whose name I know) misses Cartier's hand, falls to his knees. Back on his feet, he circles toward a couch, drops down, buries his face. Mrs. Miller takes the infant into another room.

Just Like Java / 131

The drunk, we learn, has come to dinner. Others from what Miller refers to as "the colony"—a few shacks in the distance—are expected. "How about you two taking pot-luck with us?" he asks. "The papers call us the new hate colony, how do you like that? But let me tell you, we've got a real crackerjack crowd here (the writer lifts himself, stumbles toward the bottle Miller has placed on the drain-board, goes down with a crash), they'd get a real bang out of you two."

Behind his permanent smile Cartier's face is beginning to register panic. We have an appointment in Carmel, I tell Miller, with a garage, the car needs . . .

"That's our tough luck," he says. "We get publicity, what we need is attention. You guys get fixed up and come on back. We don't live by the clock here, you'll see what I mean. We like to dance—simple pleasures—make love, sing to the little ones. What else is it all about?"

5.29.47 At Edward Weston's barn-wood chalet in an evergreen clearing, we go up the stoop of a platform porch and pull the rope of a rusting bell. Greeted by a young woman, we step into a room that undulates: Twenty or thirty cats, moving in and out, make patterns which dissolve as soon as they're perceived. "I'm Dody Warren," she says. "Edward's not at all well, you mustn't be surprised. He's been so happy, waiting for the sound of that old bell all morning."

A door opens behind her. Weston's eyes are filmy and wet. With a weak but steady smile he searches my face, then Henri's, wondering who is who. Cartier puts out a hand. Weston pulls it to his chest. "You are here, Cartier-Bresson," he says.

"Cher maître," says Cartier, *"cher maître."*

Releasing Henri's hand, he takes mine. "We'll go out and have a good look at my ocean. . . . First you will see some new things. Dody?"

She places a folio of black-and-white photographs on a low table. We gather around as she opens it to a human torso, monumentally sculptured, which turns out to be a rock worn by waves; lichen in rock-pools observed as if under a microscope; dead trees in the postures of tragic heroines; gnarled roots and splashing water; white cats, black shadows. . . .

It's a short drive to Point Lobos, where Weston leads us down a wind-blasted slope. We stoop to pass under overturned trees, pick our way through salt-rimed stumps, leap across foaming crevasses, and come to a smooth expanse of whaleback rock. On the far side of a boiling cove, sea lions are dragging themselves across a flooded ledge, barking into the wind. Weston lifts a frail arm. "My life's work!" he calls.

Cartier hides his camera in the folds of his jacket.

We drive up the coastal highway to Robinson Jeffers's tower of stone. We park in a nearby compound of suburban houses and walk a street strewn with baby buggies, tricycles, lawn sprinklers, painted ducks with wings that turn in the breeze.

Jeffers is not in the tower, but in the rough-hewn stone cottage adjoining it. Short, leathern, lean, with vague slow-moving eyes, he gives us no sign of recognition. While our visit has been arranged by mutual friends, and he has himself confirmed the time, these overtures have obviously been forgotten. To cut things short, I make a signal to Cartier, whose picture taking Jeffers has ignored, or may have not noticed. As we rise to take leave, Jeffers lifts his two hands, as if to push us back into our chairs. "No, no, you must see the tower," he says. "My wife will take you. I'd go myself, but the climb has become too much for my heart." Sun cuts the etchinglike gloom with lemon light and touches one side of his face. "I built the tower with my own hands," he says. "It was a different

California then—fields beyond, one dirt road down to the water." He makes a limp gesture toward the window. "You've seen what's happened."

Una Jeffers comes in with a bag of groceries. "This is Mr. Brenner," says Jeffers, "and Mr. Brissom." She gives us a piercing and entirely hostile glance and leaves the room.

"She'll come back to take you to the tower."

Dubious about this, we again rise. But she does come back—with a volume of poems by Frederick Mortimer Clapp, which she places on her husband's knees. "Hold it up when he takes your picture," she says. "Make sure he gets the title in." Jeffers puts the book on a table and shuts his eyes.

"If you want to see the tower," says his wife, biting out the words, "follow me!"

Over a beheaded hawk carved in stone, real pigeons are flying about. We pass under a low lintel, go up a spiral stairs to a room showing no sign of human presence; only the boom of surf, a chitter of pigeons. Mrs. Jeffers stands by, says not a word, then leads us back down. Vigorously talking to herself, she disappears.

Jeffers stands in his doorway, a shawl on his shoulders. His smile is tired. "We are too much alone here. You must come another time," he says, and holds out his hand.

On the way to the car we stop for another look at the tower. Children in Indian bonnets surround us. They all hold machine guns and rifles. "Stick 'em up!" says one.

We put up our hands. They spray us with bullets and run away.

Oakland. Fully dressed, dark sack suit and tie, propped on the pillows of a narrow bed in an otherwise empty room, Darius Milhaud extends a gouty hand. *"Vous m'pardonnerez l'indisposition, m'sieurs. Vous êtes bienvenus."* Madeleine, his wife, years younger than he, smiles at the scene and pats his leg.

"Poor Darius, he is all dressed up for you and he must stay in the bed. Come, we leave him to rest for dinner." We go into an uncarpeted room strewn with unopened packing boxes, laundry heaped in corners, manuscripts in piles, single shoes, a desiccated fern and some long-dead begonias, half-empty bottles of wine and cognac, suitcases tied with ropes and straps. "Here you will sleep. Henri we shall put in there," she says, and points to an adjoining room. "Now," she says, "to sit. You will assist?" I lift cases of wine from the seats of chairs while she removes a gooseneck lamp from another chair.

"I'm afraid," I tell her, "that Cartier and I didn't realize you've just moved in."

"*Mais non! Non!*" she says merrily. "We have been now many months—it makes almost a year. For you we have this good bed we shall bring up from down in cellar."

A door slams, followed by clumping footsteps. "Daniel," says Madeleine, "it is my son Daniel." The young man smiles wanly, tears off the wrappings of a record he's carrying, puts it on a turntable. His fingers drum the floor; the music blares. He rocks on his knees.

"Papa!" he calls. "You hear? Ravel! What a thief!"

Conversation is impossible; Madeleine goes to the kitchen. Milhaud emerges with a slow, arthritic tread and stops beside his son. "You hear?" the boy shouts. "Who does he steal from now? Ho, ho, ho!"

Half an hour later Daniel is gone, Milhaud's back in bed, cooking odors drift through the house. "*Voilà!*" says Madeleine. "All now we need is a place to sit for dining."

I clear the table of tennis shoes, yellowing copies of *Le Figaro,* half a loaf of hard bread, a novel by Julian Green, a Chinese fan and a pair of chopsticks, letters tied with a rubber band, a Hermes typewriter. I find two chairs hidden under raincoats over which have been placed sprays of dried palm and plastic baskets of rolled-up socks.

From gold-edged plates and crystal goblets, we dine superbly. Then Daniel helps me to haul my foldaway cot up from the basement. Madeleine brings sheets. I make my bed.

5.30.47 Ripples of laughter. I open my eyes. A few feet away all of the Milhauds are munching croissants.

"Darius," says Madeleine, "he has the head like Julius Caesar, *non?*"

"In his toga," says Daniel.

"Bonjour," says Madeleine sweetly. "Cartier has made such a picture?"

Clutching a sheet, I sidle toward the bathroom.

6.1.47 An afternoon on the hills of San Francisco. Stooping, checking the light, backing carelessly into traffic, Henri takes shots of some of the gingerbread mansions that survived the earthquake. When we stop for a Coke, he discovers there's no film in his camera.

"Merde," he says, "why have you not seen this?"

The day is lost. He sulks through Chinatown and through the many courses of the Szechuan dinner Darius has taken pains to order in advance; through Beethoven's Great Fugue as we sit in the Milhaud box at the opera house. The popping of champagne corks in Pierre Monteux's dressing room afterward provides no cheer.

"Forget it," I tell him, "it's a mistake anyone could make. Architecture's not your thing anyway."

"You shall not let this happen," he says. "I am not to be made like a dunce foolish."

Next morning, I was scribbling some notes over coffee when I heard his bedroom door open. "Tired, John? You would like one day without cameras heavy on your neck?"

Surprised by the note of solicitude, I waited for the kicker.

"Today I go alone," he said. "You rest."

"How you going to get into the city?"

"Friends of Daniel's will come. You stay. You rest."

The gesture was not the act of compassion I wanted to believe it was. As Daniel secretly informed me, Henri had persuaded a young

couple he'd met to allow him to photograph their lovemaking. "You are not to be told this," said Daniel, "you are not to know. It is understood they will fuck for Cartier only."

On my own, I moseyed about San Francisco, not for a moment able to look at anything for what it visibly and obviously was; everything I saw was "a subject"; the vertical city itself, tipped all angles and riding a blue sky under high-piled clouds, was neither myth or romance but "coverage." That revelation, chilling in itself, was confirmed as my day went on by another revelation even more monstrous: I missed Henri.

Back at the Milhaud's late evening, I saw that his door was closed. As I was about to climb into my dining room bed, Daniel looked in. He was wearing a fatigue jacket over a T-shirt and the bottoms of pyjamas. "Duchamp," he said. "I have been thinking. You agree with such a man? To move chess pieces on a board can be the substitute for living?"

Our bags were packed. We had come to the farthest westward reach of our travels and were about to face eastward. While Henri was loading his stuff into the car, Madeleine whispered into my ear: "Darius this morning is not so good. He would like to speak with you—alone."

I found him as I had met him—fully dressed, as formal as a corpse on his rumpled bed. He gave me his hand, shifted his weight, indicated where I might sit. "In this country I have been happy," he said. "Henri, I think, not so much. It is true?"

"Perhaps," I said.

"For me, freedom and kind persons," he said, "I need no more. I would like as I am soon leaving to make a little gift—a small opera, maybe, something it would not for young people be difficult to sing. You will think of some story that is American and joyous? Some legend to make a libretto? It must be for the joy, *un souvenir de séjour.*"

I would think, I told him.

That evening we were backstage at an ice show in Sacramento. A girl in feathers and rhinestones, with one white-booted skate curled around her neck, slid the width of the stage on her other skate, pirouetted, flew backward into the wings.

"Your Martha Graham!" Cartier shouted over the applause. "She can do *that?* On ice, it is possible to do everything, except say mass."

Reno, Nevada. Preoccupied with gambling, divorce, and marriage (weddings, a clerk in City Hall told us, outnumbered divorce decrees three to one), the transient population offered Cartier so many ready subjects in close-up, so many kinds of human extremity to feed his developing interest in American Grand Guignol, that we extended the single day's visit we had planned on to three.

Driving on to Virginia City, we spent a morning among its ghost town relics, wandered through a graveyard's tall grass and wind-smoothed wooden crosses, and came to a row of white clapboard cottages each with a tiny red light above its front door.

"Brothels, no?" asked Cartier.

A taxi from Reno, according to the company name on its side, drew up before the first of them. Two men in Stetsons got out, said something to the driver, and went up the steps. The door opened, as if by itself.

"I have this good idea," said Henri. "You will not disappoint?"

"What's your good idea?"

"We shall go in this house. You will talk to madam. She will have for you some nice girl, I will follow, to take the pictures."

"You're out of your head."

"John, this will do you much good. We are not like priests. For so long now we have been gone. This you need."

In the windows of "our" house, curtains were drawn aside to reveal two women, spit curls and bow lips, enthusiastically waving us in.

"See?" he said. "They want you."

The turning point, I thought—my sober-sided friend has involved me in a Gallic idea of a joke, and now he's stringing it out.

"You are a very funny man," I said, and started uphill.

"You will not do this?" he called after.

I kept going.

"You refuse? That is your answer?"

In the car, parked between the Last Chance Saloon and the Silver

Just Like Java / 139

Dollar on a street that seemed to drop off into the sky, I was watching a few listless tourists along the wooden sidewalks when the door on the other side was yanked open.

"I cannot work more today!" Dropping his cameras on the backseat, he sat back straight as a dummy, head up. "It is your fault! I am furious!"

The desert ahead glimmered like the first stages of a migraine headache. For a hundred miles we exchanged no word.

As stretches of sand gave way to snowfields, mountains to prairies, sociology gave way to scenery and we gave up. Henri curbed his impatience by memorizing passages from a volume of Mallarmé which, with tears in his eyes and a catch in his throat, he would recite for me; or simply by dropping his head and going to sleep. For days my notebook was blank, my journal no more than a logbook until, after a night spent in the whitewashed cells of an icy monastery near Dubuque, we came—6.15.47—to:

> Taliesin East. "When you get to be my age," says Frank Lloyd Wright, "you've made your pact with the inevitable." He stands beside a snaggle-toothed dragon of gray stone, his impresario's soft hat rakishly askew, and disperses a whine of mosquitoes with a malacca cane.
>
> Assuming that Cartier speaks no English, he addresses me. "I've been through this man's picture book," he says, "all those sad and miserable people. Does he know what a lugubrious gallery he's made? Take that one of Marie Curie and her husband. They could be attending their own funeral."
>
> Cartier, camera clicking, maintains his crooked social smile and, for the time, keeps mum.
>
> "Another Frenchman I knew," says Wright, "made the remark that this country had done something unique . . . gone from barbarism to degeneracy without having established a culture."
>
> (*This* Frenchman, I could tell him, feels the same way.)
>
> One of Taliesin's resident apprentices comes to show us

our rooms. The little suite assigned to me has Japanese-scale furniture and the air of a rock garden, with sandy surfaces of brown and tan.

"We take dinner seriously," says the young man, "no one's allowed to come late. Can you be ready in fifteen minutes?" I put on my one suit and tie and join Cartier, who's wearing his.

The room we enter is on several levels, like a nightclub. On the highest is a long table and, on lower ones, many small tables placed zigzag. On the floor proper is a grand piano surrounded by music stands. A broad window looks out upon a mile of rolling green. The ceiling is low, triangulated, and ribbed. Everything seems designed to relate people intimately in a space seemingly too large to make intimacy possible.

When the apprentices are at their assigned places, Cartier and I are seated at a table on the tier just below the main one. Wright comes in, introduces us to the several relatives who'll be dining with him at the head table. When they've been seated, the chair directly beside his remains conspicuously empty. Noise in the room begins to subside to whispers, a hush, silence. For half a minute the air is charged with a hum of speechless energy. Then, a door dead center on the highest tier is opened. Olgivanna Wright and an enormous sheep dog come bounding in and take their places beside the master. On signal, apprentices serve the meal.

Wright taps my shoulder. "The glorious young rebels of architecture," he says, "from all over the globe, twenty-two different countries. They work with their minds and they work with their hands. . . . Tomorrow they might be driving a tractor or draining a pond. It gives us a sense of family. My wife thinks servants are vulgar, the idea of servants. We've done away with it."

Since Wright does not tolerate smoking at the table, those who want a cigarette are allowed an intermission before coffee. Half the company goes out to a lawn dotted with dwarf trees where peacocks strut in the twilight among dim statues. In ten minutes we're all called back; the resident string quartet is warming up. As Beethoven follows Haydn, Wright speaks at my shoulder. "There you have the *real* Germany," he says, "the century we've lost. Will it ever come again?"

6.16.47   Peacocks. Awakened by hoots and shrieks, I contemplate the fir tree in my bedroom. Part of it's inside, part out, as though it had grown through the wall. A casement window looks on an enclosure where the birds walk about and peck, heads darting. With a slight lift of its tail, one hops onto a slanting roof and climbs daintily out of sight.

On an open terrace Henri and I are served breakfast at a table which, says Wright, was designed to save marriages. Instead of sitting directly across from one another and sharing the same space, each diner has his own area; his partner is either to the right or left. "No staring into dead morning faces," says Wright, "no blank wall of a newspaper."

In Donegal tweeds and black beret, trailing an outsize scarf, he takes us through his workshops. "I wear my houses as a turtle wears its shell," he says. We stop to examine a model of what will one day be New York's Guggenheim Museum—a spiral of concrete based on the shape of a cephalopod, perhaps a snail. "Everything I've realized working for others I've poured back into my own places," he says. "An artist should put no value on money as money. For that reason alone I've never allowed Le Corbusier to make my acquaintance."

We leave the studio to join a work gang revising the immediate landscape. As we climb a spongy rise, there's a disturbance. Everyone gathers around: One of the group has killed a black snake which he dangles on a stick, like Aaron and his rod. Wright congratulates the boy, climbs farther up the slope, sits on a grassy knoll. Calling instructions, he keeps a close eye on the digging. "Over there"— he points with his cane—"the quarry that gave us Taliesin. Used to run here as a child, barefoot in the squooshy mud. All this, everything you see, belonged to my own people."

A sharp whistle, far off: noontime. "Most of these young people are pacifists." He nods in their direction. "And they're right. War is waste, waste never to be recovered. Now it's possible we'll waste it all, return it to ashes. We kept playing with push buttons until we pressed the right one, to let the genie out of the bottle. Now there's terror before something so vast we can't find a name for it. I've been a crackpot long enough to understand what some minds have been up to. When the big joke's told, it will be on all of us." Walking ahead, he shepherds us back to the main house, waves the disciples on to the commissary down the hill.

As Cartier and I are about to say good-bye, Wright takes from his pocket a brown envelope. "Here, a little memento of your visit," he says to me. "Open it."

Just Like Java / 143

I remove a five-inch square of something I take to be rice paper, or a kind of parchment. "It's papyrus," he says, "not from Egypt, as you might think, but from India, a thousand years before the Egyptians got around to it. Who was it said history is a chronicle of misconceptions? There's your evidence."

A tomato-red Lincoln Continental drives up, Olgivanna Wright at the wheel. "My husband has many errands to do," she says, and looks at us as though we might challenge her statement. "He must now change his clothes and comb his hair."

"My wife is a follower of Gurdjieff," says Wright. "There is no escape."

6.18.47   Chicago. A young editor of *Ebony* in a bow tie, button-down shirt, offers us coffee, swivels in his gleaming leather desk-chair. "Let's look around the South Side a bit," he says. "You might not want to believe it, but for me it's always a matter of reeducation. . . . You'll see what I mean. But I've got to ask you to use discretion. A lot of our people assume a photographer is an agent of the law. Some of them even regard him as a sorcerer, someone who can steal the soul out of the body."

He guides us through hot streets bleating radio music, alleys strewn with sodden mattresses, broken pots, and gutted engines. Garbage spills out of bags and lidless containers among heaps of rags, tangled bedsprings, rusting refrigerators, stoves turned upside down. Black infants, flies crawling on their mouths and eyes, sleep unattended on the stoops of tenements. An hour of this and our guide has lost his jauntiness. "Had enough?" he asks. We find our way back to the car. The stench of stale urine and dead rats stays with us until we round a curve and catch the blue breeze off Lake Michigan.

Hours later we are in the Pump Room of the Ambassador East Hotel. *En travesti,* a black teen-ager in aquamarine silk breeches and a turban sprouting a single ostrich feather pushes his trolley toward our table: For a first course we can have shelled Maine lobster, Beluga caviar, Chesapeake oysters, stuffed California avocado, Gulf shrimp.

"It is too obvious, this country," says Henri. "India—there one would expect such." His camera sits dead in his pocket. Our meal, just as we've been told, comes flaming on a sword.

6.20.40   Detroit. Sixty-one days since we left her waving us good-bye on a Manhattan curbstone, Eli steps from a train in Michigan Central Station. As she and Henri embrace, she turns her dark eyes on me. "You have become so *thin,* Chon," she says. "Ti-ti, *look* at him. Why are you not so, also?"

6.22.47   Not far beyond Toledo we are driving beside a broad fenced-in area when in the distance Cartier spots something I can't see. "Stop!" he shouts.

I brake to a halt, he bolts out the door and sprints along the fence. Watching, Eli and I are still unable to see what he saw when, by the sudden droop of his shoulders, I know he's lost whatever he was after. Used to such missed chances and their sequel, I wait for the accusatory look that will tell me, still once more, I've bungled his opportunity. As lethal as an arrow dipped in curare, it comes.

"Mon Dieu!" says Eli, and grabs my hand. "Chon, you'd think it was *your* fault!"

Cartier's return prevents me from hugging her, but not from overhearing the blows which, in French, she rains on his head for the next ten miles.

6.23.47   Minerva, Ohio. Eli's eyes are bright. She has put a fresh red dot on her forehead. Her sari is a filmy green-blue, filamented with gold and draped in lavish folds. "Last Wednesday," she says, "I wear this to dinner when I sit with Nelson Rockefeller. Tonight, for you. . . . You like?"

The restaurant we choose looks like a country club. We

park in a row of station wagons and Cadillacs. Down a long carpet beneath a canopy, Eli precedes me to a reception desk where a woman with high-piled yellow hair cradles an armful of shiny menus. Ignoring Eli, she speaks over her head to me.

"I'm sorry, sir, we're not allowed to serve colored."

"What did you say?"

"We do not serve colored."

Refusing to budge, I spend all my reserves of invective. They buy nothing. Head high, the woman stares at the entrance door and leaves us standing as she goes to greet an arriving couple.

"Come, Chon," says Eli. "It is no matter. . . . We go." She turns to Henri. "Ti-ti, please. Tell Chon it is of no use."

In a milk bar that feels like a clinic, we dine on sandwiches that come wrapped in cellophane, french fries, ice cream served on paper plates imprinted with cows wearing false eyelashes.

6.26.47 Pennsylvania—Altoona, Towanda, endless green rain. The only restaurant we can find is a barnlike structure with a dining room decorated by enameled carousel animals and circus posters. As we are being seated, a mosquito comes zinging about my right ear. When it alights, I swat it with a road map, wipe away the fleck of blood it has left on the table.

"Is wicked, Chon, you have done a wicked thing," says Eli. "All creatures must live, all creatures are sacred."

"That pest from some scummy swamp?"

"In dharma you must believe," she says. "In dharma all things are holy, all things are one."

Cartier scrutinizes some painted elephants standing on their hind legs. Eli goes into a trance. We pick at our food.

"Mark Twain," I say. "You know what he said about Orientals?"

No one is interested.

"With them, he said, all life is sacred, except human life."

"Is wicked," says Eli, "is wicked."

Forced into a penitential silence, I drive through the damp twilight looking for a place where we might stay. No Vacancy signs are everywhere, except at a Hansel and Gretel tourist cabin, a sort of Black Forest chalet at the base of a muddy bluff. Henri and Eli can have an upstairs room, we're told, I one directly below.

Reading in bed, I smell smoke, a curiously aromatic kind of smoke. "Henri! Eli!" I call through the ceiling. "Do you smell smoke?"

"No, no," Henri calls back. "It is Eli. She is lighting sticks of punk, to drive away those evil spirits that have come out of your mouth."

Our philosophical differences were not insurmountable. Eli's presence had already transformed a grim pilgrimage into a hayride.

In Bucks County next day we came to the home of a Russian friend of Henri's named Alexei—a man, he told me, who had an eye for photographs, "X-ray, like Svengali." This information seemed neither here nor there until after dinner, leaving Eli and me to our own devices, he and Alexei disappeared for an hour to look, as Henri later told me, at some of the contact prints recording scenes from the earliest part of our trip.

After breakfast next morning, I was awaiting a chance to ask Henri how it was that a stranger was in possession of photographs I was myself hungry to see, when Alexei led us through his garden into a pasture where white-maned horses were grazing behind a split-rail fence. At the sound of our voices one of them came to be petted. "That horse I would care to ride," said Cartier. "It is possible?"

Alexei seemed to fumble for an answer. "It would maybe . . . yes, it would be possible."

"Now?"

"Now," said Alexei, and called to a farmhand who fetched a saddle.

Cartier leapt the fence. As he put a foot in the stirrup, the horse shied and skittered sideways. After three or four tries he was able to hold her still long enough to mount. She started forward, halted in her tracks, and threw him.

"She does not like you, Ti-ti," called Eli.

Brushing himself off, Cartier turned on his wife a snakelike eye and remounted. His legs clamped onto the horse's belly, he jerked the bit until she screamed. Eyes rolling, she twisted, balked, and let out a piercing cry that signaled her submission. Spurring her to a canter, Cartier circled the pasture twice. As he dismounted, the horse stood shivering, allowed the farmhand to remove her saddle, and then, with one long whinny, galloped off.

Conscious of Cartier's taut mouth and white face, we walked in silence. As we neared the house, Cartier said: "To ride a good horse is a refreshment. It is like a somersault in the clouds when you fly alone. All men can have such mastery. Cocteau said, '*Ne balancez pas si fort; le ciel est à tout le monde.*' "

"*Non, non, Ti-ti,*" said Eli, "*tu parles trop.*"

By the time we got to New England, I was home free, or so I thought.

There we stayed with friends of mine, a professor of history and his wife who had bought a farmhouse in a backwoods corner of Vermont. Setting out daily, we made sorties into Green Mountain villages and once-flourishing mill towns and, on a Sunday morning, accepted an invitation to the home of the poet Genevieve Taggard, near the hamlet of Jamaica. Among others in the vicinity Miss Taggard had asked to come for a noonday drink were Saul Steinberg and his wife, the painter Hedda Sterne. As the company settled itself in deck chairs and sling chairs, I found a place for myself on a quilted pad and reclined there in a position which allowed me to use the sole of my shoe as an ashtray.

"How do you make your foot come out like that?" asked Steinberg.

Surprised, I glanced down.

"I don't know," I told him. "I always sit like this."

"I would like to find out," he said, and drew up another pad on

© *Henri Cartier-Bresson*

© *Henri Cartier-Bresson*

which, in a few seconds, he assumed the same sort of Aztec posture I found natural.

Cartier, watching, brought his camera into play and caught us as we were. When his attention was attracted elsewhere, Steinberg and I found ourselves alone at the edge of the flagstone terrace.

"What is your feeling," he asked, "now that you have been so long with Cartier-Bresson?"

"Our trip, you mean?"

"It has been worthwhile for you?"

I thought it was, I told him, that the book we were doing should answer his question.

"I would like to make such a trip myself," he said. "In the war I have done Americans in many places, but not so much Americans in America. To do that, I would not go alone. You would consider this kind of traveling with me, next year?"

Like images on the bars of a slot machine, seventy days started spinning in my head, then stopped with a jolt. Steinberg, waiting, must have sensed my momentary absence.

"Perhaps you do not understand," he said. "I have known Cartier-Bresson." His head moved from side to side like a pendulum losing force.

Too uneasy to pursue the shadow he'd sent flying, I reached for my gin and tonic as, clapping her hands, Miss Taggard called for our attention. We were all invited to lunch, she said, and named a socialist philosopher and back-to-nature zealot who lived nearby.

En route with Henri and Eli, I pulled up at a general store for gas from an ancient domed pump with ivy growing on it. In the adjoining yard stood a sleigh with rusty runners and a bench-backed seat on which a rooster paced as he surveyed the movements of hens scratching in the dust. The only sound in the Sunday stillness was static, and an announcer's voice from Boston, the Red Sox versus the White Sox. "Ah," said Eli, "just like Java."

Through lumber camps and tarpaper communities, we came to a house built into a granite outcropping. Our host, in homespun shirt and pants, his face leathery and permanently solemn, led us into a room furnished with objects of raw wood. The stone fireplace was big enough to walk into standing up. In front of it was a wrinkled mat of straw. This, he said, was where he slept. Eli looked at me—wide-eyed, then slit-eyed. Drinks were not served. Lunch was ready at once. We took our places at a table that was no more than a broad plank resting on sawhorses. The meal was vegetarian and inscrutable: reddish mash in wooden bowls followed by greenish mash in wooden bowls, washed down with drafts of well water. Across the table Eli caught my eye. "The dessert," she said, "it will be big, yes?"

When the wooden vessels, most of them still half full, had been cleared, we sat back to await dessert: a handful of sunflower seeds poured onto a cheese board. Taking care to avoid Eli's face, I selected one. As I attempted to bite it in two, it zipped out of my mouth and landed on the floor. Trying not to yelp, I pretended to look for it under the table and managed to hold myself together until, still under the table, my eyes met hers.

In Boston, a note from Truman. "I'll wager you've lost twenty pounds," he wrote. "Perhaps I should have warned you that you were attaching yourself to an infernal machine. But hasn't it been enthralling? See America first, I say—even though it may be the last thing you'll ever see."

From Scollay Square to Louisa May Alcott, we spent three working days in and around Boston, then drove to Cape Cod where, late evening, we crossed the windy moors of Wellfleet to the summer house of friends of mine. Alerted by our headlights, our host and hostess greeted us in a vestibule off a room where ten or twelve people were gathered. Before I could tell who they were, Cartier tweaked my arm. "In this house we cannot stay!" he said. "Those people, I see among them Trotskyists!"

"Ti-ti, do not be foolish," said Eli, and demurely lowered her gaze. "Here we are guests."

Henri glared into the room as though it were a snake pit. *"C'est impossible,"* he said, *"nous ne restons pas ici!"*

Our hostess turned to her husband; he turned to me. For a long moment we were a mute tableau.

"Be calm, Ti-ti," said Eli, finally, "we are with Chon's friends."

She picked up her overnight bag; Cartier picked up his. As if they

Just Like Java / 151

already knew the location of their room, they started up the stairs. As our bewildered hostess followed, I tried to make apologies.

"These things happen," said our host, and we entered the living room where, at the moment, Dwight MacDonald was recounting in detail his recent dealings with the garage to which he'd taken his station wagon for a checkup.

7.4.47   Cartier accepts breakfast as if it were his last meal. Eli, in sari, chirps.

Our morning's task is the Fourth of July parade on main street and what else of conspicuous Americana the holiday may offer. On the scene we find: festooned baby carriages with live babies in them, Uncle Sam on stilts, Sunbonnet Sue and Gabby Hayes, fire trucks, school bands with fat tuba players, Spanish-American War veterans on canes, white-eyed mongrels in paisley waistcoats and tiny straw hats.

Cartier weaves in and out for shots of those on parade and those on the sidelines. I try to be everywhere—next to him should he need another camera or his light meter, scouting what's ahead or what may lie around the corner. Part of the parade ourselves, we string along with one marching contingent, double back to join another. Trying to see what he can't, I stop for a moment to take bearings.

"Out of my way!" With one stiff-armed blow he knocks me down and sends me sprawling among the contents of my camera bag. Back on my feet, I have one aim: to wrestle Cartier to the ground and pin him there until the hook-and-ladder, flags flying, crunches him like a beetle and flattens him to a long, thin ribbon of pulp. Spoiling for blood, my lips peeling like an ape's, I swing around. Where *is* the son of a bitch? Blind, I make for a side street and keep going.

Birds twitter in the hedges; branches shiver in the sea-washed breeze. The world, long out of focus, is all mine. Unharnessed, free, I want to sing.

Before me stands an ancient woman: matted hair, wild

eyes, a withered torso shrouded in the flimsy stripes of an American flag. I bid her good morning. She responds with a cackle, then with a tirade against someone invisible to whom she keeps pointing. Her face is caked with filth, her arms bony and red with festering sores.

Trained to see a subject in even the most pitiful of objects, I embrace the devil. On the run, I cut into the parade, grab Cartier's arm and bring him back. The photograph he takes will be famous.

Next evening, New York. Back where we started, we'd driven more than sixteen thousand miles, worn out eleven tires, four windshield wipers, three batteries, and each other. Mission accomplished, Cartier had thousands upon thousands of pictures; I had notes for them in a bundle the size of a family Bible.

In the noisy twilight of Fifty-eighth Street, I kissed Eli good-bye, shook hands with Henri, and drove off. In the backseat, Walker Evans's *American Photographs* lay face up, speckled and dusty and yet, to my eyes, whistle clean.

Accusing himself—somewhat elegantly, I had to admit—of being a "murderer by inadvertence," Cartier wrote two days later to say that in his sudden leisure he was bewildered without me and, with only one camera within his reach, "all lost." He was concerned, he said, about the right any human being has to demand instant attention, "to command like a tyrant" and remain oblivious to "damages." Perhaps individuals should only salute one another like ships at sea, he said, and so maintain their own inviolate separateness. In any case, I should be philosophical and conclude *"il faut ce qu'il faut"*—and to remember, he went on, not what happened to Emil Jannings when he walked into the The Blue Angel but to recall what Jonah must have felt when he discovered himself immured in the whale's belly. These were both instances of the destiny of displaced persons, he suggested; and then, quitting metaphor for a moment, scribbled his own conclusion: "Sorry, in a way to have misled you but *Dieu le veut.*"

Over and over again I tried to decipher this. I couldn't. . . . And then, with a chill, thought perhaps I could.

"Please John take a rest," said his postcard on the following day. "I am upset like after having committed a homicide by imprudence." Henri in a state of contrition had no place in my experience. Puzzled and, in turn, a little contrite myself, I told him not to worry about me and left it at that.

Invited once more to spend a month at Yaddo, I coveted its haven and needed its freedom. I'd hardly had a chance to tell Henri I'd be going to Saratoga on the first of August when he informed me that he'd be arriving there on the second—bringing with him Eli and thousands of contact prints for me to identify.

When they stepped from an afternoon train, I was on the platform to greet them. He was dressed in khaki, she in sari, familiar costume which did not prevent me from suddenly regarding them like creatures from another world. Was I newly aware of their aura of self-containment, their way of indicating that, having arrived, they were nevertheless forever en route?

High season in Saratoga had filled the great wooden hotels and carpenter-Gothic rooming houses. As we drove past queues of people waiting to drink their daily ration of the supposedly curative waters and other people lined up in rocking chairs on long verandas, I knew what was coming. When a group of men in black hats and yarmulkes crossed in front of us as we stopped for a traffic light, it came. "Just like Java," said Eli, and the light turned green.

"In Yaddo there are ghosts?" she asked as we drove on.

"Many ghosts."

"You have seen?"

"Only those who know where they're going," I told her. "After dark, all cats are gray."

"Ti-ti," she whispered, *"tu comprends?"*

Henri mumbled something in French.

"Mais oui," she said, *"même chose,* just like Java."

Passing the racetrack, we could hear a voice on the loudspeaker and a quickly spent roar from the grandstand. "Tomorrow," she said, "we come at the sunrise to make pictures, like Degas. You will come, Chon?"

I'd be working then, I told her, that I only went to the track to bet.

Just Like Java / 155

"Ah *no!*" she said. "At the sunrise it will be so beautiful. So many jockeys, Chon, with the shape like Truman."

When all the scenes and figures on the contact prints were named and provided with the dates on which they were taken, I invited the Cartier-Bressons to come to my room to see the whole collection spread across the floor, and to hear me read a few passages of commentary.

"Ti-ti!" said Eli, as she looked down at the pictures that crossed and recrossed the room. "*Incroyable* . . . like the wall in China."

Cartier's hawk eye, lighting up at one print, would pass quickly over whole sequences, contracting and expanding as, he must have realized, what he saw was irretrievably reduced to what we'd saved.

The particular part of the text I read to them had been chosen to indicate my general approach and its degree of American idiom. Uncertain about the latter, I was relieved when Eli interrupted my reading. "The boys in the back room," she repeated. "*Joli* . . . *les compagnons de la joie de vivre! Non?*"

Next morning, a knock at my door: Cartier, his face oddly "set."

"We must have the money," he said.

"What money?"

"The money I have paid for our traveling."

This was not our agreement, I reminded him, expenses of the trip were to be underwritten by our publisher.

"There is no more a publisher," he said. "We must have the money, for France."

"I don't have it."

"You can borrow," he said.

The car I bought, I told him, still wasn't half paid for.

"Go to some bank," he said, "wealthy friends. I insist. We must have the money."

On the following day I wrote a check overdrawing my bank account, then set about making inquiries of agencies that might provide me with a loan.

"Wednesday we come back," said Henri as I drove them to the

depot. "By September our book is *fini*, beautiful. We shall be altogether free, like birds."

"You do not work so hard, Chon," said Eli, "you lie down sometimes in grass and look at clouds. Take it easy."

The telegram that reached me on Wednesday read: SHALL NOT RETURN YADDO. NECESSITY TO PREPARE FOR FRANCE. HENRI.

This was followed by a letter. "I need dollars more," he wrote, and named an amount that made me whistle through my teeth. Would I bring these to New York as soon as possible, in cash? If, he said, I thought he was impatient, that was, he could assure me, only because his financial situation had become critical. He was "upset" to make such an abrupt demand but could see no other solution; and ended his letter, "Thanks, you bet."

One afternoon early in September I took a wad as big as a meat loaf from my pocket and handed Cartier his "dollars more." He handed me a mock-up, a sequence of photographs, roughly joined and crudely bound, which nevertheless had the appearance of a book.

"A presentation to publishers," he said. "By turning pages, they can see what has been done."

Turning pages, so could I: From thousands upon thousands of photographs, he had chosen exactly one hundred and ten. A third or more of these had been taken on the streets of Manhattan during the previous winter. The other sixty-five or seventy, taken together, constituted a study in morbidity amounting to a pathological casebook: deformed or otherwise gross figures, some of whom looked back in alarm or hostility at the man who had stalked them; others of whom, cornered by the camera, were too lethargic to care or too visibly cretinous to comprehend. The blue cardboard binding carried no title, only neatly drawn letters, "Foreword by Cartier-Bresson." Leafing through the collection twice, I put it aside and waited for the joke to be explained.

"Eli is preparing some nice tea, from Singapore," said Henri. "Friends will be coming. I have promised you will read those excellent pages we have heard in Saratoga."

Just Like Java / 157

His wife entered with a tray. "So long now we do not see you, Chon," she said. "Many times Henri says, 'Without Chon I am one without arms. I see this thing I do not understand, I turn to inquire, Chon is not there. . . . I am like his twin, missing.' "

Among the several friends they'd asked in was Truman. I read for half an hour, uncomfortably aware that my words had only the vaguest and most incidental pertinence to the photographs they were meant to accompany. As I concluded, there was a smatter of hand-clapping and an approving murmur. Eli spoke to Truman. "It's true, no? Like those words you have said already about New Orleans?"

He poked me in the back. "Let's cut this short," he said.

Out in the street, he suggested we have dinner "somewhere different." Since my car was parked nearby, I proposed we drive to a tavern I knew up the Hudson. Across town and onto the West Side Highway, I mulled thoughts that eluded conclusions. We drove in silence until Truman asked me what I "made" of the mock-up.

As much puzzled as affronted by Cartier's curious selection, I said no more than that I found it trivial and bizarre.

"That's about what I think," said T. "Where's there any room for what *you* have to say?"

The place for that, I told him, was with the pictures we took from the sand dunes of Cape Cod to the ledges of Big Sur, with the thousands of shots I had labeled and put in sequence.

The sun dropped behind the Palisades. We curved around Mohonk Circle and continued northward.

"Malcolm," said Truman, "are you quite certain in your mind and heart that there's ever going to *be* a text?"

He lit a cigarette, stared into the evergreen twilight on one of Westchester's little lakes.

"I hate to tell you this. . . ." he said and, at length, did. "This" turned out to be a visit by a friend of his to the Cartier-Bresson flat, during which Henri's mock-up was passed around for comment. Intrigued by the coincidence, Truman had asked his friend if he'd also had a chance to look at some of the text—only to be told that there was no text, except for the foreword. But, said Truman, he knew for a fact that there was going to be a text because he was acquainted with the person Cartier had commissioned to write it. Not *this* book, his friend insisted, perhaps some other book.

I kept my eyes on the road, dark enough now for headlights. "Why did you wait so long to tell me?"

"I couldn't believe it."

"Do you now?"

"In my considered opinion, Cartier will never allow anyone to be identified with his holy pictures but himself," he said. "If I can draw my conclusions, it's high time you drew yours."

Conclusion evaded me, but speculation was less pusillanimous: Could it be that, in his agent's files and available at a price, Cartier's photographs were worth, item by item, incomparably more than they would be worth published between covers, text or no text? I wrote him a letter reflecting this turn of thought and, hungry for corroboration, showed it to Truman.

"Nothing else makes sense," he said. "Put it in the box."

As I tried to deal with the long silence that ensued, I became the subject of the Kafkaesque story I'd read somewhere, or perhaps heard: I had checked in at a grand hotel, gone for a walk along the beach, and returned to find no key to my room, no signature like mine on the register, no one at the desk who could recall ever seeing the man I described: myself.

Wiped out and benumbed, I waited. When feeling returned to my arms and legs, I began to doubt my own interpretation of events and to think about what might still be salvaged. The letter I wrote next morning—a simple plea for enlightenment that perhaps did not disguise an anguished call for him to "say it isn't so"—rehearsed the steps by which we'd come to our sorry pass. All these aside, I said, I could not believe he would offer anyone the bizarre collection of photographs he'd shown me as the book he and I had set out to do.

His response was quick and curt: If I was "shocked" by the selection of photographs and its "presentation," that was too bad. The choice he'd made could not be tampered with.

The silence I kept after hearing this was no more than a clue to despair, but it worked like a calculated strategy:

9.16.47   New York. Bidden to "neutral territory . . .
like no-man's-land in a battle," as Cartier said, I join him
in the office of his newly acquired agent. A slim, govern-
esslike woman with a smile of remote compassion, she has
one thing to tell me: Every publisher to whom she's shown
Cartier's "presentation" feels there is no necessity for an
accompanying text.

"I am sorry," he says. "That is the situation."

Closed out, unable to taste the satisfaction of betrayal
exposed, or callousness confirmed, or whatever else in the
black comedy of our association has led to this moment, I
have nothing to say, nowhere to go.

"You can do sometime a book of your own," I hear Cartier saying, "poems, memories, *souvenirs de passage.* . . .
You will have much to say, John. Better now we remain in
our own right *artistes.* Better now we salute like in the
ocean passing ships."

Miles from here, a tornado gathers the million little
scenes of our travels in its spiraling cone. Its thunder, I
know, is no more than my heartbeat. Yet, to remove myself from its path, I stand up, find a door, start down ce-
ment stairs that echo like a prison corridor.

"John! Wait!"

Above, the door I've closed has burst open. The clatter
of footsteps is not stilled until Cartier, racing *brise-cou* after
me, opens his arms and pulls me into them.

"John! You have told me once of Henry James, people
who know each other this long time. They are discreet
. . . nothing! When at least they kiss, it is in the skies
lightning! We are those persons . . . it is Henry James!"

A month later, having accepted a commission to do an article on
Robert Flaherty, I went to Vermont to talk with his wife Frances.
Since the Flaherty farm was in the same part of the state as that of
the friends to whom I'd taken Henri and Eli in June, I stayed once
more with them. Up early one frosty bright morning, I left a note
with Maritta, my hostess, confirming plans she and I had made the

day before—to meet in Brattleboro at one o'clock, then drive to the village where we'd pick up the week's laundry.

Driving eastward on the same road I'd taken with the Cartier-Bressons, I crossed covered bridges slatted with sunlight and passed little cemeteries where every headstone bore a wingéd moon-face. When fishermen in hip boots casting flies waved at me, I waved back. "Just like Java," I said to a passing Chevrolet, "just like Java."

Frances Flaherty was waiting. On a flagstone terrace we sat down to coffee and croissants as she spoke of the years she spent with her husband on far-flung locations: India, Tahiti, the Aran Islands. "We were Bedouins," she said. "Always setting up camp, then dismantling everything and moving on. If we always had something to show, we always had something to regret. I worry about J.C., that charming Cajun boy you met in Louisiana? All that attention day and night, more money than he thought was in the world. And then we sent him paddling back into the bayou where we found him. Were we kind? Or were we cruel?"

I asked about Sabu.

"Oh," she said, "that was different. Sabu was on his way to becoming a star before we ever laid eyes on him. Not necessarily a movie star, perhaps a shooting star."

The sun was high and there was an Indian summer hum of insects and machines from the fields nearby. "What a marvelous man Cartier-Bresson is," she said suddenly. "How lucky you've been to know him."

I nodded.

"And what an artist! Is there a greater photographer in the world?"

"No," I said, "he's the great one."

Mindful of my appointment with Maritta, I said good-bye a little before noon and started downhill toward a covered bridge onto the highway. Without warning, something in my head seemed to shift, like loose cargo in the hold of a vessel. Rubbing my eyes, I tried to remove the sand that had suddenly got into them. Thoughts, scenes, reeled in front of me like close-ups and fade-outs in a film running out of whack. My fingers on the steering wheel felt like digits of wood. Unable to figure out what was happening, I made it to Brattleboro, parked the car, went into the first restaurant I came to and

Just Like Java / 161

sat at a counter. Before I knew I had ordered anything, there was a meal on the plate in front of me. Or was it a photograph of a meal? I couldn't touch it.

I stood up, twice my height, paid my bill, departed on stilts. The sight of Maritta brought me momentarily into focus.

As we drove westward, my head was a globe that echoed like a drum reflecting everything. Had I lost the power of speech?

"Maritta," I said, "you notice anything unusual about me?"

I could feel her scrutiny.

"How do you mean?" she asked.

"I can't say. I'm out of kilter . . . beside myself."

"Don't dwell on it," she said. "Everyone has such moments."

We passed the wooden bridge leading up to the Flaherty farm.

"That book you're doing with Cartier-Bresson," said Maritta, oblivious to the fact that she was about to drive a stake into my forehead, "what stage are you at now?"

"Oh, it's shaping up," I said. "Some problems, of course . . . the right pictures in the right order, mostly technical decisions. . . ."

"Here's where we turn off," she said, "between the two maples."

Driving alongside a village green, we stopped at a sagging gray house. Maritta went in, leaving me with fingers locked to the wheel. In minutes she was on the porch with the laundress, both of them overladen. Detaching myself, I slid out and walked perhaps ten feet.

Blue sky. Sailing clouds. A circle of unfamiliar faces looking down at me.

"You all right, young man?" The village doctor. My head was resting on his leather bag.

"I think so," I told him. "I came to see Mrs. Flaherty."

"Might as well be comfortable," he said. "Stay where you are. Wait until you're sure you want to get up."

He turned to Maritta, his right hand making circles around his potbelly.

"He'll be okay," I heard him saying. "Some little thing didn't agree with him."

ELIZABETH!!! A VISIT

Elizabeth!!! A Visit

YOU must . . . m'st . . . m'st . . . *ring* me in London,"
said Elizabeth Bowen. We had met on the edges of a New
York party and talked for no more than twenty minutes.
Her eyes were warm, but her thin smile had the unreal constancy of
something preserved by taxidermy. In love with her for years, I noted
both stammer and smile without loss of enchantment. "I'll be s-s-s-
*stop*ping at the Mandeville," she said, "or the Normandie. Déclassé
both of them, but good for a run in town. I'll give y' . . . y' . . .
you *lunch* at The Ivy."

With an old friend whose name is Robert, I got to England soon
afterward and, on the chance, wrote to her at the Hotel Mandeville,
from which my note must have been forwarded to Ireland. Answering
it from Bowen's Court, the house she'd inherited and whose history
she had chronicled, she asked me to come there, and included Robert
in her invitation.

Days later he and I were passengers on the rattling Killarney Express, Dublin to Mallow, when it squealed to a stop. Robert had met
her once before and, like me, had found her to be not at all what her
books had led him to expect. A writer whose great theme was the
pathology of innocence, she was not, as we'd assumed, the composite
of her own heroines, but a woman of commanding presence who
seemed more quietly masculine than most men and, at the same

time, as feminine as our mothers. We had long thought she was the only British writer of capacities approaching Virginia Woolf's, and that the element of comedy in her work was more robust and somehow more subtle. Of her private life the knowledge we had was, in literary circles, common: Married for many years to an educational administrator named Alan Cameron, she was nevertheless the frequent close companion of a Canadian diplomat, also long married. This relationship was regarded by American friends of hers we knew as a fairly open secret, yet one that still carried with it hints of Back Street liaison and insurmountable previous commitments. We also knew young women, some of them famous, bold enough to hint, or boast, that their claims on her attention had not gone unheeded, neither in print nor in bed. As for ourselves, had she recognized us as devotees? Or simply as reasonably presentable Americans it might be nice to know?

On the platform was a crisp and tweedy woman who introduced herself as Miss Bowen's secretary. As she drove us toward Kildorrery, she informed us that guests scheduled to depart had lingered, that since the house was not yet fully opened for the summer, rooms designated for us were not ready. For our first night we'd be lodged at a hotel in Fermoy, to which Miss Bowen would escort us after dinner.

Stopping the car without warning, she slipped out to swing wide the two sections of an ironwork gate painted white. Across a field close-cropped by sheep we could see Bowen's Court, a rectangular pile of gray stone almost big and broad enough to temper the vast banality of its design. Vaguely Italianate, it was bare of creepers or any other form of green growth, many-windowed, massively alone under sailing white clouds. As the car continued on toward a semicircular apron of steps jutting out from the house, she told us that Elizabeth would be joining us immediately for tea with the guests who had overstayed—a young couple. "Perhaps you know his father," she said, and mentioned a figure who was both a very successful novelist and a name in the high echelons of the British foreign service. "David himself is more interested in poetry," she said. "Miss Bowen tells me he's quite good."

Elizabeth emerged as we drew up. Taller and larger-boned than I remembered, she was wearing an unbuttoned cardigan, a heavy tartan skirt, fake pearls of nacreous pink on her neck and ears. Her coppery hair was combed close and drawn tight. The flat planes of her cheeks and forehead again reminded me of some Dutch or Flemish portrait I could not place. In the library she introduced us to her young guests, each of whom was as flaxen-haired and delicately roseate as the other. The late sun through tall windows struck the glass fronts of bookcases as we sat on pale velvet chairs around a table laid for tea.

"My husband Alan Cameron will not be coming down," said Elizabeth. "He wants me to say he's glad you're here. Have you been able to keep yourselves nourished in our poor postwar London?"

Photo by Elliot Erwitt, Magnum

Elizabeth!!! *A Visit* / 167

Robert, growling, lifted his hands and made a wringing motion. "I know now," he said, "how easy it would be to kill for food."

We had our first edible meal last night in Dublin, I told her, at The Dolphin, where the patrons consisted either of red-faced families sitting in graduated rows, or of rotund priests in threesomes.

"You are in Ireland," she said.

The young poet's wife, making no effort to join our small talk, seemed distracted, even hostile. While her husband followed Elizabeth's every movement with doglike alertness, the looks she turned her way had the cutting edge of scrutiny.

"While the light's still good," said Elizabeth, who was perhaps at a loss, "I thought we might drive out for a bit, to the mountains. The heather's in bloom, we may even find blackberries."

Stopping at a lookout point, we found the wind mild across a long valley which, already gathering twilight, faded into the blue distance. "That road, the one that seems to meander for no good reason," said Elizabeth, and traced its outline with a finger. "Remember Stephen Dedalus's friend Davin? Somewhere along the length of it he had his conversation with the peasant woman who invited him to stay the night."

As the others wandered off, I stayed on the spot, suddenly aware that I knew more about James Joyce than I did about my own people. This could be the very road my great-grandfather took more than a hundred years ago, trudging beside a cart through blighted potato fields toward Queenstown and a sailing ship for Boston.

"One has to remember," said Elizabeth, breaking my reverie, "the bedrock sense of place that keeps Joyce among the realists. *Ulysses* is a more reliable guide to Dublin than Baedeker."

On the way back we drove alongside a field with a skinny tower of red brick in the middle of it—a sort of minaret, uncertainly touched up with decorative bands and tufts of white marble. It looked like something brought intact from Constantinople and then misplaced. "What *is* it?" I asked.

"A folly," said Elizabeth. "Much the fashion a hundred years ago. When I was a child, my mother and I, poor relations that we were then, were invited over to Bowen's Court. A quite splendid motorcar was sent to meet us at the dock in Rosslare. Young as I was, I had much your sense of it, that one or one like it, and couldn't hold back saying how *really* foolish it looked all by itself so far from its proper home. Then one day we were invited to the house of the people who'd put it up . . . the same people, it turned out, who'd sent the chauffeur. Knowing me, my mother took precaution. 'Now we simply shan't speak poorly of the folly, Elizabeth,' she said, 'you must remember how nice they've been about the car.' It seems so sad in its funny way. One speculates on what it was meant to assert."

In the library, as we were about to lift glasses of champagne to the occasion, a maid came in. "Some young gentlemen" were at the door, she told Elizabeth, and would like permission to view the grounds. Turning to Robert and me, Elizabeth said: "Come along. I'm afraid David and Daphne have already become weary of these trippers' intrusions."

The "young gentlemen" were period pieces: languid and angular in bright woolen scarves and the flared trousers that had replaced Oxford bags, they blushed and twisted, spoke a lingo I took to be Max Beerbohm or maybe very early Waugh. The Lagonda they'd parked in the drive might have been traded in by Miles Malpractice; they themselves could have been part of the retinue of Zuleika Dobson. As Elizabeth, clearly amused, offered to show them about, Robert and I returned to David and Daphne and, if not the warmth of their company, that of the newly laid grate fire and the still bubbly Bollinger-Brut.

"Elizabeth enjoys her role," said David, "chatelaine or cicerone or whatever, but not for reasons you might expect. People she takes about think she's pointing out this and that when she's actually observing *them*. Odd as it sounds, she has this notion she has no imagination, at least none to spare, and so takes every chance to study the persons who've come with their hearts in their mouths to look at *her*. It's her way of turning importunity to advantage."

These remarks struck home. But whether they were directed at me and Robert with calculation I could not tell.

"The same with the supposedly great Irish talkers," said David. "She lets them go on, encourages them even, when the truth is she thinks them witless beyond redemption, really about as amusing as those gimcracks you can buy—paddy Irishers with tufts of grass on their heads instead of hair."

"No matter *what* you say," said his wife, "Elizabeth is as Irish as any of them."

"That she would not deny," said David. "What's your point?"

As the visitors drove off, Elizabeth returned to lead us into the spacious front hall which had recently been converted into a formal dining room. The wallpaper, pompeian red at the edges, was otherwise a fading orange-yellow. From it Bowen family portraits looked down onto the candlelit sideboard from which she served the meal without for a moment allowing conversation or her own monologue to falter. Her stammer, at first a point of troubling attention, somehow seemed to give her phrasing an emphatic bite.

"They were *not*," she said of the visitors, "quite as hopelessly Joyce Grenfell as they appeared. One of them is an expert on some phase of Islamic architecture. They all seemed to be acquainted with Isaiah . . . Isaiah Berlin. The claggy mannerisms are something that seems to have survived the supposedly new earnestness of university."

"*Elizabeth!!!*"

The scream from abovestairs hit us like a shot. No one gave a sign it had been heard.

"*Elizabeth!!!*"

Again, no ruffle of acknowledgment.

"I daresay it's quite the same at Harvard or Princeton," she said into the silence. "The official program opening out to make its sober accountings for changing times while the core of privilege remains untouched, not interested in even its own jeopardy."

Without excusing herself, she went up the stairs and, five minutes later, came down.

"Harmless as they were," she continued, "our visitors remind one how the simple fact of having written books leaves one open to every sort of intrusion and unasked encounter. This is understandable among people who have no conception of the total demand a book, any book, makes. What's utterly confounding is the same attitude on the part of one's publishers! Blanche Knopf, for instance. The fact that Shannon Airport is all but next to my door has her descending from New York as casually as a neighbor might drop by for elevenses."

Interrupted by a servant who came to remove the plates on which we'd been served a dessert of molded flan, she did not return to the subject until we were all back in the library. "Some of us may secretly invite more attention than we are ready to tolerate," she said, and drained her snifter of cognac. "Yet I wonder—would strangers make as free with Virginia . . . or Tom Eliot? Not that in his case the more brutal sort of intrusion might not be"—she waited for the word—"salubrious. The most extraordinary thing!—one takes Tom's poems as expressions of some irrepressible spiritual afflatus. Actually, he tells me, they are more apt to be the consequence of moods brought on by some very stiff drink."

This remark had a certain unintended resonance. Since Elizabeth had herself put away a number of whiskies and soda, several glasses of champagne, and several more of burgundy before we sat down to nightcaps, I found myself thinking about the road to Fermoy and the deep ditches where, even in twilight, tramps who once were kings and ghosts who once were bards propound Celtic philosophy. But she drove Robert and me through a very dark night with a disengaged precision that allayed our concerns while she pursued hers. "Bowen's Court was more or less our holiday house until just this year," she said. "The difference takes some getting used to, and the expense. So much life was lived there under other circumstances . . . when the necessary income was not a matter of twice-a-year royalties doled out from London or New York."

At a turning we could see lights reflected in smooth-running water. "The Blackwater," she said. "You may hear the noise of it as you fall asleep. Being the last of a line and without progeny, I suppose I inhabit Bowen's Court as little more than a curator. History seems to have offered me no other alternative."

On Fermoy's main street we pulled up to a doorway flush with the sidewalk. "Don't, in the morning," said Elizabeth, "attempt to pay your bill. You've had inconvenience enough."

In a dimly lit reception room we gave our names to a woman at a desk, then carried our own bags upstairs. "Isn't there more than a touch of Chekhov in all this?" I asked Robert. "Well-mannered people at cross-purposes? Unseen presences calling the tune? A house in the sticks, an axe in the orchard?"

"I'm borrowing your Pepsodent," he said, and twisted the single tap over the washbasin. "I must have left mine in Dublin."

The hotel probably had no patrons but Robert and me, and its staff was perhaps in the habit of expecting none. *"God bless you,"* loudly sang a chambermaid in the empty corridor next morning, *"and kee-e-p you, Mother Machree."* After breakfast in a dining room where tents of white napery stood expectantly on every table, we went out to stroll along a sad row of pastel-colored shops with nothing in their windows, until Elizabeth's secretary came to drive us to Mitchellstown to see the Saturday pig fair. This was meant, most likely, to give a bucolic dimension to our visit. But Robert, born and bred in Manhattan, found the naked little pink-eyed creatures revolting, and we were soon on our way to Bowen's Court.

There, seated on garden benches, we were chatting with David when his wife joined us.

"I've been up to see Alan," she said, "the darling man looks simply terrible. I don't think we should leave this house."

"What do you mean?" asked her husband.

"Just that," she said, and sent toward Robert and me an accusing glance. "He's so alone here, so *alone.*"

"Alan's been terrible for years," said David. "Aren't you forgetting why Elizabeth took him away from London in the first place?"

"Drink is *not* what I'm talking about," she said. "The dear man is deeply, *deeply* ill. Can't anybody *see?*"

David turned to me. "Let me have your address," he said. "My book's awfully thin, even for a first volume, but I'd like you to have it."

At lunch Elizabeth and Robert met happily on the subject of Stendhal, but not for long. Daphne's presence, oppressive as Cassandra's, was beginning to put a pall on everything, including the omelet and the watercress salad. Her husband's way of dealing with it was to keep his wineglass full. Mine was silence. Elizabeth's, an early return to her study. "Who's for a walk?" asked Robert, but not until we were alone. Heading into a scattered flock of sheep, we started across the greensward to the gate, then stopped to take snapshots and look for four-leaf clovers.

"David's pretty seriously in love," I said. "You and I are a nuisance he's decided to be good about, for Elizabeth's sake. His wife suspects we've caught on and makes no pretense."

On one knee, Robert aimed his camera.

"He may not exactly be Elizabeth's *cavaliere servante*," I said, "but don't you agree something's up?"

"Lift yourself on your right elbow," said Robert. "I'm trying to get your mug and the house in the one frame."

In the library at teatime my eye was caught by a curious porcelain object with an electric socket in its flower-printed bottom. "Eudora Welty sent it," said Elizabeth. "It makes chocolate. One is supposed to keep it at one's bedside."

It looked like a Bavarian stove in miniature.

"The first night I tried it," said Elizabeth, "it gave such a sinister chuckle I had to pull the plug to shut it up. Eudora'll be delighted to know you're here, I'll be writing her."

Elizabeth!!! *A Visit* / 173

Carefully, she refilled our cups. "What a perfectly remarkable woman to have come out of that circumstance," she said, "Mississippi." And did not elaborate.

At five o'clock the Irish sun had the slant and antique light of October in New England. Elizabeth supplied us with walking sticks and led us around the stone walls of a garden, then into the garden itself. "You can see what once it was," she said, her voice weighted, her smile without nuance. We ambled through a low maze of undergrowth among which a few hardy perennials had put forth ferocious blooms. The great house beside us, implacable and bare as Cromwell's hat, bore no relation to its surroundings. The fact made me suspicious: Had Elizabeth's *Bowen's Court* recorded the life of the place or, indeed, provided it?

"We dare not tarry," she said. "The Hennesseys are expecting us at six."

Repairing to our rooms, we washed in hot water we poured from jars into basins, changed clothes, and met on the front steps. On roads so hedged as to shut out the view on either side, we had to squeeze to half our size to allow tarpaulined lorries to pass on our right, and slowly tailed farm machinery that crept out of bushes and took up half the macadam. The house we pulled up to was small and dark-eyed, surrounded by wide-branched trees. In the living room around a low fire were several men and women, including a man who, we were told, was the amateur golfing champion of France, and a stiff-backed and meticulously coiffeured woman who said, "We had to drive over in the Morris. These idiotic little roads were simply not designed for the Cad."

Elizabeth's attempts to bring me and Robert into the conversation were subtle but useless. Mutely nursing our highballs, we listened to talk of the waywardness of servants, the madcap antics of someone named Maud, the deplorable state of the weather in Brittany during the month of July. *"There,"* said the stiff-backed woman, "we do *ninety* in the Cad whenever we bloody well please." She turned to Elizabeth. "Darling, haven't you done something extraordinary to your hair?"

"It's had a wash," said Elizabeth.

* * *

As we were driving back, I asked, "Are they the brandy Hennesseys? the five-star ones?"

"Members of the same family," she said. We'd come out of blinkering hedges onto a roundabout. "We might, don't you think, lower a curtain on the episode?"

Awakened next morning by a shaft of sun and a flight of swallows, I was halfway across the cavernous Long Room to the bath when I ran into Robert. We exchanged a pyjamaed stare.

"You come here often?" I asked.

"Stuff it," he said. "I love this place. She's beautiful."

Early afternoon, I found Elizabeth alone, taking the sun on the stone steps. "Sit down," she said. "It's been a perpetual surprise to me to find how very seriously Virginia Woolf is read in the United States. Your educated young seem to know her better than Thomas Hardy. Don't you think it's curious that Lily Briscoe should loom as large as Tess of the d'Urbervilles?"

"Not really," I said. "Young people like the shape of a book like *To the Lighthouse,* patterns they can make out, as if no one else had discovered them. Would Virginia Woolf herself have had any awareness of what you've been saying?"

"I'd venture, yes. The popular success of a difficult book like *The Years* in America was something no one could have foreseen. Yet she was obdurate, refused completely to believe that Americans were, at least in her sense of the word, civilized."

"How do you account for that? Her own godfather, after all, was James Russell Lowell. Didn't she know he was an American?"

"*Americans,*" she said, taking care to make the term abstract, "are a Fleet Street invention, a fiction of the popular press—which everyone deplores and, of course, reads daily without fail. Virginia was no exception."

She looked at me; I looked at her. "Americans I've met are generous," she said through her unwavering smile, "a quality we tend to assign to backward peoples, or the unlettered."

Sheep with black faces looked up at us from across the graveled driveway. Except for sporadic murmurs of talk or snatches of song from the kitchens, the house was still.

"Virginia's curiosity was shameless," said Elizabeth, "and of course there were always those among her acquaintance delighted to feed it, especially among the more outrageous young men she'd take care to cultivate. The tidbits they'd put on her plate amounted to nothing more than entertainment, I suppose, but they were of a nature decidedly anatomical. Virginia was not one to be satisfied with the merely romantic agonies of the *jeunesse dorée*. She wanted to know exactly who did what with whom and where, particularly if it was not in bed."

A low cloud darkened the landscape and caused her to put on the cardigan she'd kept on her shoulders. As I stood up to help her work an arm into a sleeve, she said: "Cyril Connolly must have been especially useful. Cyril has the peripheral vision of those who find advantage in snobbish distinctions and, of course, the outspokenness of a libertine. He once brought Virginia here, in fact. . . . But I think the deeper demands of her voyeurism were supplied by John Lehmann. He, no doubt, would invent what he could not certify."

"Wasn't William Plomer also part of that picture?"

"Yes and no," she said, "and truly no. William has a kind of dignity that allows him to forego opportunities others seize. . . . Dignity may not be the word—"

"*Elizabeth!!!*" The shout was abrupt, a cry strangled.

"There's something large and mellow about William's nature inimical to the coterie," she said. "I've always felt in my heart, when I should come into trouble, I'd turn first to him."

"*Elizabeth!!!*"

"He's South African, you know. Perhaps that helps him to remain one who can keep his own good distance in the midst."

She disappeared into the house out of which, a few minutes later, came Robert.

"I have a feeling that Daphne is the only one who knows what's going on here," I told him. "Like the obstreperous kid who insists the emperor is naked. She sees what she sees and won't be hushed. Her concern for Alan Cameron is a way of countering her concern about her husband's lovesickness."

"Don't you be fooled," said Robert. "Elizabeth knows. She's quietly keeping things 'up' . . . it's a function of style, *her* style. At the same time, she's being protective."

"But what's she protecting?"

There was impatience in the glance he gave me, and pity.

"*Us,*" he said.

Elizabeth, returning, said: "I'm sorry Alan is still not able to come down. He sends you a message. 'Tell them,' he says, 'that I like the sound of them.' "

Sound of them. The echo came from the vast facade behind us. "That cloud from Iceland means to stay," said Elizabeth. "I'll hurry our tea along. I want to drive you to your train myself."

On the way her silence enforced ours. The station platform was bright with other people heading for Rosslare and the overnight boat to Fishguard, where the London express would be waiting.

"My dears," said Elizabeth, "you know I loved your being here." And she kissed us in turn. Her permanent smile was gone, replaced by an expression of naked bewilderment, as if she were about to make a confession, or already had.

Unprepared for the welling up of feelings out of all proportion, we climbed aboard. Eyes wet, we stayed at the windows to wave. In the widening distance she stood like a statue and, only once, waved back.

A few nights later Alan Cameron died in his sleep. Soon Bowen's Court was sold. Empty and bare for a little while, it was then bull-dozed out of existence. Surviving her house, Elizabeth promptly re-vised its story. "Loss has not been entire," she wrote. "When I think of Bowen's Court, there it is. And when others who knew it think of it, there it is, also."

Elizabeth!!! *A Visit* / 177

THE SITWELLS IN SITU

The Sitwells *In Situ*

Jane, Jane,
Tall as a crane,
The morning light creaks down again. . . .

So she had written, and for the irreverent young poets of Britain she became "the Old Jane." Why? The outspoken extravagance of her personality, perhaps. Perhaps because of the alliance she formed with her brothers to combat, as she tirelessly said, all manifestations of the philistine. Possibly because of a style of life that seemed more congenial to fashion than to literature. Coming onto the scene not as an aspirant but as a sponsor, with a magazine of her own to serve as a showcase for herself and her brothers, she advertised her privilege from the start. She had been painted by Sargent, Wyndham Lewis, Tchelitchew; portrayed as St. Cecilia and again like a corpse on a catafalque in famous photographs by Cecil Beaton; caricatured on the stage by Noel Coward. Exotic and prominent, she made an easy target.

Yet her talents were genuine, her intuitions canny, her mission timely. Her suite of poems, *Façade,* had brought the most playful elements of *Symbolisme* into a drab period of English poetry. Before anyone else, she recognized and published the poems of Wilfred Owen, and spotted the genius of Dylan Thomas before the nets of literary trawlers could catch it. In her crusade against the parochialism of the stately home and the semidetached villa, she had shaken out banners proclaiming "another diapason, a new vision" approaching the barbarous. Her natural state was one of lèse majesté and she

maintained it with appropriate hauteur. Continually embattled, she was also myopic, striking out at friend and foe alike.

My first contact with Edith Sitwell was both routine and daunting—a letter from her in response to one of mine requesting biographical data for an anthology I was helping to edit.

"I object strongly to any autobiographical details appearing before my poems," she wrote. "My private life is my own, and can add nothing to the interest of the poems. I was born, and I shall die. That is all that concerns the general public.

"In the case of a prose book of mine, in the American edition, an extraordinary biographical note of me appeared (I had especially asked the American publishers not to put in biographical details, and they have since expressed their regret for doing so). In this note, practically every detail was wrong. It was *two hundred years wrong* in one case! The note said we have lived here for six hundred years. We have lived here for eight hundred years!—And I was not 'brought up at Renishaw Park'—which is the local golf course!

"I dislike intensely any intrusion upon my private life. I do hope this does not sound as if I were being disagreeable to *you*. Far from it. I am sure you will understand and respect my feeling. . . . Apropos of 'Still Falls the Rain'—no, the last line is not a quotation from anyone (direct or indirect). It is mine. The poem was written after the two worst raids on Sheffield—which were very, very bad.

"Oh dear! I *do* hope the earlier part of my letter does not sound curmudgeonly. Indeed it is not meant to be so.

"I am grateful to you for choosing some of my poems which I feel to be the best. If you only knew how rare such a choice is—but perhaps you do!"

I became acquainted with her several years later. By that time she and her brother Osbert had made the first of their reading tours across the American continent and I had become director of the New York Poetry Center, a position which led to my taking on the management of Dylan Thomas's professional affairs and, inevitably, involvement in his personal affairs.

When I got to the Center one afternoon in October 1950, the girl at the switchboard put a hand over her mouthpiece. "You suddenly

The Sitwells In Situ / 183

have about a thousand dearest friends," she said. "Want to take a call from one of them?"

At my desk, I picked up the phone.

"John Malcolm?"

"Speaking."

"Tennessee here. I'm told there's not a seat left for Miss Sitwell tonight. Could you squeeze me in?"

Curbing an impulse—Tennessee *who?*—I promised him the last house seats I'd been hanging onto.

In black tie, I got to the Hotel St. Regis at seven thirty and waited in the lobby until the elevator doors opened to reveal a tall, thin woman in a gold-threaded turban and a flowing black pelisse. In her arms she carried what looked like royal robes. "I'm afraid they weigh a most fearful ton," she said, and held them out. "It's so very kind of you to fetch me."

On Fifty-fifth Street six or seven people were waiting for taxis. As occupied cabs kept sailing by, the group got larger, the doorman's whistle shriller, his dance in the street more frantic. Finally, one empty cab pulled up. Before I was aware that she had left my side, Miss Sitwell was settled in its backseat. I fumbled after, tangled in brocade. The taxi pulled away under the cold stare of the stranded multitude. "Well," I said, "how did you manage *that?*"

"Oh," she said, "*you* know how it is—a little word here, a little word there. And it *does* help to be known as a particular friend of the people who own the hotel."

The precious stones on her hands were as big as plums. A cloth bag, a sort of governess's reticule, lay heaped in her lap.

"I must say, you quite startled me at the lift," she said, "you look so exceedingly like a friend of ours. Perhaps you know him—John Lehmann? You must come of the same stock. Would you know if that is the case?"

"I'm Scots-Irish," I told her, "born in Canada."

"Of course," she said, and placed a loaded hand over mine. "I might have known. One of *us.*"

I was still puzzling over the meaning of her remark when we arrived at the Poetry Center and edged through the crowd to the Green Room.

"Dylan Thomas," she said. "I've been told there's this American woman who's been causing the most fearful rows. Do you know her?"

I had to admit I did.

"Can it be serious, do you think?"

Trapped, I made a judicious face and shrugged my shoulders.

"That wife of his can be a Gorgon, as many a little adventuress in London has learned. She's been known to attack with her teeth, my dear—anything. With my own eyes I saw her reduce a most eminent dinner party of mine to a shambles. Mr. Eliot had to sit by while she *demanded* Mr. Hayward to lick from her bare arm the sherbet she had been careless enough to spill."

Her stare forced me to respond. "Did he?"

"She got as good as she gave. He'd lick the sherbet off of any *other* part of her, he said, but not at my dinner table."

An usher came to announce curtain time.

"Oh, dear, let me see," she said, and started to grope in her bag. "Spectacles can be so tiresome. . . ." After I'd helped her into the medieval trappings, she waited in the wings while I made my introduction. Then, stork-straight, she walked on to prolonged applause, nodded to left and right, rummaged through her bag, changed her glasses, and embarked upon her reading. But only for twenty minutes. Alerted by the sudden silence, I listened as she told the audience that she would take a short rest, that she would return to finish her program. Swiftly off stage, she made directly for the Green Room and stretched flat out on a sofa. Alarmed, I stared down at her.

"Is there anything I can do for you?"

"Tell me," she said, "what do *you* think will come of all this?— one hesitates to mention the word romance—this, this *dal*liance of Dylan's? What one hears on quite acceptable authority is that his gray lady—everyone knows who *she* is—has brought the whole story to Caitlin and that they've ganged up."

"Ganged up?"

"Just that, my dear, women beware women. It's an old tale with many a telling. I know you are discreet because you must be. I shall press you no further. Dear Dylan. The trials of genius. If you'll give me a glass of water now, I shall return to the arena."

Afterward, she sat at a table in the lounge and autographed books.

Just as she was about to be borne away by a covey of heavily jeweled women, she turned. "We are to be friends now, aren't we? You shall come to England ₄and I shall give you a luncheon party. You'll remember that I stay in the city until August. Pray, make it before then."

Before then she came, genuinely "by popular demand," back to the Poetry Center, from a stay in Hollywood where arrangements were underway with the director George Cukor to use her *Fanfare for Elizabeth* as the basis for a movie.

Her room, when I called for her at the St. Regis, was bowered with lilies, roses, hyacinth, amaryllis. It looked like a greenhouse and was almost as hot. Still unopened boxes with florists' labels on them were stacked along the walls. "Such kindness and such deplorable waste," she said. "Do you suppose I might dispatch them to some hospital?"

She crossed the room and reached for the knob of a closet door. "Mercy! I simply cannot get used to the shocks one suffers in this city. Ever since I saw blue flames *leaping* from a keyhole when I attempted to insert my key I've been careful to touch nothing unless totally gloved." She started to check the contents of her capacious cloth bag. "Well, now," she said, "I believe this Christian is ready to be thrown to the lions."

I lifted her long mink coat from the back of a chair. Since she was taller than I am, I had to hold it high. "Thank you," she said. "Americans are the only persons left with any sense of manners. I find it true here and I found it just as true in California. But I must say the appalling degree of informality there leaves one at a loss." She worked her left arm into the sleeve. "Perhaps not so much informality as it may be the effects of drugs. . . . I find no other way to account for the behavior of Hollywood servants. They come into one's room madly smiling, purring like cats, and all but jump into one's lap. Most unsettling."

We were alone in the elevator. "Now you won't breathe a word if I tell you a little secret? I've just had notice that Oxford is going to present me with a degree, Honorary Doctor of Letters. Isn't that charming? To think of the ab*use,* the *cal*umny I've had to endure from the pip-squeaks and blackguards who've come down from there. It almost restores one's faith in the scales of justice."

In the Green Room she fished in her bag and produced a lozenge. "Utterly vile," she said, examining the pill as though it were a species of beetle, "but I still have a touch of bronchitis and my throat feels like sand. I'm quite convinced I got it from Ethel Barrymore. An enchanting woman *but,* my dear, a breath you could trot a mouse on."

Her reading, once again an alternation of amateurish fumblings for books, papers, reading glasses, with a thoroughly professional address to the text in hand, lasted for an unbroken hour.

In Liberty scarves and Queen Mary hats, inverness capes and fedoras, mink, seal, Persian lamb, half of her listeners crowded around afterward as she sat at a table to autograph her books. The Poetry Center had never before drawn an audience of such affluence or of so broad a composition. Carson McCullers squeezed my hand. "Oh, that was lovely," she said. "I almost forgot where I was." Martha Graham, for the second or third time, introduced me to Agnes De Mille, and cast her eyes on a particularly formidable trio of well-upholstered matrons. "I doubt they came for the love of literature," she said, "but they seem not to be disappointed." My iconoclast friend Ankey Larrabee, in tennis shoes and an oversize trench coat, stood glowering. "Pretty high camp," she said, "you wouldn't hear *that* much talk about gold in the Klondike." The painter Theodoros Stamos grabbed my elbow. "I come for poetry," he said. "I get vaudeville. What's this place turning into?" Charles Chaplin, white-haired and dapper, parted the crowd with a small smile and moved toward the exit.

In London that summer en route to Dylan Thomas's home in Wales, I asked the operator in my hotel to call the number Edith had given me, the number for the Sesame, or Sesame Imperial and Pioneer Club, on Grosvenor Street. As the phone there rang for a long time without answer, I heard the operator whispering to herself. "Open Sesame, open Sesame." Then, as we continued to wait, she spoke up: "I don't suppose Americans know what that might mean, do they?"

The Sitwells In Situ / 187

A click, and the call went through. "Dr. Sitwell speaking," said Edith and, as good as her word, went on to say that she would arrange a luncheon party in my honor a few days hence.

When I got to the Sesame at the appointed time, the hall porter directed me to a purplish dim anteroom to await her arrival. Already on hand were several muffin-shaped ladies in squashed hats and strips of attenuated fur, and a wet-lipped young man with a black beard.

"What's on her agenda *today,* do you suppose?"

The woman on my left was not speaking to me but to the woman beside her.

"No telling, but it's always a show and she does get away with it. I come to watch. I leave word with the porter that I'm expecting my sister from the West Riding. The dear soul must wonder why she never arrives."

The bearded young man and I exchanged a congenial glance.

"A week ago she came in wearing the sort of wimple one sees in rustic pageants. She *does* resemble someone stretched out on a sarcophagus—marble hands and a look, one might say, of untried virtue."

"It's true? She has never married?"

"Never. There's a brother, if you know what I mean."

Dr. Sitwell loomed in the doorway. She was wearing a broad-brimmed hat of black straw, a cape of purple velvet. I stood up, as did the young blackbeard. "Peter," she said, "you won't mind going in to join the others while I have a few words with my friend from America? They'll be at table, awaiting the arrival of Mr. Hayward. You may be asked to assist with the chair and the taxi. Such a bore but there's nothing for it, there's a dear."

She sat down beside me and threw open her cape. Her chest was layered with big Boadicean plates of silver hung on chains. "I call it my shining armor," she said, "a gift from my lovely Millicent Rogers. She lives in New Mexico. Now, let me tell you whom you are about to meet. We'll be eleven: dear Maurice Bowra—you know of him, I'm sure—and Arthur Waley and Roy Campbell. . . . Then, for your age, kindred souls I thought—David Gascoyne, if he'll indeed venture this far without Miss Kathleen Raine. You *know* who she is."

"I know her poetry."

"You'd agree that what she produces is not so much the poetry of a lady as it is the poetry of a lady's *maid*?"

Before I could demur, she was off: "Women are hopeless as poets, except perhaps for Sappho whose accomplishment, in my poverty of Greek, I have no true way of assessing. Christina Rossetti had a modest moment or two . . . and I suppose one must recognize your Miss Dickinson. But perception, in her case, however deep, cannot excuse incompetence. And, to be fair, one could never accuse Marianne Moore of wallowing in the depths of being female."

Her hat, like a careless umbrella, kept bumping my shoulder.

"Oh, yes," she said, returning to her roster of guests, "and there's Peter Russell, the one with the beard I sent ahead, and for variety's sake Lord and Lady Moulton and the very nice Mrs. Kilham Roberts. I so much wanted Tom Eliot but he's engaged. He tells me he'll be seeing you in any case. Have I not kept my promise? Let us go in."

Our table was located in the center of a large dining room. I was seated at Edith's left, David Gascoyne beside me, Maurice Bowra opposite. Dry martinis and pink gins were brought in on a tray while we waited for John Hayward.

"I've been reading the most remarkable new poet," said Edith, "his name is Sydney Goodsir Smith—Scottish, wouldn't you know, perfectly thrilling in English and I suspect in dialect as well. You've made his acquaintance, Maurice?"

"Just far enough to agree with you," said Bowra. "But I must say I find the Scottish pieces a form of deprivation. One had thought that sort of double allegiance had ended with Christopher Grieve."

Into the momentary lull spoke Campbell. "All well and good," he said to Lord Moulton, "but to find one's translations outselling one's collected poems is a bit thick."

"That is bound to change, dear Roy," said Edith. "Saint John of the Cross, if I may say so, is not everybody's dish of tea."

John Hayward, having endured the ordeal of being trundled into a taxi in Chelsea and lifted out in Mayfair, rolled his wheelchair into place.

"So good of you to come, John," said Edith, and addressed the table. "This part of London is intolerable in July. If they're not ripping up the paving stones with diabolical little drills, they're splitting one's eardrums with shrieking motorcars and klaxons. One would as soon be caged with a flock of maddened yaffles."

She leaned my way, her hat for a moment tenting both of us. "You've noticed how the whole room is positively *eaten* with curiosity," she said. "They can't imagine who we all might be."

A year later we met at the Sesame again for an afternoon drink which, in her case, meant four double whiskies. "How I *do* love America," she said over the third of these. "Anyone who doesn't must be *mad.* . . . All three of us shall be there this time, if perhaps not all at once. And just as well—there's a tendency, you know, to regard my brothers and me as some sort of aggregate Hindu god with three sets of arms and legs protruding from the same spirit. Sachie will be going first. I've told him to be sure to ring you at once."

As it turned out, his call would not be necessary.

I was at this time well into a critical biography of Gertrude Stein. While I had spoken at length with Alice Toklas and other people important in Gertrude's life, I had not yet seen Virgil Thomson. By great luck, I found him aboard the *Ile de France* when I sailed from Southampton.

An entry in my journal reads:

9.19.52   With Virgil T., find a windowside perch in the lounge where we can watch the patterns of cutwater on a running sea. He says I must not make the mistake of taking *The Autobiography of Alice B. Toklas* literally. Alice's memory is bad, he says, I'd be wise to accept Gertrude's version of her companion's recollections merely as "convenient" impressions. I should also be aware that many of the quarrels and personal disruptions referred to in that book were the consequence of boredom. When Alice got fed up with "sitting with the wives" while Gertrude explored visionary realms with the husbands, she'd plot palace revolutions, then carry them out with "Spanish finesse." Edith Sitwell and Pavel Tchelitchew, for instance—Alice had little affection for either. When, to all appearances, they were settling into a favored place in the Stein circle, Alice was conniving "to give them to one another" and thus be rid of both at once. As for the Sitwells as writers: "Among the three of them," Gertrude liked to say, "they had just enough material for one first-rate man of letters."

The faint blast of the ship's whistle tells us it is noontime. With talk of absent Sitwells ringing in my ears, I leave Thomson for an aperitif, as coincidence would have it, with Sacheverell Sitwell and his wife Georgia—the consequence of a note to my cabin when they spotted my name on the passenger list.

Tall, with a statuary face, Sacheverell has Edith's deep-set eyes and a bearing peculiar to certain Englishmen: a ramrod verticality with an ease of movement made possible by bespoke tailoring. She is pretty in the way girls of the twenties with permanent waves and bow lips were pretty, and is running slightly to plumpness. He wonders if his lecture will find a sympathetic audience in Boston. I ask what he's lecturing about. "Poltergeists," he says, "there's been so great a resurgence of interest in the subject, I fancied Americans would like to know something about it— with very explicit and intriguing examples, of course."

With nothing to go on, I suggest it will. "After all," I hear myself saying, "Boston is not very far from Salem."

9.21.52   At sea; last night out. Georgia and Sacheverell are waiting when I get to the main-deck foyer. They have reserved a table for the entertainment after the captain's farewell dinner. We enter the Café de Paris where a glow of red and orange neon colors everything, like a fever made visible. Our chairs are of tubular chrome, upholstered with maroon Leatherette, placed around a rickety card table spread with fringed cloth on which sit a saucer of peanuts and a plastic ashtray. In shiny dunce hats and glittery tiaras of cardboard, men and women are pelting one another with cotton snowballs while an enthusiastic but inadequate group of musicians clumps through a repertoire of twenties jazz tunes and songs from Broadway musicals. Sustained conversation is impossible, but between sets I listen to Sacheverell.

"My sister adores America," he says, "but her last tour brought dollars in an amount to make taxes troublesome. 'One more triumph like that,' she told me, 'and I'll face ruin.' " A snowball bounces off my head. "One doesn't want to perform for charity quite, but one must anyway be prepared to sing for one's supper. Then, again, three Sitwells in one season may suggest an invasion. I thought I'd do poetry only on demand, as Osbert does. Would you say that the demand is perhaps as much for the performer as for the poet . . . on the order of Dylan Thomas?"

What he wants from me, I sense, is not so much information as encouragement. Nothing I can offer seems conclusive.

"Don't look now," says Georgia, with a nod toward the entrance, "but that perfectly charming Mrs. Samuel Goldwyn seems to be hovering in some distress, as if she'd mislaid something."

Sacheverell brushes a little mound of snowballs from the table. "What *we* offer must seem remote, perhaps even baroque."

"*He's* with her now. They seem only to be observing," says Georgia. "What a curiously matched couple. There's not a smarter woman on the ship."

Joining the dancers on the dime-size floor, we two-step from one standstill to another. Georgia, it seems, is in a pet. She speaks of her trials at the captain's table—a woman from Montreal who sours every meal with whining remarks about the snobbishness of the English. "Every bloody meal since we left Southampton," says Georgia. "After all, I'm from Canada myself, but so far I've kept that little piece of information *to* myself. Tonight when she started up, I could *not* put up with it a moment longer. 'My good woman,' I told her, 'I'll thank you not to clank your chains at me!' "

As if to enforce the point, she clanks her own armload

of golden talismans as we circle in place to the limp strains of "Amapola." When we return to the table, Sacheverell rises to his full guardsman's height.

"What do you know about Cleveland?" he asks. "Osbert says he's never been."

Among items of mail awaiting me at home was a note from Edith: "Meanwhile," she wrote, "my brother Sacheverell and his wife are arriving in New York on the 22nd of September. He is going on a lecture tour. He does hope very much to have the pleasure of meeting you. I will not give him a letter to you, as that, I think, is always so tiresome. But it would be most kind of you to communicate with him.

"I wonder if you know Sacheverell's poems. Of course he *is* my brother, but that will not prevent me from saying that I believe him to be one of the greatest living poets—with such a wonderful sensuous beauty, and on such a huge scale. I am sending you his *Selected Poems*."

By the time that curiously arcadian volume had arrived, so had she, "excited at being here," as she said in a letter from New York, with a postscript about Mrs. Dylan Thomas: "Caitlin has been very active lately—but more in the verbal way than by strong-arm stuff." She and her brother Osbert would stay in the city briefly—she en route to Hollywood; he to Florida, with their joint appearance at the Poetry Center scheduled for December 18, an event for which all seats were sold well in advance. To make things easy for all of us, Edith suggested we dine *à trois* that evening in their hotel suite.

Meeting Sir Osbert for the first time, I was surprised only by the sense of perpetual apology that marked his manner and deportment. His smile was wan, his eyes sad, his voice subdued. Whether this was his natural disposition or a consequence of his illness (I'd been told it was Parkinson's disease), I had no way of knowing. I could feel the tremor in his hand as he shook mine, and his movements even across the width of a room were slow and painful to watch. Yet a flicker of good humor that continually played about him forestalled pity and invited one to give it larger opportunity. About their friend Evelyn Waugh, he was wry: "Fancy leaving calling cards at a hotel

Photo by R. Thorne McKenna

desk," he said. "Evelyn apparently wants to dismiss the telephone, along with everything else that tells him the world has changed. Bumbershoots and bowlers may still be de rigueur in St. James's but on Fifth Avenue I'm afraid they make one look like an unemployed busker."

Patient with his sister's inevitable rehearsals of real or imagined assaults upon her person, her reputation, and her peace of mind, he neither interrupted nor contributed to her litany of injustice and imposition. When the waiter who had already made several trips to the room returned with menu cards, she gave him a motherly pat on the arm. "Nathaniel," she said, "I shall have no dessert whatsoever, you may bring me a double brandy."

"I recommend the fraise soufflé, John," said Sir Osbert. "You'll find it sheer heaven."

This scene—setting, costume, personae—was duplicated three months later, as my journal reminds me:

"Besieged!" says Edith, "I am eternally be*sieged* by poetesses. Would you believe that the maddest of them once made her way to the very doors of Renishaw?"

"What did you do?"

"I had the servants pack her off, of course, to the Sitwell Arms. That's an inn, our home for the unwanted. If only I could do as much here. They stalk me in the lobby, they send me their wretched female caterwaulings special delivery and have the gall to ask how I manage to get published!"

Nathaniel arrives with martinis on a tray. Edith lifts one, holds it high. "To the last of the Eumenides!"

Osbert, unable to raise his glass more than an inch or two, bends to the table and sips, audibly. I ask Edith about Hollywood.

"A sleeveless errand, I fear, and my last," she says. "They've proceeded to reduce everything I've done to shrieking vulgarity. Henry the Eighth did *not* use napkin rings! Nor, I might add, did he batten on the thighs of small beasts in the repulsive manner attributed to him.

The Sitwells In Situ / *195*

That simpering Charles Laughton! The idea of him holds them in thrall. I do not intend to stand by and allow them to turn a glorious history into the antics of buffoons."

Throughout the meal Osbert is subdued—to such an extent that Edith apparently feels called upon to explain.

"You find us in the greatest distress, John. Queen Mary . . . the Queen Mother's death has reminded us once again that the world we've known has vanished. Osbert was of the greatest comfort to her in the days of the war. Only last year he sat with her to view the coronation."

"We were very close," says Osbert. "Her Majesty was so emotional."

Since they were in residence at Renishaw that summer, I did not see them when I went to England and later made a side trip to Wales in an effort, entirely unsuccessful, to dissuade Dylan Thomas from making another trip to America. When Dylan died on November 9, Edith and Osbert were on their way to New York aboard the S.S. *United States.* Responding to my radiogram to the ship, they sent one in return, asking me to meet them when they would disembark on November 12. At Pier 90 before daybreak on that date, I waited for hours until they were cleared and then could but embrace them and perhaps by my presence make the fact of Dylan's death tangible. There was no more than a flick of tears among the three of us. Still, it was some time before we were able to speak.

"Come to us," said Edith, "as soon as you can—today?"

I left them in the care of the man from the steamship company assigned to see them through, made a late morning's visit to Caitlin Thomas at the house in the Village where she was staying with friends, then rejoined them at the St. Regis. There, in an obsessive trance of recollection, I told them all I could remember of the four long days of Dylan's dying.

"I know what a mother must feel who has lost a child," said Edith, "a dreadful numbness, a surrender nothing will relieve."

A week later, on the evening when she would read at the Poetry Center, she came, unescorted, into the Green Room and dropped her bag onto a chair. "The most scandalous thing is about to be perpe-

Photo by R. Thorne McKenna

trated," she said. "I can*not* understand why the poor woman's bones cannot be allowed to lie in peace. If one *is* that way, as I happen *not* to be, one *is* that way. It is the proper concern of no one but oneself."

I didn't know what she was talking about, a fact that must have shown in my face.

"I'm speaking of Miss Emily Dickinson," she said. "One of your so-called scholars—a woman, mind you—has looked into some musty closets and come up with perfectly astonishing evidence that the great love of her life was not that Reverend What's-his-name at all. The great love seems to have been a female."

"What sort of evidence?"

"Circumstantial, as I suppose it would have to be. Whatever, it has sufficiently impressed the editors of one of your glossies to lead them, quite without justice I should say, into publishing details of a most unsettling nature."

An usher beckoned me to the doorway. "Tell her highness it's five minutes to curtain," he said.

"Some of our dearest friends in England have had to suffer just such unnecessary exposure," she went on. "Perhaps I don't have to tell you who they are?"

My look was blank.

"Perhaps I do. Of what earthly use is it to know that Emily Dickinson was of a Sapphic disposition? The emotions are the same, whatever their objects. Sensible people know that, don't you agree? My own life, I can tell you, has been so much a matter of what could be construed as illicit anguish that I can understand it all."

The idea that I write an account of Dylan Thomas's life and death in America came from Edith and Osbert on the day when, for them alone, I had detailed the circumstances of his collapse. Then my one concern was to get away, to put space and time between me and the event, to accept its inevitability and perhaps come to acquiescence. After handing in my resignation as director of the Poetry Center, I spent weeks by myself on an island and came back ready, or so I thought, to resume my teaching and get on with my book on Gertrude Stein. What I hadn't counted on was delayed reaction, in my case severe enough to put me into a hospital bed for two weeks and keep me immobilized at home for two more. Back on my feet, I was able to carry out my remaining duties for the Center and, one day in March, to accept the Sitwells' invitation to lunch.

When I joined them in the King Cole Room, Edith was wearing a hockey player's sweater under mink and an Ottoman empire turban ribbed like a pumpkin, Osbert a dark blue suit with a faint chalk stripe. As we studied the menu over martinis (Edith would eventually put away three of these), he recommended an entrée with a French name. Edith said she'd never heard of it. Neither had I. "It's what Americans call pot roast," he said, and we all ordered it.

Talk came around to Gertrude Stein. "She was forever wrong about people," said Edith, "in, I think, every conceivable way. If she told you someone was the very dearest friend of someone else, you could be certain those people were deadly enemies. . . . But, since she lived on gossip and those little mischiefs of Alice's, I suppose that didn't matter in the end. Osbert and I had simply to learn to accept everything she told us as something quite opposite to what she made it appear. Oh, the trouble that one made pursuing *petits maîtres* . . . and showing herself as eccentric when eccentricity was simply *no* part of her simple nature. All the same, I did so admire that early work of hers—the *Geography* . . . what is the rest of it?"

"*Geography and Plays.*"

"*That's* the one. I thought it was something worth hailing, and so I did. We became friends at once, then Osbert and I brought her to England and went about with her while she proceeded absolutely to s*educe* the brightest young men of Oxford and Cambridge."

Surveying the crowded room, she nodded with mechanical smiles to people at nearby tables who appeared to recognize her. "John!" she said with sudden vehemence. "I do *hope* you are going to give us a full account of Dylan. We urge you, we implore you. Now *are* you?"

I was hesitant, I told her, to write anything for general publication, on two quite different scores: The experience was still too painfully close to me; much of the story, no matter how truthfully told, would be open to morbid interpretations—not scandalous in the way of salacious anecdotes people had made up, yet in itself something that would make a fairly sobering record.

"Then," she said, "you must do precisely what Osbert has done.

The Sitwells In Situ / *199*

You must write *two* accounts—one to set the record straight as only you can, another to be put aside until persons to whom it might give offense are dead and buried, as I've already decided to do with my letters to Pavlik Tchelitchew."

Osbert nodded in agreement. "When indiscretions become historical," he said, "they become discreet. Parts of my autobiographies will not be accessible to anyone for another hundred years. You could make the same sort of arrangement with the Library of Congress, under a similar injunction. Whatever, you *must* do it, John. It would be a shame if you were to let the story get away from you because of scruples that do not apply."

When our waiter presented the bill, he and Osbert went into conference. Edith, whispering, leaned toward me. "A most dear friend takes care of all our expenses. Isn't that lovely?"

Osbert wrote down a figure for the tip and signed the tab. The waiter bowed, then stood to let us pass.

A few weeks later I got a call from the State Department asking if I would serve as the American delegate to an international congress of poets to be held in Belgium. Glad for the free ride this would entail, I said yes and, later in the same day, got a letter from Edith inviting me to Renishaw, not on her behalf but Osbert's since, she said, she was dealing with matters that would keep her in London. "Do propose yourself to lunch," she wrote, "any day excepting the 10th and 11th when I have to record *Façade* for the Decca company.

"Oh dear! *What* is this about dear Dylan? If you are having fresh trouble, I am sure you ought to go to a lawyer. Caitlin has been giving hideous trouble. I'll tell you about it when I see you. One of the trustees told me he dreaded to open the papers each morning and evening.

"P.S. It is great fun. I am 'Dame Edith' now. The Queen has created me a Dame Commander of the British Empire—a fearful slap for the Pipsqueakery."

Early in August I sailed for Ireland, spent a short time in Dublin, and en route to Renishaw, flew to Manchester—from which point the entry in my journal for August 13, 1954, provides detail:

In the xanthic glow of Manchester Central, I board a train that smells of plush and disinfectant. In Sheffield late morning, I hire a taxi for the cross-country passage to Renishaw Hall. The driver, an ape-size man of fifty in a blue serge suit, says he has no idea where that might be. But the challenge of finding it, and the size of the fare I agree to, appeals to him. As we start off, I'm less concerned about the route than the fact that an exchange of notes and telegrams with Sir Osbert has still not established my arrival time.

The countryside is bland and suburban: cropped fields rolling gently, punctuated by rows of semidetached brick villas, roadside stands advertising Tea Within and Coaches Welcome. In less than an hour, helped by people we stop to question, we've come to the wrought-iron gates of Renishaw Park. We follow a drive that cuts across a golf course, climb a slope lined with ancient trees to a clearing from which we can see the great Jacobean house. Its hundred eyes are vacant, its yellow facade scabrous, flaked and pocked like the bark of an old elm. We swing into a semicircle of gravel and stop at a stone apron extending far out from the main door. There, immensely alone on his two canes, a shawl across his shoulders, stands Sir Osbert, shyly smiling. (How long has he been waiting like this? My heart breaks in two.)

Gripping a cane in each hand, he leads me into an entrance hall which glints like an armory: spears in racks, suits of mail, breastplates and helmets, objects of silver and brass, an enormous longbow that could have been used only by some Brobdingnagian archer. "That's Robin Hood's bow," says Osbert. "I hope you're not famished. We'll lunch as soon as you've had a chance to wash up."

Servants pick up my bags and I follow them up a long staircase under a graduated series of oil portraits. The room to which I'm assigned is of modest size, a large part of the space taken up by a bed heavily canopied and tasseled. To

The Sitwells In Situ / 201

sit on it, I have to hoist myself up and let my legs dangle. There's a big brass container with a spout like that of a gardening can on the glass-topped bedstand which also supports a porcelain washbasin and a big pink rosebud of soap. Since the container is filled with hot water, I pour it into the basin and make my ablutions without interrupting my survey. Above a shiny chest of drawers hangs a pencil sketch of Lady Ida in a gold frame. A few yards from the foot of the bed, there's an armoire with mirrored doors which reach almost to the ceiling. The windows, framed by serpentine growths of vines, look out upon a drop-step series of formal gardens in which stand obelisks of green and heroic figures of stone. The last and lowest of these terraces is a semicircular enclosure of unmowed grass where some cows are grazing. Beyond this is a little lake separated from the gardens by a fissure in the landscape, which reveals itself only when a subterranean rattle and a swift upward drift of steam indicates the passage of a goods train.

Changing into what I trust is appropriate costume for Sunday in a country house, I find my way downstairs. A maid in a starched pinafore guides me to the "red" drawing room. Waiting there, I poke about in its vast Pompeian redolence, open leather-bound tomes of etchings, study the familiar Sargent portrait of all of the Sitwells: Edith about nine, standing beside Sir George who is in riding clothes with his arm around her shoulders; Osbert about three, playing on the floor with the infant Sacheverell and a black pug dog; Lady Ida—the compositional center of the painting—posed, wan yet upright, in a sequined dress and a hat with a transparent brim. The portrait hangs in the middle of a wide wall, above the Renishaw Commode by Adam and Chippendale—reproduced in the painting itself—and nicely modifies the mythological Sturm und Drang of figures in other large canvases ranging around the room.

Osbert comes in. Careful of his steps, he maneuvers himself to a point where he can simply drop into an upholstered chair. Behind him comes a little woman who seems to be wringing her hands even when she is not—his secretary, Miss Andrade.

"Miss Andrade is my good angel," he says. "She takes down everything I say and never ventures to tell me how foolish it might be. Then she types it up and has the effrontery to hand it back to me. Shall we have some sherry?"

In an apparent agony of shyness, Miss Andrade pours from a decanter. "It's a shocking experience to lose the use of one's ten fingers," says Osbert, "especially when one has reached the carelessness of senility and is ready to tell everything. But Miss Andrade is my fingers now. Pity she will not admit of censoriousness; at least not to me."

"Sir Osbert," says Miss Andrade, "you know very well that you censor yourself more strictly than anyone else ever could."

"I was not aware that you had noticed," says Osbert, just as luncheon is announced. "Now, John, I must ask you to observe our little ritual. You and Miss Andrade will go ahead and settle yourselves. I shall follow at my own pace, just as soon as I can pull these wretched bones together."

We proceed to a dining room at one end of which, on a marble-topped table supported by four Atlaslike figures, sits a bust of George III beneath the scalloped whiteness of an Adam ceiling.

"It would be well to stand clear of that end of the table," says Miss Andrade. "The dear man is not always able to stop when he wants to."

In silence for a minute, we hear the thud of quick, heavy steps from the distant drawing room and the intervening hallways. Osbert comes hurtling through the doorway like an express train, quite unable to stop himself until he hits the table and is jolted to a halt. We sit down—not at the candelabraed banquet board that occupies the center of the room, but at a small table with a view of misty gardens.

Contemplating the poached salmon, I ask after Edith. "My sister prefers to summer in the city," he says. "She finds Renishaw too cold. She stays at her club until it shuts down for August, then moves to Durrant's. That's an old coaching inn off Manchester Square rather like a bed-sit boarding house for what used to be called gentlewomen. Lately she's been occupied with a new recording of *Façade* she's making for the Decca people." He attempts to lift a sauce boat of mayonnaise, but has to return it, rattling, to the table. Miss Andrade takes over.

"Miss Andrade, perhaps you'll show Mr. Brinnin about the gardens a little later on?" He turns to me. "Miss Andrade has become our resident cicerone, perforce. The house is open on Wednesday afternoons to anyone who wishes to visit. She's had to learn much that I seem to have forgotten."

"Is the part of the gardens you used to call 'the wilderness' still as it was?"

"More overgrown, I believe, and perhaps more forbidding than ever. Miss Andrade will take you. You'll understand what I mean when I say we all three were hatched there. Edith's Colonel Fantock, of course, and Sachie's wanderlust. It was the first place we could get to, away by ourselves. If we could run *that* far from tyranny, we thought, someday we might go further. Quite early on Sachie made up his mind to see every notable piece of art and architecture in the world, and so he has. Down the garden path, you might say, to Machu Picchu and the Caves of Ajanta."

When we've had our coffee, Miss Andrade rises. "Would it be convenient," she says, "if I were to knock you up about four?"

I allow that it would be. She disappears, leaving me to help Osbert into his black overcoat and see him into the car in which, a lap robe over his knees, he is to be chauffeured to Chesterfield station to greet his longtime friend David Horner.

Promptly at four Miss Andrade does indeed knock me up. We begin our *giro* in the dripping rose garden, move

on to peer into the brambles of "the wilderness," circle Sir George's pretty folly of wedding-cake architecture—a Gothic temple now overgrown with ivy—and return, chilled, to an enormous tea tray set out in the glow of a banked coal fire.

Not until I'm back in my room and the twilight is beginning to deepen do I become aware that there's no lamp to switch on, nothing to dress by but the last flickers of daylight in the mirrors of the armoire. The great house is without electricity.

At precisely seven forty-five—the appointed hour for cocktails—I'm in my dinner jacket and total darkness. But the staircase, at least, is lit by candles in sconces. I descend to find David Horner in the library, pouring martinis. Osbert introduces me to his friend, who is tall, with a middle-aged suggestion of Rupert Brooke handsomeness and an air of being much at ease in his clothes and the place. Just back from New York, he has come by sleeper plane. "Deliciously comfortable," he says, "but deplorably expensive. One could cross in the *Queen Mary* for the price. But seventeen hours *above* the Atlantic is much to be preferred to five days *on* it. How have *you* traveled this far?"

"On a small Dutch ship," I tell him, "Hoboken to Cobh in eight days."

"How many would you say she carried in First Class?"

"Exactly forty," I say, "with about eight hundred in Tourist Class"—as yet unaware that I've frustrated the first of the feelers he will put out in an attempt to "place" me.

One wall of the room is hung with tinted etchings of horses. Osbert notices my glance. "You've been surprised, no doubt, by our little equine exhibition? We try to keep the house more or less as Sir George left it, so we must put up with his filthy beasts, as well. I don't abide them in reproduction any more than I could when I had to mount them."

As we enter the dining room, firelight from the grate makes flying shadows on the four walls and in the fluted niche where the eyes of George III maintain their marble stare. Osbert apologizes to me, as an American, for the prominence given to "your" old enemy. "One of my ancestors," he says, as if to explain everything.

The blaze in the grate is hot and high. Only the fire screen placed at my right shoulder keeps me from turning the color of the steamship-round of roast that comes in on a trolley; and I'm much relieved when we return to the milder climate of the library for demitasses and snifters of Napoleon.

"Do you share our fondness for Palm Beach, Mr. Brinnin?" asks David. "We found it most amusing when we were staying in Hobe Sound not long ago, but now Osbert thinks Sarasota and is *not* to be dissuaded."

"You must know my friend Chick Austin," says Osbert.

"Only as the man who was the power behind that first production of Gertrude Stein's *Four Saints*," I tell him, "in Hartford."

"Now he's in charge of an exquisite little museum in Sarasota. Americans seem not to know of it. Even to me it sounds unlikely, but it does quite splendidly exist."

At midnight we repair to the entrance hall, there to light tapers at one large candle. "Now that you know your way," says Osbert, "perhaps you'll consent to lead us upward and onward."

Holding my flickering taper high, I start up the drafty stairs under the glazed eyes of the portraits. Assembled on a landing, we say good night and, lights diminishing in several directions, find our rooms. In mine a little forest of candles is burning on the night table, on the lower shelf of which is a volume of essays by Stephen Spender. Four pages of this and I'm left with barely enough strength, between deep breaths, to lean over and say, "Out, out . . ."

8.16.54   An instant flood of daylight. A tall maid has whipped the draperies across one window and is about to do the same to the other. Then, without a word, she reaches down, picks up my shirt, pants, socks, underwear, and carries them out. (Where is she going with my underwear?)

In a moment another maid comes through the doorway backward, bearing a wide tray she places on my bed. One red rose in a tiny vase is surrounded by slices of orange, boiled eggs, sausages, six pieces of toast in a silver rack, pots of jam, marmalade, tea, hot water, milk, and folded like serviettes, all the morning papers from London. I eat more than I have appetite for and read everything—data from the blotters of the Bow Street police headquarters in the *Daily Mail* and long columns advertising used Bentleys and Rolls-Royces in *The Times*.

The first maid returns with my garments—now pressed, brushed, and in the case of the socks, turned inside out. She arranges these neatly on the silent valet. "Your bath is drawn, sir," she says, "might I show you where it is?" I follow her along thinly carpeted corridors and up a little stairs to a dim room in which there's a tub big enough to float a canoe.

Back in my room, I've started to put on walking shorts when, without knocking, Osbert comes in to inquire into the state of my health, then hobbles to his study. I go downstairs, find the dining room, and bend down to pass through the low wooden door leading to the gardens. The sun is mild and high as I wander through copses, hedges of yew, topiary labyrinths, past Neptune and Diana to the lowest of the terraces. There, seated under one of the two Giants, I open a volume of Yeats and read Crazy Jane to a cow.

On my way back up through the gardens, I find Osbert seated in a trelliswork of exhausted roses. The high sun in the windows of the house gives them a piercing glint from which we have to avert our eyes. "Renishaw," he says, "one wonders what will become of it. Other houses like it have become circus arenas. Death duties, it seems, are designed to pauperize. The poor heirs lose all their dignity in trying to keep them, opening them to tour buses, garden clubs from America, film companies that want them for backgrounds—" The swift *huff-huff* of a train on the hidden track interrupts him. "We've at least been spared that. Frieda Lawrence's daughter once got it into her head that Lawrence had used Renishaw as the residence of his wretched Chatterleys. When she got in with some cinema group, she telegraphed me, proposing I make it available for a film version of the story."

"Did you?"

"The matter ended before it began. I wired back telling her that her request was as gross as it was libelous. That stopped her. Our victories in courts of law are well known. Now, if you'll give me your hand, we might go to our sherry."

A day at Renishaw, I begin to understand, proceeds in unspoken agreement as to what one is supposed to do and where one is supposed to be—as if one had entered a kind of machine-for-living designed to operate with grace and precision on a timetable fixed by custom and ignored at peril. Repetition is essential; variation *de trop*. The hiatus between breakfast and luncheon is clearly the time for correspondence, meditation, self-entertainment. When sherry is served in any of the several drawing rooms at noon, it's presumed that you have changed from *déshabillé* or sports clothes into something suitable. After lunch you are expected to disappear without discussion of your intentions or reference to your appointments. At teatime you reconvene, but only long enough to insure the observance of amenity, not on any account to linger. Dinner is the main and climactic ritual. Dressed formally, you are congenially gregarious and "on" from martinis at seven forty-five to brandies at midnight. Then you are induced to say a crisp good-night, seek your room, and proceed to bed.

In London a few days later I obeyed Edith's injunction to "propose yourself" to lunch and was quickly answered with an invitation. Durrant's Hotel, with its murky plush Writing Room, wooden coat-stands, napkins in napkin rings, did indeed have that slightly grubby boarding-house air that Osbert had prepared me for.

Edith was wearing headgear of some sort—in no way would it qualify as a hat—from which drooped a silken wimple, tending to make her look like a figure on the porch of a Romanesque church. Our whiskies were double, our lunch something as inscrutable as pemmican buried in gravy, snowy potatoes, and watery carrots. Over a hapless plate of plum duff, she told me that, later in the afternoon, she'd be setting off for the Decca studios to hear the first playback of her new recording of *Façade*. Would I join her there?

At four o'clock, approaching the address she'd given me, my taxi kept to a stately pace behind a big, high-bodied antique Rolls-Royce. The figure visible through its rear window was wearing a wimple. We drew up together. As the chauffeur stood at attention for Edith's descent, I joined her and we passed before twenty or thirty employees lined up as if for a military review. Inside a studio which was heavily padded and draped for, I assumed, acoustical reasons, we were escorted to the first of some six or seven rows of folding chairs where we sat side by side, the murmuring congregation behind us.

At a signal the recording began with a flare of trumpets scored by William Walton. In a few seconds Edith's voice, strong in timbre and nimble in its shifts of tempo, glided and raced through a series of verbal fox-trots, waltzes, hornpipes, and pavanes. By this time, having removed her dark glasses, she held them folded against her cheek in an attitude of entranced attention. Between the last line of one poem and the first of another, she placed a finger lightly on my wrist. We exchanged glances: Dame Edith was pleased.

The performance ended with an abruptness deftly planned, bringing shouts of pleasure and a long round of applause from the audience behind us. As tea was rolled in on carts, the company surrounded Edith in an aura of congratulation and smiling deference.

A photographer who'd been hanging about, camera poised, sent one of the employees over to ask if she would pose for him. No, she said, she did not care to be photographed. Looking hurt, the emissary retired. A few minutes later one of the Decca executives approached her. In a whispered conference he apparently made a second plea. "If I must," said Edith, "I suppose I *must*." She turned with an impatient twist and, lips pursed, chin jutting out, stood sulking beside a piece of recording equipment. The photographer, cowed by this unexpected behavior, asked very politely if she would be good enough to remove her dark glasses. She snatched them off and, simultaneously with the shutter's click, shook her head. The man's shoulders drooped as he gave up and went his way. Those who'd witnessed this tantrum pretended they had not—and I wished I hadn't.

When it was time to go, a group of executives escorted us to the waiting car. Edith waved graciously as we pulled away; everyone lined up waved back.

"Well," she said, "did you see what I did to that obstreperous young man?"

"I'm afraid I did."

"Persons who have no consideration for one's stated wishes should not be rewarded for their insolence."

The August afternoon was gray and humid, yet Edith had continued to wear her long mink coat. As we settled in for the drive back to the city, she lifted a big furry lap-robe from its rack beneath the glass partition and tucked it about the two of us. Then she produced from the seat beside her a pair of outsize fur gloves of the sort worn by members of the Lafayette Escadrille and put them on.

"Now, John," she said, buckling her wrists, "there's been so much talk. What did Dylan *really* think of me?"

"Why do you feel the need to ask? He was deeply fond of you, always grateful to you. . . ."

"Why then was he so frightfully shy of me? He *was* shy with me, you know."

"But he was also shy with many other people, even frightened of them, especially people he thought were grand." I hesitated for a moment, then spoke the truth. "He thought you were one of the grand."

She placed one great mitt on her chest and, her deep-socketed eyes fixed in astonishment, glared into my face.

"Me?—grand!!!" The Rolls in its hush slid through the gates of Hyde Park.

* * *

The Sitwells In Situ / 213

A tourist in Italy, a delegate in Belgium, I spent two weeks on the continent and was back in London on September 7 when, midmorning, the phone at my bedside rang.

"Edith here, John. Is it too frightfully early? I've been trying you for days. Now say you're free to lunch. It just happens to be my sixty-seventh birthday and I'm having a few very dear friends to the hotel. Half past twelve?"

En route, I bought Michaelmas daisies at a sidewalk stall. "I'll have them placed at our party table," she said as I handed them over, then introduced me to those gathered in the vestrylike Writing Room: "My old friend Mme. Wiel . . . deaf as a post, as everyone present knows . . . my dear secretary Elizabeth . . . Mr. Geoffrey Gorer, you've perhaps met before? . . . Mr. Gordon Watson. Mr. Watson is the greatest master of the piano Australia has yet produced." I bowed to each, found my place in the circle, accepted a pink gin.

"Evelyn Wiel and I have just plunged to our deaths in the lift," said Edith, addressing the company, "at least we thought we had. We had to shriek like baboons to be extricated. It seems that without knowing it I had got the hem of my skirt caught in the opening and was about to be dragged to perdition. *How* we survive all that is imposed upon us in this age we live in quite escapes me."

Mme. Wiel, turning to me with an enthusiastic smile, bent to my right ear. "I am from France," she said, jerked back her head, and stared into my eyes as if to say, *What* do you make of *that?*

"Mme. Wiel is from France," said Edith. "In spite of her handicap she has the most acute sense of what is going on around her always. Any one of us might covet her perceptions."

A starched cap appeared in the doorway.

"Now, when we go in," Edith told us, "each of you will find a name on a card . . . I *had* thought we might do a proper party and astonish the room with paper hats and crackers, but the thought came too late, I'm afraid, so we'll simply have to declare our festivity with the bubbly."

My place card put me on her right. As I hovered to see that she was comfortably seated, she addressed the table. "Americans are the only people with a *thought* for manners," she said. "The nonsense repeated in this country about their supposed crudities takes on the proportions of a national scandal. Geoffrey, you must agree. Have you ever once found in America anything but the most respectful of attentions to one's person?"

Mr. Gorer, with half a nod, addressed his soup.

Putting down her spoon, Edith leaned toward me and spoke in a stage whisper. "I'm so enjoying what the queen has done. I daresay that some lips have been sealed, and for *good*. I do not refer only to those jackanapeses who've persecuted me and my brothers since we first dared to tweak their long noses, but much, much, more. You see, we've never really been accepted by some of those who, by any *fair* accounting, should be happy to wipe our boots. Even when we were young, the county took every opportunity to cut us dead. You know, of course, that my brute father allowed my foolish mother to go to prison? Early on, we children simply made up our minds not to suffer. That decision in itself made us strong, kept us together for battles that lay ahead. You can understand why I make no attempt to hide my gratitude to Her Majesty."

A slight commotion at the table signaled the arrival of champagne. Geoffrey Gorer's toast was simple: "To our dear Edith," he said.

"To our dear Edith!" echoed Mme Wiel, in a clear solo.

The late-in-life love affair of the Sitwells with America showed no sign of ebbing. While plans for Edith's epic movie about the Tudors would soon fall through and Osbert's worsening physical condition made travel hazardous, they continued to make winter voyages across the Atlantic. Meanwhile, encouraged by them and driven by a need of my own to "set the record straight," I was coming to the end of my labors on a book I would call *Dylan Thomas in America*. To the manuscript chapters of this which I had submitted to them, they responded with helpful details and often with surprise. The Dylan they knew and the man I knew were obviously two distinct figures— the one a burning genius beset with the impositions of mortality; the other a poet in whom a talent for self-destruction had, at the moment of his triumphs, disguised his decline.

While they were easy with Americans, Edith and Osbert could

never quite dispel the aura of exoticism in which Americans seemed to see them. Reading their poems in many of the same halls where Dylan's voice still echoed, they received a somewhat more awed sort of adulation than he did, and took this simply as their due. I next saw them when they came to Massachusetts where, for the first time, I could formally entertain the brother and sister who had so often beguiled and entertained me. When, one cold bright day in March, they concluded their visit to Wheaton College, I was on hand to drive them the short distance to Boston.

Osbert sat with me in the front seat, Edith in back. "How very nice of you to swoop down and rescue us," she said as we cleared the campus. "Not that we've been in distress, but that we were in mortal peril of being killed by kindness. I've begun to understand *quite* what it must have been like for dear Dylan—all those lovely young women in what seems to be a perpetual state of rapture. Osbert? *Would* you believe that one of them came up to me with a copy of *Planet and Glow-Worm* in her dear little hand? It was like seeing one's long lost child."

Coasting along the shore of a lake shining in cold moonlight, we came to a village with an oval green surrounded by white clapboard houses. "Very pretty," said Osbert. "Wooden dwellings of the sort are quite unknown in England. We tend to think they belong only to empire outposts—Singapore, perhaps, or Simla. This motorcar, do you have a particular name to describe it?"

"We call it a convertible," I told him. "If you unlatch it there and there, and press that button, the top rises and disappears like an accordion into a boot."

"Mercy," said Edith.

"Dylan had his own name for it. He called it the *in*controvert-ible."

Stopped for a red light, we found ourselves beside a rickety struc-ture with a long band of crudely lettered paper pasted to its windows: Fresh Ground Chuck 39¢ Cukes 10¢ Idahoes 5 lbs. 89¢ Lobster-in-the-Ruff.

"Extraordinary," said Edith. "Fancy one's lobster arriving in court costume!"

* * *

My party for them next day was scheduled for five o'clock. Greeting them in the lobby of my apartment house, I showed them to an elevator. When the doors parted on my floor, we waited for Osbert to precede us. Dropping his cane, he stooped to retrieve it before I had a chance to and was halfway out when the doors started to close. Edith shrieked. The doors sprang apart. "O, my *dear,*" she said. "I thought you were going to be cleft asunder."

Among perhaps thirty people overcrowding my living room, the Sitwells took their places as though these had been previously assigned—Osbert lowering himself into an upholstered chair on one side while Edith, her left hand with its burden of oversize rings uplifted to her chin, sat in a straight chair on the other. When the party was well along, and anyone who cared to had had opportunity to join either of the circles that had formed around the guests of honor, a friend came into the kitchen to help me with drinks. "It *has* to be an act," he said, "the sovereign sibling holds court while her brother holds council. Do you think they rehearse it?"

The afternoon was mild, the descending sun reflected on the Charles River and on the golden dome of the State House atop Beacon Hill. People began to step out onto the balcony for the view, among them Robert Lowell.

"He looks," said Lowell, "rather like a deposed king, don't you think?"

"Gertrude Stein had the same impression. She said he looked like a king's uncle."

"I wonder if Dame Edith knows as much about Swinburne as she pretends to."

"Why do you say that?"

"I mentioned in passing a phrase from his 'Hermaphroditus,' and she drew a blank. Yet she's supposed to harbor this lifelong devotion to the old pervert."

"Don't you get the feeling that her relation to things, everything, is less rational than theatrical?"

"More than one person," said Lowell, "has said the same thing about me."

When we stepped back into the room, I noticed that Edith was holding out her hands so that the wife of one of the Harvard masters

The Sitwells In Situ / 217

could examine her rings. "They're *so* lovely," said the woman, "but I should think you'd never get used to the weight of them. Have you—got used to it?"

"That same question was asked of me not long ago by Miss Monroe," said Edith. "Marilyn Monroe. At my age, I told her, one has got used to the weight of many things—the least of which is one's ornaments."

A man's voice broke in. "Dame Edith, what did you make of Marilyn Monroe?"

"*Make* of her?" (In an instant, she had become Lady Bracknell). "I found her to be a perfectly gracious and intelligent young creature, with a great natural dignity. They brought her to me at the Sunset Towers expecting it would all be a lark—publicity, you know, with reporters and photographers to record the moment. Chalk and cheese we were supposed to be, me in my black robes and this sweet little sex symbol kissing my hand or something of the sort. But we fooled them, we simply talked by ourselves as persons of good sense and intelligence do, and had a perfectly lovely time."

When they were ready to leave, Osbert had to be helped from his chair and into his overcoat. He and Edith bowed to the company, all of whom stood to witness their step-by-step departure. Robert Lowell and his wife escorted them to their hotel.

In July, the envelope I took from my mailbox bore a return address written in script that covered half the back of it:

> *from* Dame Edith Sitwell D. B. E.
> D.Litt. D.Litt. D.Litt. D.Litt.
> Renishaw Hall
> Renishaw
> > near Sheffield
> > England

"My dear John," she wrote. "I am perfectly *aghast* when I think how long it is since I have been meaning to write to you, and *should* have written to you.

"You must *please* forgive me. I arrived back dead with fatigue, and since then the unceasing hard work, worry, plaguing and pestering have been beyond any words.

"We are longing to see you, and are so very happy that you are coming to England in August.

"Osbert will be here (and waiting for you). I shall be in London, (and waiting for you). For the first 12 or 13 days I shall be at the Sesame Club . . . and after that, at Durrant's Hotel. . . .

"We enjoyed every minute of the various times, all too short, that we spent with you. And your party was the happiest to which we went.

"How is the book going? I must say I can't think why we don't both die of overwork.

"Love from us both, and we look forward to next month.

Edith"

As the car Edith has sent from Renishaw to Chesterfield to meet me rounds the gravel drive [I wrote in my journal] Miss Andrade appears on the steps to escort me upstairs to "the pineapple room." This turns out to be a spacious chamber with a big bed—with the intricately carved finials from which the room takes its name. One of the walls is nothing more than a bookcase filled, floor to ceiling, with volumes in many languages by one or the other of the three writing Sitwells. Chairs are placed at windows, overlooking the drive, curtained with a fabric of red and white in a hide-and-seek pattern which, studied closely, reveals a thousand tiny heads of Victoria Regina. Teatime has already passed, says Miss Andrade, but a tray is being prepared for me and will be sent up. Dame Edith is resting. Sir Osbert is in the rose garden where he is expecting me.

Downstairs within a few minutes, I make my way to the dining room, bob through the little rabbit-hole doorway, and find Osbert seated on a bench. He lifts a tremorous hand, makes room for me beside him. He and Edith have read my manuscript, he tells me, and have found it "enthralling."

"I daresay we've known more about Dylan than anyone else over here—except, of course, the ubiquitous Margaret, Lady Bountiful—but we were still not prepared for the sort of death march those years turned out to be. Quite early on in the book, one gets a devastating sense that his descent was final, that he was helpless to break his own fall. Was that your intention?"

"Not in the least," I tell him. "I had to watch him die, die in the hospital, but it wasn't until the book, not the life, was finished that I understood, really for the first time, that I'd gone to the airport one day in 1950 to meet a dying man. The hidden thing, I think, was the fear that had already gripped him, the terror. I don't believe it was anything less . . . and he would try to escape it by just the kind of self-exacerbation that could only result in making the terror more real, and finally unshakable. He saw the gates of hell, you'll remember, and they were real. But he also saw mice and roses, and they weren't."

Long thin shadows from the trellises reach to "the wilderness" and deepen its air of perpetual gloaming.

"One small thing, John," says Osbert. "That letter you quote, the one where Dylan says that Edith's parties are magnificent opportunities for self-disgrace. Do you think you might omit the passage? It would make her unhappy to see it in print. She's become perhaps unduly sensitive about the subject of Dylan. I think she has quite rightly suspected that there have been deliberate attempts to deny the importance of their relationship, to belittle the fact that she was his first champion."

"Of course."

"I would take that as a great favor to myself. Edith would not presume to alter the work of another writer. But anything that might feed the sort of harpy mentality we've always had to deal with would only cause her to suffer."

Slowly, we make our way inside, Osbert still dependent on his cane yet notably more steady on his feet than he was this time a year ago.

"When you find a moment," he says, "have one of the servants show you to the east gallery. I've acquired a Sickert I think may be one of his best. We'll meet, then, in the library, at seven. Edith prefers to dine early these days, because of the chill."

Alone in the library, as I study a wall of John Piper drawings which depict Renishaw from many angles, my glance falls on one of the dead-eyed stuffed ducks that the editors of *The Harvard Lampoon* are in the custom of presenting to celebrities in the spirit of their magazine.

"John, my dear, welcome," says Edith from the doorway. "You've seen our trophy. Droll, would you not say? But I'm not *entirely* certain that the joke isn't on the dear boys themselves."

After dinner the duck's eyes shine like buttons as we settle in the library for brandy. A maid brings a large sandalwood box of cigars and, at Edith's request, "pokes up" the coals. Osbert asks me if I've seen "Tom" Eliot in London. I tell him no, but that I've been to tea with John Hayward in the flat they share.

"A curiously successful *ménage à deux* that. You'd share our opinion?"

I take his question to be rhetorical or, at least, one I could not be expected to answer.

"Something deep in Tom's nature," says Edith, "must propel him constantly toward expiation, to choose his companions from the strange and damaged souls of this world. We knew Vivienne. We saw *that* martyrdom to the bitter end. Then there was that hopelessly lah-di-dah vicar he moved in with, all airs and flutter, and then our poor dear wretched John. One can only wonder if his *secret* life is fulfilling to some other degree."

Reluctant to rise to this bait, I do not have to.

"Because he *does* have a secret life, you know," says Osbert, "as on one occasion it was revealed to us many years ago, and in a circumstance as amusing as it was bizarre."

"Vivienne's dinner party!" says Edith.

"About 1927 or thereabouts," continues Osbert, "we'd gone to dinner with him and Vivienne. Joyce and Nora and the Fabers made up the rest of the party. We'd had ample warning, I suppose, though Vivienne's whines and complaints about Tom were so many and so unceasing that we'd learned to take them all *cum grano salis*. This time it was Tom's lack of interest in anyone, including *her,* to be sure, except an individual she referred to as a retired policeman whose function or whereabouts she never made clear. In any case, when dinner was over that evening, some of us remained at table while the others took to the drawing room. The wine, I remember, was particularly good. I think we stayed behind to enjoy a bit more of it. There we were, Joyce and Mr. Faber—lingering as one will and without much need to talk, when a panel of the room we'd never suspected of being a door suddenly opened and . . ."

"Jack-in-the-box!" says Edith.

"Jack-in-the-box, there he was—the policeman! In a bowler, no less, and quite bug-eyed in his cups. We must have looked at him with as much astonishment as he at us . . . and, of course, if *he* wasn't speechless, we *were.* As though he'd stepped directly out of that good-night scene in 'The Waste Land'—'Goo' night, Mr. Eliot,' he said, tipped his bowler, repeated his 'Goo' night' all round and then vanished into another panel that closed behind him like something you'd see in a dream. After that, we could never quite doubt Vivienne's complaints. Who the man was was never said and we never asked."

9.4.55   Far-off bells remind me it is Sunday morning and set up expectation that Edith will soon be off to mass.*

---

*One month ago to the day, Edith had been received into the Roman Catholic Church, with Evelyn Waugh and Roy Campbell as her coreligionist godfathers. The event, well publicized in England, was one I had anticipated on the basis of a letter that came to me in Italy and which I had lost. The decision had given her courage

Comfortable over coffee and the remains of a many-splen-dored breakfast, I write letters on stationery crested with an etching of Renishaw Hall, keep an ear cocked for the sound of tires on the gravel drive beneath my window. But the car does not move from Sir George's stables, now used as a garage. As the morning passes, my disappointment deepens: Where again might I see a replica of Elizabeth I on her way to a pew in an outpost parish of the Church of Rome?

Just before noon I find her in the "red room" where she is not so much seated as perched. In mink coat and turban, a big black handbag on the floor beside her, she looks like someone waiting for an overdue train.

"Good morning, my dear John." Her voice is crisp. "Come sit. We can chat by ourselves."

"Do I take it," I ask, "that you've already been to mass and back?"

"Oh, dear," she says. "I was too weary even to order the car around."

"When I was a Catholic," I tell her, "I went to mass."

"Now, you must not reproach me. Conversion at my age entails a certain degree of sophistication when it comes to churchgoing and the simpler claims of the catechism. Will it make you any happier should I tell you that my confessor will be coming to see me about teatime? Now that he's got me, he's quite panting after Osbert. What about *you*? Would you permit him to do what he might to bring you back into the fold?"

"Not a chance," I tell her. "When I broke, I broke clean."

---

to meet the difficulties of her life, she wrote, and with courage had come peace of mind—a statement enforced by her sober tone and her moving, unselfconscious references to "our Redeemer" and "the blessed Mother of God." She wrote like someone who, having learned a new language, is limited to the straightforward and simple.

Dubious about religion as therapy, at least for someone of sophistication as broad as hers, I was nevertheless impressed with her new humility, touched and no little surprised that she had felt a need to describe the experience of conversion to me.

"He's really the most ingratiating of men . . . but I can see he's not the one for you."

She bends over, sends a conspiratorial glance about the room and, lowering her voice, says: "I have something *wonderful* to tell you but, mind, you must keep it in the *strictest* confidence. I have your word?"

I give it.

"Our dear Alec Guinness will be received into the Church at Christmastime." She sits back, head high, with a tight smug smile that suggests she's bagged the man herself. "I don't have to tell you, do I, that I had con*sid*erable to do with it? My main worry now is Osbert. Distress is driving him into the arms of a healer, someone I cannot but believe a mountebank, one of those creatures who make a career of battening on the hopes of the incurable. He's going to London tomorrow, to submit himself to the supposed charms of this Svengali. The most curious thing, John, it's been observed that in his sleep my brother shows no sign of that dreadful trembling whatsoever. I'm afraid that fact has overimpressed him and started him on this unfortunate pilgrimage."

In silence for a moment, I stare at the Sargent family-portrait some twenty feet away from me.

"There we are," says Edith. "Would you believe . . . *to* this day I can feel my father's arm about me? How I loathed the touch of it."

Osbert, in city clothes, came to my room next morning with a book. "A little souvenir of your visit," he said, and held out a copy of *The Scarlet Tree.* "You may find parts of it amusing."

"You're driving to London?"

"I've found an individual there," he said, "who I've been told might help me. Perhaps Edith has spoken to you about him, a professional healer who does *not* require that one make a confession of faith. My sister is convinced, for no earthly reason, that the man is a charlatan. In the way of it, he may well be. But I cannot see what I have to lose by assuming otherwise, except a few pounds sterling, of course. *Au revoir,* then, until we meet in New York in the winter."

I did not so much shake the hand he offered as simply hold the tremorous weight of it.

"Don't let them take Dylan away from you," he said. "They will try, you can count on it. But don't let them."

With Osbert gone, Edith in her room, the servants in their quarters, the house became enormously empty, beautiful and foreboding. Wandering at will, I lingered nowhere, oppressed by grandeur retained as if for its own sake, and for nothing else. Since Edith would not be coming down for sherry until noon, I found a bench outside and sat there making longhand copies of some poems of mine she had asked me to leave with her.

At lunch she was subdued, unassertive—even, for the first time in my memory, humble. "I have come to the conclusion, dear John, that I may be in need of guidance."

The statement caused me to look up.

"*Not* spiritual guidance," she said, "professional guidance."

On her mind were difficulties, "troublesome beyond conception," she had encountered in the process of putting together a comprehensive anthology of poetry commissioned by an American publisher. "I know some of your poets," she said, "Robert Lowell—that most extraordinary poem of his called 'The Ghost'—and that quite mad polar bear Roethke, and dear Charles Henri Ford and José Villa, and I've shaken hands with Allen Ginsberg. But for the whole picture I'm at a loss. When well-meaning persons direct me to this not-to-be-missed poet or another, I say, of course, I'll put him or her in Volume *Two.* But, you see, there is not going to *be* any Volume Two."

Her smile was uneasy.

"I simply use the idea of it as my excuse, my bolt-hole. Let me make a little pact with you: Stay in England for the month, look over what I've done, and give me the benefit of your judgment. For a reward I'll have you come with me to the premier of Benjamin Britten's *Turn of the Screw. And* to the new version of *Façade* I'm doing with Peter Pears. Now think it over. You can give me your answer at teatime."

Edith out of character was touching, but not persuasive. Too often, she had advertised her ignorance at the very moment when she was smugly calling, "Touché!" Faced with bad reviews, her strategy was to attack the reviewers, not for opinions they'd expressed but because they were insignificant—meaning only that she had never heard of them. "Whoever *he* is," she would conclude her riposte, "whoever *she* is," completely unaware that nearly all of her readers or listeners knew exactly who "he" was and who "she" was. It had long been obvious to me that her view of herself, shared by those for whom the sibylline outechoed the asinine, was not amenable to correction, and I preferred to keep it that way. I was tempted by her offer, I told her later that afternoon, but had to say no, simply because I had an itinerary putting me at the mercy of arrangements made long ago by my travel agent. I flew to Naples two days later and from there took return passage that brought me early in October to Boston, where a letter from Renishaw was waiting.

"I am in no wise exaggerating," she wrote, "when I say I am deeply moved by your 'Cradle Song.' A most extraordinary poem. I suddenly sprang into life after reading it—having been dead for some time.

"I haven't been able to get Osbert to settle anything yet. He is horribly depressed, and really life is unbearable. Why this should have had to happen to somebody so good, so kind, I don't know. We loved having you here. It is the only thing I have enjoyed for ages."

Osbert's long search for a cure brought him to New York the following March. He had heard of a new operation by which symptoms like his had already been "miraculously" alleviated, but found that the American surgeons capable of performing it were reluctant to take him on, at least for the present. This I learned one day in May when, just before he was to sail back to England, I accepted his invitation to "a little bon voyage luncheon" with him in the Plaza's Oak Room.

There when I arrived, he looked like a man without troubles, least of all physical ailments. Barbered with precision, manicured to a gloss, he sat in his own Plantagenet elegance, his eyes clear, his cheeks ruddy. "I've been trying not to laugh aloud," he said. "When you've had a chance to look about, you'll see why."

Taking my time, I looked over my shoulder. At a table nearby sat two women, fashionably dressed, whose idea of fashion included head coverings which were either a milliner's version of a parlormaid's mobcap, or the real antique thing itself. "The excesses of the French Revolution," said Osbert, "seem to have reached the Plaza. *Sans-culottes* will come next."

"You look wonderful," I said.

"Thank you. But I must still remember not to let my hands stray from the table. Have you finished reading my autobiographies?"

"Every last word," I told him. "Why haven't critics pointed out the fact that it's social comedy, always on the verge of becoming hilarious?"

"I don't know. But that's the particular thing I've always wanted them to say first," he said. "You have to understand class hatred in England. Laughter in the next room, *if* that room happens to be a drawing room, is regarded not only as offensive but as illicit."

"Haven't I read that you are about to become a Commander of the British Empire?"

"At my age, a paltry honor, I'm afraid."

He would within the month make his pathetic *marche-à-petit-pas* to royal investiture through the halls of Buckingham Palace and, paltry honor or not, accept it.

My book on Dylan Thomas, published in England at that time, received the kind of attention usually given to news events—an editorial in *The Times;* headlines in provincial papers; a diatribe in the scandal columns of the *Daily Express.* But not until a few months hence, when I would find myself stalked by reporters from the Ocean Terminal in Southampton on to every hotel, railroad station, and airport on my itinerary, was that fact really brought home to me. Meanwhile, the reviews I read in the literary journals and "serious" newspapers were, in range and tone, predictable save one, that by Edith Sitwell in *The Sunday Times.* Like many others it was not so much the judgment of a book as a commentary on the phenomenon of Dylan Thomas with, in her case, vituperation directed at those people in America she believed responsible for his death. Since Edith had herself proposed the writing of my book and had seen it in all stages of composition, there had been ample opportunity for her to register objections she may have harbored. But this was private knowledge and did not make for ease when, as I soon learned, the review was often regarded as an attack upon me. By midsummer all reports of the book were in. On balance, heaped with praise and spattered with calumny, I made plans for England—en route to Belgium where, once more, I would represent American poetry at the Biennale Internationale de Poésie.

A letter to Edith, admitting my distress over reactions her piece in *The Sunday Times* continued to evoke, and letting her know when I'd be in London went unanswered—ominously, I thought—until I had passed through the city on my way to Belgium and, within the week, returned. "I was so glad to get your letter," she wrote from Renishaw, "but, as you will see from the enclosed envelope, I got it only *after* you had left for Belgium. . . .

"*Osbert says can you come here before you leave?* If so, *do* telegraph.

"*Do* come if it is humanly possible.

"I hoped I had made it perfectly clear in my review that I understood *perfectly* your reasons for writing your book about Dylan. I also thought I had made it perfectly clear that I value your friendship greatly. I *had* to say that I think the women—with the one exception of the lady who stood so nobly by Dylan in that dreadful last phase, and who truly loved him—had behaved disgracefully. That has no bearing on you, at all. Also the people who helped him drink himself to death—well, of them the less said the better.

"Infuriated—as we all were in England—by the possessive attitude of the people who degraded and helped to kill him—by their self-glorification—I was determined to show their conduct as it really is, as a matter for deep shame.

"That has nothing to do with you, who tried to protect him.

"People, of course, would try to make mischief between us. I wish, now, that I had written about it to you at the time. But I was battling with mobs of very angry persons, all pulling in different directions.

"Nothing did, or has, diminished my very real affection for you. Did I not make that clear? I thought I had.

"*Do* try to come."

* * *

Renishaw Hall in September 1956 was not a happy place. Routine was unchanged; the rituals were observed. But a cornice of the domestic facade had worn so thin as to threaten the collapse of the whole edifice.

Arriving late afternoon, I was just in time for tea, which we took in the library where a coal fire burned blue. "I've been saving these until you'd get here," said Osbert, and pointed to a pile of ten or twelve issues of *The New Yorker* beside his chair. "A good number of the cartoons elude me. You'll have to explain very patiently, perhaps in the morning?"

His face was heavy, with baggy eyes, pronounced creases; and the buttons of his cardigan were tight to the point of bursting. Edith, in a black turban ringed with medallions of gold thread, was wearing her long fur coat. They had developed, I noticed, a habit of staring at one another, expressionless as cats.

"Osbert has missed his lie-down," said Edith. "Now that you're here, we must see that he takes it." As he reached for his cane, I stood up, ready to help him out of his chair.

"No, no, John," said Edith. "I've already rung for Mary, who knows just what to do." Mary was a housemaid. In minutes she had him on his feet and headed for the doorway. His little steps were still echoing when Edith collapsed into her chair with a long sigh and put both hands over her eyes. The coal fire hissed in the silence.

"One moment more and I would have screamed," she said. "I'm afraid Father Caraman instructs me in everything but the control of my own nature. Osbert endures the devil's own without a twinge, as you can see for yourself. To have to witness that is horrible enough, to have to see him abandoned to his affliction is intolerable. That David Horner!"

She made a noise like a prolonged growl, her teeth clenched.

"He's been our house guest for twenty-six years, and his behavior has become *des*picable!"

Embarked on a diatribe lasting for ten or fifteen minutes, she cited chapters and verses of her pent-up resentment. The gist of it was Horner's reluctance to assume the role of male nurse and his protracted absences from Renishaw which, as far as I could interpret, she deplored as much as his presence. "In a matter of weeks now," she

said, "we shall be off, the most unholy three, to a winter in Italy I shall not survive without recourse to violence!"

A sound of footsteps in the corridor; a figure in the doorway: David Horner, holding a cat with dilated amber eyes. "Still a cup of tea for us?" he asked.

Awaking next morning, my fortieth birthday, I drew open the curtains and contemplated the long topiary vista as though it were the future itself. Promptly at eight the arrival of the maid sent me back to bed, where, from the vast breakfast tray, I lifted a note placed beneath a silver bud-vase holding a yellow rose.

> My dear John, [it read] very many happy returns of the day.
> It was lovely that you were able to get here.
> Bon voyage.
>   Love, Edith.
>
> P.S. If anyone else tells you I was trying to attack *you* in the *S. Times*, tell them they had better say it to *me* when I come to America!

I made one more summer visit to Renishaw and there saw Osbert for the last time. My last sight of Edith occurred by happenstance.

Invited by the State Department to give a lecture inaugurating the auditorium of the new American embassy building in Grosvenor Square, I flew to London in mid-January 1961, fulfilled my assignment, and a few nights later went to the Royal Festival Hall to hear a performance of Verdi's *Requiem*. Before taking my seat, I was dawdling among others who had come early when, alerted by a commotion nearby, I looked up as the crowd parted to make space for a wheelchair being rolled toward the door to the royal box. The shrunken figure in the chair was Edith, her smile fixed, her eyes glazed and without focus. As, bowing continually like a grotesque mechanical doll, she passed within touching distance, I bowed.

But that picture gives way to another one three years earlier and more congenial to memory—Edith in a spectacular hat of white ostrich feathers, presiding as hostess at "a tea party (to celebrate Sachie's new book)," as she wrote on her invitation, and dominating a crowded room without moving from her chair. On hand were not only all the familiar members of the London literary establishment from C. P. Snow to Cyril Connolly, but a number of the "angry young men" of British letters who, unlike their predecessors, had apparently forgiven Edith her eminence and accepted her friendship.

Ready to leave the party, I was about to say good-bye to her when one of these young men blocked my way. Standing apart, I watched as he leaned toward Edith and took her hand—a hand weighted with stones that were as big as eggs and rough as uncut quartz—and vigorously shook it. A wrinkle of pain crossing her face, Edith withdrew her crumpled fingers and forced a smile.

"Shall we agree," she said, "that when next we meet we shall simply *bow?*"

And so, three years later, on the threshold of the royal box, we simply did.

MUSHROOM PIE IN THE RUE CHRISTINE

Mushroom Pie in the Rue Christine

O
UT of ink and envelopes, I went one summer day in 1946
to a stationer's, made my purchases, and lingered to examine a shelf of books that stood in the back of the shop
like an afterthought. Secondhand and dusty, the choice it offered
seemed nondescript . . . until I picked out a copy of Gertrude
Stein's *Geography and Plays,* a book published privately in Boston
twenty-four years earlier. The price on the still-crisp pale blue jacket
was $2.25. Unbelieving, I carried the book to the cash register and
asked the price. Examining it front and back, the clerk gave me a
slightly contemptuous look, and said "Two twenty-five."

Later that afternoon, cutting its still-uncut pages and turning them
with as much reverence as I'd take with the first folio, I browsed for
an hour and more, at times pausing to read an especially furry or
silken passage aloud.

That evening I picked up a newspaper: Gertrude Stein had died in
Paris at the age of seventy-two. Skipping dinner, I went to my desk
and put down the following lines so quickly that they seemed to have
been waiting in my head to be discovered and transcribed:

LITTLE ELEGY FOR GERTRUDE STEIN

Pass gently, pigeons on the grass,
For where she lies alone, alas,
Is all the wonder ever was.

Deeply she sleeps where everywhere
Grave children make pink marks on air
Or draw one black line . . . here to there.

Because effects were upside down,
Ends by knotty meanings thrown,
Words in her hands grew smooth as stone.

May every bell that says farewell,
Tolling her past all telling tell
What she, all told, knew very well.

If now, somehow, they try to say—
This way, that way, everywhichway—
Goodbye . . . the word is worlds away.

Come softly, all; she lies with those
Whose deepening innocence, God knows,
Is as the rose that is a rose.

Sent off next day to *Harper's,* the poem was quickly accepted, pub-lished promptly, and I thought little more about it. Seven months later I took from my mailbox a thin brown envelope addressed in script that looked like the trackings of a tiny spider: "May I thank you for the Little Elegy," read the letter, "it touches me very deeply. At intervals during each day since a friend sent it I find myself drawn by its exquisite form and tender understanding to reread it. Tomor-row I am showing it to a friend who translated Brewsie and Willie to Gertrude Stein's complete satisfaction. He will probably ask if you would permit him to translate it. Would you object to it appearing in one of the literary reviews—either Fontaine or Confluence—to both of which Gertrude Stein contributed. I must tell you that their contributors are most inadequately paid.

"With appreciation and admiration. A. B. Toklas."

The translation was soon made, but not very well, I thought—a judgment confirmed by Miss Toklas: "Your exquisite lines have re-ceived very rough treatment indeed," she wrote. "On the other hand Gertrude Stein, when I complained of the translations of her early things, used to say, some of it has to come through. I am sorry you didn't come to see her for she so much enjoyed meeting young Americans, more particularly those who were to write. If you come to Paris while I am still here please let me know so that I may welcome you to Gertrude Stein's home."

Gertrude Stein had long been for me an object of veneration qualified by puzzlement. Sixteen years old, the first thing I had ever published was an imitation of the *faux naïf* mannerisms that identified her reportorial style. And when I was nineteen, the first thing I did on my first day in Paris was to make a moony-eyed pilgrimage to the courtyard of the legendary rue de Fleurus. If it would be the last thing I did, I was already determined to solve the puzzle of Gertrude Stein, if but for my own satisfaction. These notes from Alice B. Toklas were not only unexpected felicities but a form of encouragement she could not have suspected.

"One of your students," she wrote a few months later, "is bringing you a wee souvenir of Gertrude Stein. It's a tiny wood carving that Gertrude had already when I came to Paris. She was devoted to it and always had it near her, so it seemed best that you should have it."

"It," I could see for myself a few weeks later, was, an octopus astride a horse carved in teak or mahogany and worn so smooth it turned in the hand as smoothly as an egg. I took it as a message and it became a talisman. Within three years I had made a draft of a critical biography of Gertrude Stein and come to a point where only Alice B. Toklas could confirm or dismiss certain notions I was pursuing.

Informing her of this in a note, I asked if she would see me should I come to Paris in the late summer. Yes, she said, but only in the terms of our acquaintance. She could be of no help to me in the general matter of Gertrude Stein or her work. Set back, and contemplating her implied chastisement, I was wondering what next to do when I got a letter somewhat softening her initial response: "It occurs to me that it was not probably made clear to you . . . that my reasons for not being able to be of any assistance to you was that if your book is to be a critical study . . . the manuscripts at Yale would be all you would need—and if it is to be an anecdotal history it would be necessary for me to refuse. The fact that I survived the latter experience once is not sufficient temptation to attempt it again. Perhaps you would let me know just what your project for the book is—it would then be possible for me to say what you would hope to gather from such a barren field as you would find."

I did tell her, and she invited me to come to the rue Christine, but not without a cautionary word: "It is best that you should hear again that there is very little likelihood that you will find me able to be of aid to you."

As my journal reminds me, I got to Paris when I said I would, but first had other things to do:

9.7.50   A walk to 27 rue de Fleurus—to stand in its courtyard as, nineteen years old, I stood hoping Gertrude would come out in her brocaded jacket and deerstalker's cap with Basket on a leash and say good morning length what is length when silence is so windowful you must come this evening Pablo will be here with Olga and Scott perhaps not with Zelda O dear and how we do like to see them come and see them go and of course the new Russians you will find it amusing climate and the affections I have often been quoted as quoting that.

The atelier seems to have been converted into a garage. The courtyard is paved with finely crushed gravel and decorated with funerary pots with artificial trees in them.

All that radiance dimmed. Gertrude four years in her grave.

9.8.50   *Dans le métro*—"*surtout les apparitions de ces visages*"—I find the way to Père-Lachaise. The chief clerk is absent from his office and his assistant has no idea of the whereabouts of Mlle. Stein. Wondering what tack to pursue, I linger.

"*M'sieur* Oscar?" asks the clerk.

"*Oui.*"

Delighted, he produces a map and pencils an "X" to mark the site of the grave of Oscar Wilde.

"*Très beau,*" he says, "*le sculpture d'Epstein—Jacob Epstein.*"

Flowers I bought by the Madeleine are wilting in my hand when I get to Epstein's pre–art-deco art-deco stone. Tempted to add them to the five or six handfuls of blossoms already placed there, I do not.

Back at *le bureau,* I get the man properly in charge to re-mark my map. He points me in the direction of a newly opened part of the cemetery where the stones are modest and uniform, bearing the names of *maquis* who died in the very last days of the Occupation. Gertrude's gravestone is marble, a polished gray rectangle perhaps four feet high and three feet wide. Her name is cut into one side of it, "Alice B. Toklas   San Francisco" into the other.

Men on a scaffolding are building a mausoleum that will soon throw Gertrude's resting place into perpetual shadow. As I place my flowers, they put down their tools, fold their arms, and stand solemnly at attention.

On my third day in Paris Miss Toklas answered the note I'd sent telling her where I was staying—in the form of a *pneumatique* for which I had to go to the nearby *bureau de poste.* Suggesting three different times when I might come, she also answered a question I'd posed: "Yes the rue de Fleurus has changed. We thought 27 had a few months after we left it, immediately before they altered the pa-vilion. In that short time it had ceased to resemble the memory of the home we had lived in for so many years, which made us more than ever pleased to have been forced to leave it and live here."

Later, on the phone, she said: "Sunday would be particularly con-venient. I'll expect you at four and a half. We'll be alone."

At four that afternoon, with marzipan strawberries in a basket woven of bluegrass, I set out on foot for V rue Christine. The street number, white on a blue ceramic plaque, was affixed to a wall beside an open gate. Beyond was a bookbinder's yard smelling of glue and sawdust, at one end of which was an outdoor stairs. On the first landing I pressed a button that set a bell clanging deep inside.

Miss Toklas opened the door. "Welcome to Gertrude Stein's home," she said. She was so small that I looked down at the top of her head. Bent, dark, Hebraic, she led me through a dim hallway

hung with Japanese prints and unframed paintings in serried ranks—
most of them from Picasso's early cubist phase of complicated mono-
tone—into a drawing room full of Spanish-looking furniture, onto
which fell a cheerless northern light. Bibelots of wood, glass, and
marble—the "breakable objects" Gertrude favored—lay on every flat
surface. The paintings on each wall were as striking in their familiar-
ity as historical figures with whom I might have just come face to
face.

Miss Toklas sank down into the black pillows of a horsehair sofa
(the one they'd bought in London in 1914?), motioned me to the
chair opposite—a slipper chair, the seat of which was worked in need-
lepoint, stitched, she said, from "doodles" made for her by "Pablo."

"You'd care for one of these?" I took the Balkan Sobranie she offered and stood up to light hers. "There was a young man here not
long ago who claimed to know you." She took three quick puffs, like
someone smoking for the first time. "Does he? His name is Truman
Capote."

I was on my way to Venice to see him, I told her.

"Now, *there's* a quaint one," she said. "A bit presuming, a little
off-putting, at first—that voice and those curious little airs. I don't
mean airs in the snob sense. I mean in the way he can't help con-
ducting himself. But it strikes me there's a head on those shoulders.
Would you say so?"

I would.

Mushroom Pie in the Rue Christine / 241

"So much about him reminded me of Gertrude Stein's young men—the pose of languor, the mix of wit and silliness somber people find so confusing or threatening. Dear George Antheil. He affected a similar haircut when he was your friend's age . . . You know the Man Ray portrait? The same smooth open face you'd find on some *affiche* for baby powder, the same big doll's eyes. And to think what became of him—*Les Six* to Miss Lonelyhearts!"

Basket II, a dun-colored poodle with vacant, melancholy eyes, came to be fondled. "He's been full of moods all day," she said. The dog gave her a long-suffering look and rolled over.

Alice B. Toklas then proceeded to obliterate all my preconceptions. Neither mousey, murmurous, dovelike, or supernumerary, she was tough, spirited, quick-witted, biting. She threw away wicked lines before I could catch them, pounced with a cackle on a foolish idea or an inflated reputation, kept a straight face as she spoke judgments that sizzled like acid on a grid. Still uneasy about the reticence and ambiguity of her recent letters, I need not have been. Questions I'd thought perhaps silly, naïve, impertinent, or redundant were all carefully entertained. Warming to the past without sentimentalizing it, she confirmed what I knew and opened up whole new areas of investigation. When we'd talked for nearly four hours, she rose, put on all the lamps in the room, reached into an armoire for a fifth of Cutty Sark, placed the bottle on the low table between us, and asked me to help myself. Sinking back into the big pillows, she put both arms straight up in the air. "Good heavens," she said, "why didn't you tell me you'd be like this? How old are you?"

I was born, I told her, thirty-four years ago that minute, or, at least, no more than a few minutes from whatever time it was.

"I should have given more credit to Joe," she said. "Joe Barry, he's the only one who tried to give me anything like a useful report of you. You were the one who introduced him to the works of Gertrude Stein."

Searching, I found no image to fit the name.

"Gertrude was deeply fond of him," she said. "She made him Jo the Loiterer in *The Mother of Us All* . . . all because he got arrested for loitering . . . she loved the sound, 'arrested for loitering' . . . when there was some sort of political trouble in Ann Arbor. On your return from Italy you must come to lunch with him. He's married to an intelligent American girl. Would you be particularly interested in a mushroom pie?"

Awakened next morning by the cooing of pigeons in the grillework of my balcony, I went downstairs and found the usually dour concierge all smiles.

"*Pour m'sieur,*" she said, and handed me a bouquet of white flowers tied with white ribbons, along with a large manila envelope, folded once, in a way that obscured the words in the upper left-hand corner: "War Department Official Business." Pinned to a ribbon was an old-fashioned calling card. One side was printed, the other handwritten: in script, "A happy birthday to you—Alice Toklas," and verso, "Miss Toklas San Francisco." The envelope enclosed two pamphlets: *An Elucidation* and *Have They Attacked Mary He Giggled.*

Flowers in one hand, literature in the other, I started for the sidewalk café where a friend from Boston was waiting.

"I'm thirty-four years old," I told her. "Look what I've got."

On the following Sunday, relieving me of my raincoat, Alice spelled out our schedule: We would converse until four, have a nip of Cutty Sark, and be ready for "a little tea party" at five. She had invited friends of Gertrude's—Francis Rose the painter, Max White the novelist, George John the poet. She settled into the horsehair sofa; I perched on Picasso's chair. "Now," she said, "have we disposed of the shadow of Leo Stein once and for all?"

At five sharp came George John—gangling, boyish, and bearded. Of all the anonymous GIs who rang the bell it was he, said Alice, whom Gertrude most wanted to come back, and he did. In a few minutes Alice answered the door for Max White. Bald like me and open-faced, he had a Kansan accent, an almost rustic manner of speaking, and was obviously familiar with the flat and with Alice. Half an hour later came Sir Francis, preceded by obbligatos of his high and slightly squeaky voice from the moment Alice opened the door until, with a prissy hand over his knees, as though he were smoothing a skirt, he sat down. He was wearing a well-cut but stained blue suit, white socks, a pink shirt, and he lisped. He spoke about people he and Alice knew and we did not. "If it came to *that*," he said, "Huilan and Mme. Oui would simply give him what for and clear *off*. Daisy, I'm sorry to say, has been awfully odd since the disaster," and went on about these obscure figures without addressing anyone else.

As George John and I quietly recalled the great events of our muddy midwestern childhoods, Sir Francis maundered on about "Bubi" and "Bebe" and "Cecil" until Alice pulled things together with a salon finesse that united us over the delicacies she had prepared but which left us with nothing to say. I was about to take my final sip of tea and head for any place less confining when she lifted the pot, filled my cup, and sotto voce, said, "You stay on."

"Oh, dear *me*," she said when the others had left. "I'm afraid Francis was in one of his dressmaker's moods. He can be amusing, but oh dear. Shall we go back to the beginnings of Baby's friendship with Bernard Faÿ?"

Happy for everything she offered, I wondered, as she launched into still another monologue, whether she was serving Gertrude's memory, or merely putting off that moment when she would be left alone.

Basket whimpered and moved toward my chair. I scratched his head and massaged his back as Alice talked on.

Back from Italy a week later, I found a message at the concierge's desk: "It seemed prudent to engage the Barrys to meet you at one on Monday," wrote Alice. "So I will be expecting you then, indeed if you arrive early enough perhaps you could come a bit earlier say a quarter to one so that we may have a moment to go over some of the answers to the so happily unformidable questions. The whole subject of Leo fusses one, in itself and for your feeling it is a controversial subject, requiring defense and proofs. If you can't come early could you possibly give me a moment after the Barrys leave, though you should be warned that they have the habit of staying on. In any case a moment must be contrived and you will help me find it.

"Lunch will be ready for one o'clock unless I hear from you that you prefer it later."

Still reaching for the identity of the Barrys, I unpacked one bag, bought a hot bath from the chambermaid, and hurried to the rue Christine.

"I'm giving you my own mushroom pie," said Alice. "It takes watching. You'll forgive me if I disappear from time to time. Now, a cassis? Or would you have a taste for something *italiano*?"

She poured vermouth at a sideboard and, for a moment, stood looking at the wall. "The problem of Leo," she said, "one can't ignore him, I suppose, although I must say nearly everyone of common sense *has*. . . ." She handed over my aperitif. "Once it was easy to assume that his perpetual crankiness was a symptom of dissatisfied wisdom. It was not, of course. Everyone knew his own Leo, particularly in America . . . I don't mean the village idiot or the idiot savant, oh dear no, but the obstreperous student . . . the one who rejects the text because he simply can't understand it and instead of admitting his own ignorance says that the text is wrong and writes his own. Leo kept writing his own, poor man. Then, when psychoanalysis took over, he didn't have to write it any more because he *was* it."

In all I'd learned, I told her, I'd found no evidence that Gertrude ever spoke of her brother with a shred of the contempt and invective he directed toward her.

"Nowhere, never. She said all she had to say in that piece of hers called *Two*. When she was finished with that, she was finished with him, and so she remained."

The doorbell rang. "That will be Joe and Naomi," she said. Into the room came a young woman with lively dark eyes and a short, conservatively dressed man with a mild smile. He held out his hand.

"John, it's been a long time. . . ."

Joe Barry was Joe Bernstein, my old-shoe compadre on the vanished barricades of Ann Arbor.

"Little could you guess," he said, "when you put a copy of Gertrude's *Useful Knowledge* into my hands ten years ago it would lead to this."

Opening the kitchen door, the housekeeper murmured something to Alice. We went into a small dining room and sat down to a clear soup followed by a pie big enough to house four and twenty black-birds.

On the eve of my sailing, I saw Alice again. "I've told you more than I thought I would . . . or could," she said, "but when it comes to the genius of any particular work of Gertrude Stein's, you'll have to find your own way."

"Sometimes," I said, "just the slightest knowledge of a place or a circumstance provides the essential clue. 'Ladies' Voices'—once you know how it came to be and what it means to demonstrate, it's no longer the exotic fragment you first thought it was."

"Exactly," said Alice. "And that is true of Baby's whole life. She had a perfectly simple approach to what she was about. Sherwood Anderson said she worked like a farm woman baking pies on a wood-burning stove. About her writing when she was writing it, she was untroubled. The doubts when they came came from the outside, when everyone knew who she was. The critics who understand her understand her intuitively and don't have to be told. Donald Suther-land—you've read his book, of course."

Of course, I told her, adding that I'd found it the most brilliant as well as the most frustrating attempt to explain the metaphysics of Stein, mainly because its critical choreography gave Sutherland all the adagios and made everyone a spectator, not at Gertrude's performance but at his.

"So you might say," said Alice. "One finds it very satisfying none-theless. Since he posed no questions, he was not concerned with what people think of as answers."

Sensing my uneasiness at this turn of our talk, she took my glass and, without asking, refilled it. "In another year or so," she said, "you may understand better what I mean. There are people, some of them of the utmost sagacity, who have given up on Gertrude Stein when they found that the problems were no problems, the puzzle no puzzle at all. The challenge disappears and the critic disappears with it."

"I'm afraid I had better disappear right now. My boat train leaves for Le Havre in six hours."

When she went into a bedroom to fetch my raincoat, I had one last chance to look at the raw cubism of Picasso's days in Horta de San Juan and Céret.

Alice saw me to the door. "You'll come again, God willing. I don't travel, you see. Except in the past."

"You've cracked Alice, I hear," said Thornton Wilder in New York. "How did you accomplish that?"

By accident, I told him, a little poem I had written.

"You think you've got something to say? You going to take us through Picasso, Hemingway, all that?"

"I'm finding out, what I have to say."

"Tricky," he said. "First, you have to understand it's all *there*. Either you'll plough into the Stein thing itself or you'll tell stories. And the stories have all been told."

My model, I said, was his own introduction to *Four in America,* the best thing ever written about Gertrude Stein.

His horn-rimmed glasses glinted; his evangelical eyes drilled into mine; he did not smile. "Then," he said, "you're ploughing me. Okay. But don't talk *about* Gertrude. *She* did that. *Do* her."

Taking my hand, he cracked every knuckle before he let it drop.

Wilder's injunctions were useful in ways others were not, mainly because others tended to doubt the testimony of Alice B. Toklas: Virgil Thomson because her memory was "selective" and reduced to "convenience"; Edith Sitwell because of her misapprehension of the true natures of people: Carl Van Vechten because, about the memory of Gertrude she had become proprietary to the point of miserliness. Accepting these cautions while refusing to be cramped by precaution, I could only follow Alice's admonitions and find my own way.

In the sad, senile decline that would soon have her immobile and given to periods of aphasia, Alice B. Toklas was still Alice B. Toklas, even in the briefest of notes. "It is a disappointment," she wrote the following year, "that the day of your arrival [in Paris} is the one on which I leave for Spain. We will not meet this time, will there be another time?

"Last year with friends Spain was revisited . . . and all the lovely memories revived. It was a miracle to have lived it again in this life.

"Good luck to you as Gertrude Stein used to say."

I did not see her again until 1958, when plans we'd arrived at for meeting in Acqui Terme and then to make, as she put it, *"uno piccolo giro"* to Portofino had to be canceled. Ready to depart for Acqui, a spa near Milan, to take the cure, she was overtaken by an infection that left her unable to walk or even to stand. So we met in Paris, over double whiskies and biscuits, in the cheerless light of the rue Christine. My book, *The Third Rose: Gertrude Stein and Her World,* was on the press then, a fact which for all her earlier trepidation and hesitant generosity she did not seem to take in. On this occasion, instead of waiting for conversational leads from me, she introduced points we had never before discussed—the shadow that Gertrude's admiration for certain collaborators under the Occupation had cast upon her judgment; her "constitutional inability even to boil an egg"; her almost blithe acceptance of her death. "She chose a way of dying as she did a way of living," said Alice. "When the doctors refused to operate, she said, 'Well, I guess there's nothing more to say but thank you and good-bye.' "

One year later, I heard what I wanted to hear. "Your book," she wrote, "was a great and successful undertaking." That she then thought I was a Mr. Binner, that the book had got confused in her mind with the whisky called Four Roses, that she addressed her letter to a street on which I had never lived, were, as I squinted at that spidery scrawl, matters of no consequence.

MR. ELIOT, I PRESUME

Mr. Eliot, I Presume

THE aging bridegroom photographed under palm trees, a red bandanna on his straw hat . . . the rumors of dancing lessons and plastic surgery . . . the smirking references to late risings and last stands—toward the end, our image of him underwent a change, our idea of his monastic rigor. But, for most of his life T. S. Eliot seemed awesome and remote, a figure whose choice of exile chastised our complacency. Except for scholars and poetic disciples who went to Russell Square like oblates to the Vatican, few Americans ever saw him. In poetry he called for self-effacement, and conducted his personal life with the same reticence. Yet privacy and apostasy did not inhibit the growth of legend. His influence was so broad, the austerity of his presence so widely assumed, that he came to be regarded as something close to a latter-day divine.

When he was awarded the Nobel prize in 1948, a man from Missouri sent Eliot a recording, "You Came a Long Way From St. Louis," by the dance band of Ray McKinney. Acknowledging the gift, Eliot wrote to say that he was particularly cheered "by the concluding line of the lyric—'But, baby, you've still got a long way to go.' "

Unprepared to accept this broad hint that there might be another side to him, I was not sure I wanted to. There were so few other monuments to look up to, that to find this one winking from his pedestal and joking with a stranger disturbed the right order of things. At least, this was my reaction in 1950 when, new in my job as director of New York's Poetry Center, I felt I had to find a way to break through Eliot's well-known reluctance to appear in public and add his name to the roster of other celebrated yet still less eminent poets the Center had begun to present.

When I confessed as much to an acquaintance at lunch one day, he said he might be able to solve my problem. When was I going to England? Richardson Wood was a Rhodes scholar who'd known Eliot at Oxford and had subsequently met the man with whom he currently lived, the critic John Hayward. Cautioning that an uninvited phone call or any other gesture that might border on importunity had to be avoided, Wood said he'd open the door for me. He'd give me a letter which, as soon as I got to London, I'd post along with a note of my own saying where and when I could be reached. "Then," said Wood, "you simply sit back and await developments, if any."

This is what I did, and got a letter from John Hayward answering for them both: Eliot would see me in his office on the following Monday, Hayward in the flat they shared on the day before. And so it was that a taxi took me through the gray soup of a London Sunday to 19 Carlyle Mansions, Cheyne Walk, Chelsea. I knew that it was the house in which Henry James had drawn his last breath, and as my taxi rounded a semicircular driveway off the Embankment, I could see that it was a Victorian pile of very red brick overlooking the narrow part of the Thames where muddy-footed swans waddle in tidal flats. The bell I pressed looked like a belly button set in brass. "Come up in the lift and walk right in!" a voice called down. Stepping into a gilded birdcage, I ascended, creaking, and walked through an entrance hall into a room accented by pieces of French furniture and warmed by a dozen lighted lamps.

"How d'je do," said a Quasimodo figure in a wheelchair. Grotesquely bent, he had a big head, thick lips the color of raw liver. "You'll have to get used to me," he said, "just like everybody else."

The hand he offered hung like a broken wing.

"Make yourself a drink." He pointed to a table on wheels. "And one for me, some whisky and a little water. You can have ice, if you insist."

His head was as shaggy and broad as Beethoven's, his back curved like a sea lion's.

"Sit where I can see you," he said. "Dick Wood tells me you're a friend of Dylan Thomas's. How does it feel to be an American friend of Dylan's? Over here, everyone's his friend . . . at least everyone thinks he is. Poor Dylan. Isn't his idea of a friend anyone who'll stand him a pint of bitter and a packet of Woodbines?"

I'd done that, too, I told him.

As the flat—warm, spacious, expensively ordinary—echoed with the absence of its other tenant, Hayward read my mind. "Tom will be away until dinnertime," he said. "You'll be seeing him tomorrow. Let me show you around." He made a ninety-degree turn and pointed his wheelchair in the direction of a closed door.

"His," said Hayward, indicating the room we had entered. Its walls looked as if they'd been uniformly stained with nicotine. There was one bare bulb on a chain, an ebony crucifix over the single bed. The wardrobe closet was open: crow-black silk ties on a rod, a scarlet water-silk sash, three glen plaid suits, others in shades of gray and black; a Prince Albert hanging by itself. "The confessional," said Hayward, "here we have our bedtime chats. He tells me *everything*."

We continued down a hallway. "My pigsty bed-sit," he said. "The housekeeper won't touch it, and I can't. You believe what they say about orderly minds, disorderly desks? I'd be living proof"—his laugh was like a hiccup—"*if* I had an orderly mind. That's his chair, the straight-backed one."

We had regained the living room.

"And *that,* if you're interested, is his umbrella." It lay horizontal on a table beside a dish of sixpence and shillings—"for the number nine bus," he said, "or the Sloane Square tube station. Tom likes to see what's going on in the streets."

"Don't people recognize him?"

"He doesn't think so. I hope he's right. On the day *Time* magazine came out with his face on the cover he walked for hours looking for wherever he might find it, shamelessly taking peeks at himself."

When the doorbell rang, he showed me where to press the buzzer. "That earnest young man from Toronto, I expect—a Canadian who writes rather nicely about the Pre-Raphaelites. Would you meet him at the lift and show him in?"

The Canadian, a bearded image of Dante Gabriel Rossetti, had barely sat down before the bell rang again.

"Hilary," said John. "He knows the way. Sit down and hope for the best. Hilary likes to talk."

The newcomer was a well-known critic and erstwhile poet who had also written notable biographies. Once introduced, he poured himself a drink, draped himself over Eliot's chair, and conveyed his annoyance at the presence of me and the man from Toronto by pretending we weren't there.

"How's Tom?" he asked. "Set for Switzerland? I've got some stories for him."

"He'll be in this evening," said Hayward. "How did you entertain yourself in the south of France?"

His question started the critic on a disquisition—names we knew, nicknames we had to guess, events and places in which the fritillaries of British letters chance to meet. Shifting in his chair, he sent a slightly defiant glance toward me and the Canadian. "I must say I *quite* liked it, for a fortnight, anyway. Delicious debilitation. How *are* you, John? Have you looked into the new Hemingway? If not, don't bother. Unless you happen to be bonkers for big fish, and brave little boys."

Cutting into his monologue, Hayward nodded toward me. "Here's the man," he said, "who's been taking care of Dylan in America."

The critic made a losing effort to smile.

"What *is* this sinister devotion of Tom's to Switzerland?" he said. "Oh, I know what he *says*, about it being the only place that still is what it was and all that. Myself, I should think . . ."

Since each of us had different things to talk about, nothing prevailed but the critic's confidence that the Pre-Raphaelite scholar and I would soon be gone.

To make the first move, I stood up.

"Let me show you the way," said Hayward, and wheeled himself into the hall. "As you see, Hilary's full of himself. Come back. I want to hear about Dylan's American woman. It's serious this time, I understand. Won't there be hell to pay?"

Next day, mindful all day of my four o'clock appointment, I distracted myself in bookstores and museums, corrected my watch by public clocks, prepared as best I could a face to meet the face that I would meet. Ten minutes before the hour, I'd completed two circuits of Russell Square and was about to make another. My joints were stiff, my hands cold.

Inside the Faber & Faber offices on the dot, I stated my name and mission to a woman at a desk. Another woman emerged from an inner office hugging a sheaf of manuscript to her chest. "I'm Valerie Fletcher," she said. "Mr. Eliot's asked me to see you up."

Unaware, as I returned her efficient smile, that I was in the company of the future Mrs. Eliot, I followed her to an elevator which barely accommodated two people. We rose with a jerk, stopped with a jerk, and the door clanked open.

Eliot stood waiting in the hallway. Lean-faced, slightly furrowed, deeply bent, he was wearing a glen plaid suit with a vest and a watch chain. We shook hands and went into a room not much bigger than the elevator. As we sat down, I had to twist my knees to keep them from jutting into his. At the edge of his desk was a tray. On it were two mugs of tea and a bleak dish of buns so highly glazed they looked ceramic. He spoke in distinctly separated phrases, with a curious humming noise that served him as a form of punctuation.

"Richardson Wood . . . Dick," he said. "I don't quite understand . . . what his business actually involves. Hmmmm. I knew him as a Rhodes scholar, when he was pursuing . . . hmmmm . . . some rather audacious notions about sixteenth-century literature . . . hmmmm. . . . Now I believe he pursues notions . . . hmmmm . . . about the functions of enlightened capitalism?"

His assumptions were correct, I told him—our friend advised industrial corporations, sometimes governments, on the profitable and humane uses of natural resources.

"In other words, he maintains good conscience . . . hmmmm

Photo by R. Thorne McKenna

. . . while making good money." His smile broke the ice. "You
might tell him that I hope to see him and Millie in New York. I
shall be there in October."

Encouraged, I learned that he'd also be spending a few days in the
Midwest and a week with what he referred to as "surviving members"
of his family "not far from Boston."

"Your Poetry Center," he said, as though helping me to come to
the point, "we have nothing quite like it over here, at least not on
your scale. From what I've heard, and what I've seen for myself
. . . I get the New York papers to see how they advertise my play
. . . your presentations are regarded almost as theatrical events. To
us, that seems most curious."

Handed an opening so clear and wide, I made my pitch and stated my price.

"I think," he said, "I might be able . . . hmmmm . . . to come to you in December . . . in fact . . . I should be grateful for the opportunity. Money, I must tell you, is no small consideration."

This information (*The Cocktail Party,* a surprise hit of the past season on Broadway, was still running) was strange enough to make me squint.

"Absurd, of course," he said, "but it's impossible to take sufficient monies out of this country to pay for my visit. And my solicitors . . . hmmmm . . . inform me with some emphasis that I may not spend a penny of the royalties . . . hmmmm . . . rather nicely accumulating in New York. So, you see, I need all the help I can get. Your tea must be cold. Let me ring for Miss Fletcher."

I don't mind cold tea, I told him, and drank up.

"Your shining stars are the Sitwells, are they not?"

The Sitwells, I had to admit, had never been on the Poetry Center's roster. Their American audiences, I told him, were ladies' clubs and the vague cultural circuit managed by high-powered agencies.

"If we do have a bright particular star," I said, "it's Dylan Thomas."

"Does he behave himself?"

"No."

This late in his life (he was sixty-one) Eliot had given less than a handful of readings in the United States and, I believe, had read only once before in New York. The response to our announcement of the event suggested that many people thought his reading at the Poetry Center might well be his last. On the morning after we had named his date in *The New York Times*, fifteen or twenty requests were made for every seat available. Pursued and badgered to use my influence to produce tickets, I found that people who'd never read a sonnet since the seventh grade were suddenly lovers of poetry whose devotion I was implored not to dismiss. Whatever else he might have been in the eyes of the world, T. S. Eliot in 1950 was for New Yorkers a hot ticket.

About a month before the event, he wrote from Chicago: "I would not want to have my address in New York generally known but will, in due time, inform you what it is. My overriding concern is the problem of dress. Shall I put on evening clothes?"

I wrote back to say he might dress as he pleased, that most poets came as they were, while a few others thought that a reading became something more of an occasion if they appeared in black tie.

"I think it would be better if I were *not* to put on evening clothes," he wrote, "because I have accepted an invitation to a cocktail party of the English Speaking Union and some other literary organization on that very afternoon, and it would be too much of a rush if, between one engagement and another, I had to find a way to change my costume."

On the appointed evening early in December, I got to the Poetry Center an hour before the reading and found myself barred from even entering the building. Crowds on the sidewalk were being kept in check by uniformed policemen, one of whom, as I attempted to identify myself, looked at me like a Thurber dog confronted by an insect. Rescued by an usher, I was finally able to muscle my way to the Green Room, where Eliot was chatting with a man of cherubic countenance who turned out to be his American editor, Robert Giroux.

Eliot's face seemed weighted with weariness, and when he stood up, I thought he was even more deeply bent than he'd been in London. But his sad, lingering hint of a smile suggested he was at ease with the circumstance. "Do you suppose I might read 'Prufrock'?" he asked. "Or would that be altogether too familiar to a sophisticated audience?"

As far as I was concerned, I told him, to hear him read "Prufrock" would be a very special pleasure.

"I want to make a good appearance," he said. The directness and humility of this left me with nothing to say.

When I presented him with his check, he gave it a glance. "Are you entirely sure you can afford as much as this?"

Since the figure was the one agreed upon, I took his question as a form of solicitude, or an indication of embarrassment. In any case, the check went into his pocket and in a few minutes he was on stage, not quite smiling into the waves of an ovation that kept him standing, bowing, unable to speak.

In the wings, entranced by the particular nuances he gave to words I'd long ago memorized, I felt again what had occurred to me in the course of our talk in London: He was a man trapped, condemned to live up to an image he could not live down. By all accounts I'd read or heard, he was masked and Parnassian—an oracle who spoke in many voices, all his own. In actuality I had found him to be gentle and open, with a slow-fused kind of humor and a slightly wicked sense of conspiracy he seemed to want to share. Had he, in life as in poetry, carried his conviction about the self-effacement of the artist too far?

When the reading was over and Prufrock in his seaward swoon was one with Thomas Stearns Eliot in a black three-buttoned suit on a bare stage in the city of New York, the audience recognized the conjunction and called him back again and again. As I surrendered him to ushers who would lead him down fire-stairs to a waiting car, he turned.

"I don't think John Hayward would believe all this—from me, at least. Shall we see you in London? Perhaps he'll believe *you.*"

En route to Wales that next summer, I stopped in London for a few days. Still mindful of protocol, I sent a note telling Eliot where I'd be staying—in a fleabag bed-and-breakfast hotel near Euston Station—and again sat back to await developments, if any.

His response was prompt: a call I had to take in the raincoat I used as a bathrobe, at the hall porter's desk, since there was no phone in my room. Would I care . . . hmmmm . . . to join him for lunch on Saturday at . . . hmmmm . . . one o'clock and go on to a cricket match? Beside the porter's desk was a big neon-lighted tank in which tropical fish were swirling about a scummy castle set in feathery weeds. I'd be delighted, I told him (my mind was swirling like the fish), but that I was going to Wales and had no way of knowing when on Saturday I might get back. Should it be only a matter of missing lunch, he said, I might come when I could, a bus from Paddington would bring me almost to the door.

In Wales on the following Friday Dylan Thomas was at my side when, my fingers cramped with reluctance, I wrote out a message to be wired to Cheyne Walk saying I was detained.

"Pity," said Eliot in his office on Monday, "it was a lovely afternoon for cricket. I'd have liked to have shown you some of the finer points. Officially, I'm out of the city weekends. Actually, I stay fairly close to home."

"Incognito?"

He smiled. "It's not difficult to remain incognito on a cricket green in Chelsea. We'll plan for another Saturday. How did you find Mr. and Mrs. Thomas?"

I found them, I did not say, as Dylan himself described them— "Cait and dog"—or report their thunderous skirmishings in the bedroom overhead, the slamming doors, the wincing cries, the running feet on the stairs.

"Fine," I said. "The place is beautiful, the situation . . ."

The glance he gave me was sly.

"Oh, there were a few awkward moments," I said, and did not

rehearse the barrages of flying china, the hair-pulling wrestlings across the dining room, the slambang confrontations in the vestibule.

"Mrs. Thomas, I have reason to know," he said, "sometimes takes occasion to show her Irish character."

(Irish character! What, in the name of Brennan-on-the-Moor, did he think *mine* was?)

On his desk, no doubt placed there by design, was a copy of the anthology of modern poetry I had edited with Kimon Friar. He picked it up and riffled through the pages. "I'm pleased," he said, "to find you've given generous space to Isaac Rosenberg. He tends to be neglected here . . . in the same way David Jones is . . . by everyone but a few writers who learn from him, and use him, and keep very quiet about it. Sassoon and Owen get most of the attention when it comes to trench poets. To my mind, Rosenberg's the best of them. It's also good to see you've made a feature of Mr. Frost's sonnets. I don't think anyone else *has*."

That was Friar's idea, I told him.

"Those passages from Miss Barnes. Who thought of including them?"

"Both of us."

"Would you be free one afternoon, to come to a screening of the film that's been made from my play?"

I was booked for Paris on Thursday, I told him.

"I'd like to know what you might think of it. Curious. I've learned more about writing for the theater from the making of this cinema than from working in the theater itself. Nothing I could have predicted."

"Faulkner once told me he liked working with movies because the writer has no more status than any one of the technicians. He says he likes the impersonality of it."

"I believe I've felt something like that," he said. "One becomes objective in the presence of so much formidable paraphernalia. On the stage *Murder in the Cathedral* tends to become a sermon. And since it is so often put on in chapels and churches, that seems quite proper. Actually, it was written to be performed at Canterbury, as a fairly solemn religious celebration and not at all the entertainment

Mr. Eliot, I Presume / 261

people have made of it. On the screen one cannot assume the advantage of the three actual dimensions a theater or church provide. The nature of the movie audience is to give its attention wholly to what is seen and yet remain passive, to stay in a sort of *rêve éveillé*. Still, it's mandatory that things move, even when those things are moral distinctions."

The office, the whole building, had suddenly become quiet. Five o'clock.

"You must know young Lowell," he said. "Should I take the stories I hear about him seriously? Or with a large grain of salt?"

"Both."

"Then, his delusions are, as one might put it, real?"

"Most likely. But so are other people's—about him."

"No doubt," he said. For a moment I wondered if he'd caught the note of chastisement I had let slip. "It might be much easier, would it not, and perhaps more charitable, if we took him simply as goofy?"

His grin was bony and wide.

"Excuse me for a moment," he said, "then maybe you'll walk me to the Baker Street tube station."

Alone in his book-lined cubicle, I thought: He'll go home now and—as I'd learned from John Hayward—eat a meal from a tray on his lap, read the papers, perhaps correct proofs for *Sailing the Channel* or *Hints for Seaside Gardens,* or compose jacket blurbs for other such titles his company publishes. At bedtime he and John will have their "confessional" chat under that bare bulb, that crucifix on the wall, and he'll be back in this little office in the late morning. If, as Joyce said of him, he was the one who had abolished "poetry for ladies," he may also have done in for all time the figure of the poet as a creature of impetuous stances, wicked curls, and wide-caped broodings. A holy man—by nature? Or by default? In the way of Henry James's exhortations to "live," how hungry he seems, how carefully he's made the likelihood moot.

"Now, then," he said from the doorway. "I think we might descend. What shall you be doing in Paris?"

In December I wrote to ask if he'd come to the Poetry Center again in May, and to say I hoped he'd assure me that the fee was adequate.

He would come if he could, he said, depending upon family matters. As for the fee: "Be assured," he wrote, "that I regard the honorarium you mention as generous, particularly when I recall the pleasure of an audience of such warmth and attentiveness as that which you provided a year ago."

In a postscript—referring to a trio of British poets (Kathleen Raine, David Gascoyne, W. S. Graham) I had brought to the Poetry Center and for whom I was then trying to arrange an American tour, he said: "You cannot, I suspect, be bearing lightly the burdens that your importation of three temperamental British poets must impose. I trust you have learned to deal with such things without incurring the penalties they are all too likely to exact."

At five A.M. on the agreed-upon date in May—after a midnight ride from mid-Connecticut with Dylan Thomas, followed by a bar-hopping tour of the West Village—I was standing at the entrance to the Hotel Chelsea trying to convince Dylan that he ought to call it a night and go to bed. Four hours later a phone call from Eliot brought me from my own bed in something less than clearheadedness. "I should be pleased," he said, "if you would arrange to have Marianne Moore admitted to the backstage area tonight. . . . I've already taken the liberty of telling her I'd see her there."

I'd be glad to, I told him, and forgot about it until that evening. Once more, a reading by T. S. Eliot had proved to be an event of such magnitude that crowds of people without tickets had joined those with tickets in numbers that made passage to the Green Room an inch by inch progress. I found him there alone.

"How did you find Los Angeles?" I asked.

Lowering his head, he seemed to be giving the question more thought than it called for. "I don't think," he said finally, "I've ever felt so far from home in my life, perhaps because I'd never quite believed what I now know to be true. My friends were kind, but that in itself did not alleviate what appears to be . . . hmmm . . . some grotesque condition of the spirit."

In a tricorne hat and Mary Jane shoes, Marianne Moore was ushered in. Embracing like biblical figures, almost without touching, they spoke softly to one another and sat down side by side. Excusing myself, I left them until curtain time.

Mr. Eliot, I Presume / *263*

* * *

One afternoon in the following August I got to Carlyle Mansions at three, not without some wonder as to why, having been asked to come to tea, I was bidden to arrive so early. I had still not caught on to the fact that John Hayward was the most indefatigable and, in the eyes of some people, the most malicious gossip in the parishes of literary London.

Before I could sit down, he said: "I understand there's bloody hell to pay. Dylan's liaison has been discovered."

"Which one?" I asked, and bit my tongue.

"The American woman who followed him over last year. Caitlin and the gray lady, you know who I mean, they've joined forces to send her packing. From what I hear, Dylan's still not aware his mail's been opened for months. No idea why things have come a cropper. Have you?"

I'd not seen Dylan, I told him—a fact that allowed me to forestall further questions to which, in this case, I had all the answers. He chose a new tack.

"Tom tells me you've been to Ireland . . . to Bowen's Court, no less. Is Elizabeth still devoting body and soul to that hopeless old blimp? If you're hungry, don't wait. Help yourself to one of those." He nodded toward a wicker caddy laden with platters of small sandwiches, pound cake, and pastries. "The story goes that she took him to Ireland to keep him out of sight, as if he were an idiot nephew. Is he—out of sight?"

I was glad for the sound of footsteps in the hallway.

"Tom," he said.

Carrying a black briefcase, Eliot looked into the room—warily, I thought—then advanced as I rose to shake his hand.

"She has not yet made her entrance, I see," he said to John, and sat down with an audible sigh. "Perhaps John has told you that a lady relative of mine from the States will be joining us. She's sailing off tomorrow. . . . This turned out to be my only opportunity to see her."

"Tom's loyalty is excessive," said John, "what you Americans call a complex. In his case, obsession with the tribe."

Eliot, with a mildly reproving glance, seemed to be waiting for his

friend to make more of a familiar contretemps. "I have so few connections left," he said. "This one, as you'll see, is a lively relic of
vanishing Boston, a tiresome little soul but otherwise harmless. She
tells me considerably more than she understands."

"And all over again," said John, "she'll tell what Tom's nephew
said to Tom's niece when they saw cousin True or Charity—those
sorts of names they have—riding her bum down the steps of the
Church of the Advent on Pentecost Sunday. Mind you outstay her,
we'll have a drink."

Reclining in his tall-backed chair, hands clasped at the crick of his
neck, Eliot stretched out his legs and gave me a thoughtful smile.
"I was speaking with Stephen Spender a while back," he said, "those
troubles you had getting him to come to one of your poetry evenings,
because of the McCarran Act."

I nodded.

"Was it true you had to get Archie MacLeish to intercede with the
White House?"

"We had the same sort of trouble getting Dylan into the country,"
I told him. "It was bad enough when they found out he'd signed the
Stockholm peace petition. But when he admitted he'd accepted an
invitation to read his poems in Czechoslovakia, they began to see a
criminal pattern."

"Insanity," said Eliot. "As far as I can tell, Stephen Spender was
a member of the Communist party for about twenty-five minutes fifteen years ago. Surely everyone knows he must now be the most
effective anti-Communist we have?"

"If they do, they don't care. They stick to the letter. . . ."

"Some curious obsession seems to lie behind it," he said, "but with
what? Does anyone seriously suppose there's anything threatening in
what's left of the sad rags of official Communism?"

"There may be no logic," I said, "but there's power."

"Isn't it a kind of Bible Belt fear based in ignorance? Xenophobia
calling the tune for national policy?"

He leaned forward and with two fingers lifted the wicker caddy.
"A gooseberry tart? Fortnum's best. I don't suppose a public letter on
the subject would have much effect. But I must say I've had some
thoughts about composing a very angry one."

Mr. Eliot, I Presume / 265

Throughout this exchange my surprise and consternation on hearing liberal sentiments from the mouth of a supposed archreactionary must have shown in my face, at least enough to keep him observing my response with the twinkle of someone pleased to have been "found out" in his own heresy.

At the sound of the doorbell he went to the landing and returned with a small, neat woman wearing a navy-blue suit with a lace dickey and a bird's nest of a hat. She was *finally* all packed, she said without prologue and a bit breathlessly, how *do* people manage? If one *knew* the trials of travel beforehand, one would not travel, would one? She was returning on the *Parthia,* she said, the one Cunarder on which First Class accommodations cost nothing so outrageous as what they charge for the same accommodations on the *Queens.*

"Would we then be correct in assuming," said Eliot, "that we are the happy witness to your Parthian shot?"

Blinking for a moment, she declined to be interrupted. Not only that, she went on, but a small ship, particularly when it was British, seemed always to attract a nicer type of clientele. "I bless you for putting me onto it, Tom . . . or don't you remember? When you answered my boat letter to the *Media?* I'd never heard of either one of them. Of course, it makes a much *longer* voyage, but there's nothing of that cabaret atmosphere some people expect on the ocean, and—"

"Do have another," said Eliot, and gave me a slow wink as he lifted the caddy and pointed to some squares iced with chocolate.

"—I do so like my rubber or two in the afternoon. Coming over the captain himself made our fourth every day. Every day, that is, when we weren't plowing through the fog."

Lights on the Battersea side of the river had come on when, at long last, Eliot saw her to the door. At John's suggestion I poured three hefty whiskies and squirted soda into them. "Bon voyage," said John in a stage whisper, and raised his glass. "To the world's nicer types," he said, *"au revoir* from the scrofulous. Talking does no good. This holy devotion to kinship can be carried a sticky little bit too far. For God's sake, sit down."

* * *

A year later in the same room, I found John heavier, more painfully twisted in his movements, more slurred in speech. Yet he was
as eager as ever to draw me out about where I'd been and whom I'd
seen and then to elaborate upon my most guarded reports with acid.

"So you've survived still another visit to the Thomases," he said.
"They still playing rugby on the bedroom floor? Dylan lost his trousers, Tom tells me, on the way to a reading for the Queen Mum, had
to take the podium wearing Louis MacNeice's. Then they sent him
back to John Davenport's flat wrapped in some poor soul's mac he
nipped from the cloakroom on his way out."

Disappointed to learn that Eliot would be in Scotland during the
brief time I'd be in London, I left him a letter.

"I am indebted to you," he wrote a month later, "for your kind
letter of September 10th. I had known of course from John Hayward
that you were here and am deeply sorry that our paths did not coin-
cide. After my week in Edinburgh I went at once to Switzerland for
a fortnight's holiday.

"It is kind of you to ask me once again to read at the Poetry
Center. If I hesitate to accept, it is due only to the fact that, as you
are aware, my repertory is modest and having already appeared there
twice I am uneasy about turning up again so soon with a programme
that can hardly be much different from those I have already presented. But I have always been very happy with the audience you
provide, and if you really believe you want me again, I shall indeed
be pleased to consider it.

"My next American visit will likely occur in the fall of 1954; I see
no way of getting there before. Would I be welcome then? To my
deep regret you say that you are determined that this will be the last
year in which you will be arranging these occasions. Yet I can well
understand how such activity must have its term.

"I do wish that you could have remained longer in London. I
should particularly have liked to have taken you to see my play when
it arrived more or less intact from its premier performance in Scotland."

When Dylan Thomas died in New York two months later, rumor
and counterrumor put so morbid a shadow on his deathbed that I felt

obliged to tell his British friends the facts of his dying as I knew them. Among the letters I sent off within the week of his death was one to Eliot and Hayward.

Midsummer of the following year, I wrote to tell them the days I'd be in London. John at once named a date for another of our crepuscular rehearsals of lives and times; Eliot's reply came from his secretary. "Mr. Eliot has only now come back from a period of recuperation in the countryside," she wrote, "and has asked me to tell you that he hopes to be well enough to see you in the late summer. Because of an attack of tachycardia, he has been confined for weeks in hospital. This episode was apparently provoked by over-exertion and while there is nothing else wrong with him, organically, his physician has strongly counselled that he remain quiet for a good length of time. Consequently he has cancelled all social and public appearances until October or so. This should not deter you from making your presence known when you are in London because he would very much like to see you."

"What *is* tachycardia?" I asked him one day in August.

"A condition where the heart beats at twice or more its normal rate," he said. "It seems sometimes like five times that, actually, but the doctors insist it's not as alarming as it always must seem to the patient. One has the feeling one is harboring some runaway machine. I can't say I've ever gotten used to it."

Caged in his office, he seemed more hunched, more stiff than ever. Yet his smile—half pain, half mischief—made him appear quite himself and added to the feeling that the patient whose symptoms he described was not T. S. Eliot but some figure who might deserve our objective scrutiny but had no special call on our sympathy.

"I hope John has told you how deeply moved I was by your letter, the one about Dylan Thomas's last days. Written as it was, so close to the event, I don't think you can be aware of what a document it is."

"Thank you," I said.

"We were quite in the dark over here. No one believed the reports in the paper, and of course there were stories making the rounds, some of them not very pleasant, to say the least. So you see it was a comfort to have your witness, if there was indeed any comfort to be had. You may have heard that I've done what I could on this end. Mrs. Thomas asked me if I would assume the chairmanship of the group setting about to raise funds for her and the children and I've been happy to do it."

We concluded our meeting with his promise that he would make still another appearance at the Poetry Center in the following spring. I did not know that, in order to allow him to make good on his promise, I would have to resort to chicanery.

The Poetry Center was part of the Young Men's and Young Women's Hebrew Association, an organization that went much further than its Christian counterpart in promotion of the arts, particularly the performing arts. To some members of the Jewish intellectual community, the hospitality it had repeatedly extended to Eliot seemed, at best, anachronistic or, at least, politically naïve. His poetry contained distasteful, if not slanderous, references to Jews to whom he gave fictitious names; and he had suggested in a famous lecture that a history of intellectual irascibility and religious intransigeance on the part of Jews would obviate their inclusion in his own particular vision of the City of God.

Eliot's first two appearances at the Poetry Center had gone unquestioned, even by Jews well acquainted with his poetry and with his spoken sentiments. But when news of a proposed third reading was out, several individuals on the periphery of the Center's activities took it upon themselves to chastise the board of governors and to present them with a tally of Eliot's sins of commission. His name, they felt, should be removed from our roster—not as an act of vengeance but as a matter of policy. The question they put to me was simple: On what basis might a Jewish organization countenance sponsorship of a man whose anti-Semitism was evident both by literary inference and by overt statement?

In spite of my private conviction that Eliot was perhaps not so much anti-Semitic as he was the unwitting victim of the myths of his class and kind, I was defenseless. If Eliot were actively anti-Semitic, I thought, why had he accepted our invitation in the first place? If he were covertly anti-Semitic, why were his friendships with Jews constant and his admiration for Jewish writers outspoken? But I could not bring myself to argue my convictions against the claims of those whose feelings I regarded as inviolate.

To resolve the matter, I was told, it would be necessary for me to obtain from Eliot a statement making his position explicit. Trying for days to find the words that might bring this about, I got nowhere. Every letter I sketched out came, in the end, to nothing but, "Dear Mr. Eliot, are you an anti-Semite?"

Stymied, I was saved by the ingenuity of a colleague. "I *have* it," he said. "We sponsor a petition. We send out a call to a dozen writers here and abroad, Eliot included, asking them to state their feelings about the Soviet persecution of dissident Jewish intellectuals."

Within hours a letter to Eliot was in the mail to England. Within ten days I had his reply. "On" to the ruse, as he let me know later, he accepted its threadbare pretext, then ignored it as he composed a document (here published for the first time) leaving no doubt about his personal feelings or his view of recent history: "As one of the poets who has enjoyed the generosity of the Poetry Center and the kind attention of its audience, I am glad for the opportunity to respond to your letter of the 12th instant. But a mere statement of my approval of the need to take a public stand against the present anti-Semitic policy of the Soviet government is far short of what I feel writers should do—for what humane person could refuse to lend force to such a protest? I think we should go on record with sentiments much deeper than that.

"The one notable distinction between the current anti-Semitism in the Soviet Union, and the anti-Semitism of Nazi Germany is, I think, this: that the Soviets have 'benefited' from the errors of the Nazis, and are much more clever propagandists. The Nazis persecuted Jews for being Jews, and so brought down on themselves the antipathy and censure of all the civilized world. The Soviets hold back from any open doctrine of racial superiority because this would too egregiously countermand their published principles, and confuse the workings of their foreign policy. Just as they have denigrated and silenced their more important Christian victims—not on the basis of their being Christians, but always on some trumped-up notion of incivility or treason—so the Jews who are condemned to death, or worse, are always accused on some other pretext, than that of being Jews. But in the end there is no difference.

"In all anti-Semitic drives by governments there is a discernible pattern of *policy* and *hysteria*. The hysteria of the masses is whipped up by cold deliberation. Yet there is a quotient of hysteria even in the deliberation itself. True anti-Semitism—as distinct from anti-Semitism in Moslem areas, which tends to carry with it the old burdens of familiar racial, nationalistic and religious opposition—is a force wholly inside of one country, or of a ruling clique against the Jews who happen to be its own citizens. It is a symptom of the deepest dilemma, chaos and of the malfunctioning of the economy and in the religious pretensions of that nation; and is used to the point of exploitation by rulers as a radical remedy which, in the end, only aggravates the disease of which it is a symptom. These remarks provide a more reasonable ground for the conviction which I have long held, that any country which denies the rights of its own citizens or makes pariahs of any body of its own nationals—and most especially the Jews—will sooner or later have to pay the full price for so doing; and even the 'uninvolved' people whom it governs will have to expiate the crime of having allowed such a government to lead them."

Commotion and clamor once more attended his reading in May, but he bore them with a sort of elegant weariness. In the half hour we had to ourselves that evening, he refused the Chivas Regal we kept on hand to cheer or fortify our speakers, accepted a cigarette, and began to draw me out about the operations of the Poetry Center and poets who'd recently appeared there. Puzzled, he said, by the lack of serious critical attention paid to older men like Robinson Jeffers and Conrad Aiken, he wondered if they had been part of our program. They'd been invited, I told him, but both had declined—Jeffers because he was not well enough to make the journey from California, Aiken because of an admitted terror of exposure to any audience, much less one as large as ours. Djuna Barnes? he asked. She had also refused, I told him, but pointed out that Dylan Thomas liked to read a chapter from *Nightwood* on those programs of his drawn from other writers than himself. Obviously pleased to hear this, he spoke of the "pathological reluctance" on the part of critics to deal with a book of the "deepest puritan persuasion" simply because it was based in a society sexually aberrant.

Knowing he'd been to Washington recently, I asked about Ezra Pound. "A very sad case," he said. "I found myself forgoing visits I might easily have made, simply because the man's megalomania would have made them pointless. From what I could tell, he seemed capable of rational discourse in the early part of a day but grew less so as the day went on. To be in his company was less to attend him than to observe him—the deterioration, painful for the visitor and of no earthly help to Ezra, though the faithful Olga Rudge insists otherwise."

When the reading ended, somewhat anticlimactically, with "The Cultivation of Christmas Trees," he went off in the company of his publishers. Starting for my office, I was passing through the lounge when I found Marianne Moore, black-caped and pensive, alone in the dispersing crowd. "Did Mr. Eliot know you'd be here?" I asked.

"The opportunity was private," she said. "A friend offered me a ticket at the penultimate moment."

"How are you getting back to Brooklyn?"

"The subway," she said, "is usually sufficient."

I offered to drive her home.

In her flat on Cumberland Street she poured orange juice for us both, then wound up a little pink elephant and set it laboring across the floor.

"Mr. Eliot was responsible for the trance in which you discovered me," she said, "a state not often induced by one's own publisher. But on this occasion I went only for the poet . . . a decision I would not have believed so consequential. We've been allied for many years. He knew my mother."

The tiny elephant, running down, hit a table leg and toppled over. Picking it up, she turned the key in its back and sent it going in another direction.

"We came, Mr. Eliot and I, into this world almost at the same time—mere months apart to begin with and now, I suppose, 'of an age.' He was the first to give all care to my possibilities."

The elephant crashed into a baseboard and collapsed.

Now chronically ill, Eliot was also in love. I had learned of the illness firsthand, but knew of the romance only by inference at the point when it was about to lead to marriage and the transformation of a life of reclusive asceticism into a perpetual honeymoon. The aged eagle, as he termed himself, was about to drop a ruffled feather or two, spread his wings, and more precipitously than anyone could guess, take off. But only two people in the world were likely to have known this when, in May 1956, he came to Cambridge, Massachusetts. Phoning me at home, he invited me to an evening at a house off Brattle Street where, he said, he would "lend his presence, if not much else," to a reading of a new play by his old friend Djuna Barnes.

As my journal entry for the twenty-second of that month suggests, he resumed for Cantabrigian literati the role expected of him:

> Accepting T.S.E.'s invitation, find the house (it belongs to Bunny Lang's sister) where he is to "lend his presence" to a private, i.e. "public," reading of Djuna Barnes's *Antiphon*. Flanked on one side by Eliot, on the other by the Scottish poet Edwin Muir, with I. A. Richards next to him, she sits serene as the pythoness in a white turban while amateurs read a script static and obscure—like something of huge presence dimly perceived through clouds of chalk. The hard chairs we sit on get harder as the late May twilight fades to dark and the lamps are turned on. Eliot in pinstripes brings a deacon's gravity to the proceedings and sets the tone—that of a tribunal preparing a verdict. In a less funereal convocation, the play may show more life, but I have my doubts—and a feeling that, somewhere in the droning stillness, so does Miss Barnes.

Eliot's pronounced solemnity that evening may have been due to other causes. Three weeks later, aboard the *Queen Mary* en route to England, he was stricken with still another attack of tachycardia, confining him to sick bay for most of the voyage, then causing him to be removed from the ship to a London hospital.

Mr. Eliot, I Presume / 273

"Now he's in Switzerland, without his brolly," said John Hayward, and nodded toward the conspicuously big-handled umbrella lying on the hall table, "where it's apparently been raining without cease since he got there." He accepted the whisky and soda I poured for him. "Do you think I might make it to America in one of these new jet airplanes that cross in a matter of six or seven hours? You think they could handle a body like me?"

Of course, I told him, and wondered how they would.

"Tom's now developed something called emphysema," he said. "It's rapidly become apparent he needs a nurse more than I do. And I have an informed suspicion that the ever-adoring Miss Fletcher is ready to assume the role. You know her?"

"The young woman in his office?"

"There's somewhat more to that flower of the Yorkshire marshes than meets the eye," he said. "The perfect secretary has begun to see herself as the lady with the lamp."

This remark, inscrutable at the time, I recalled four months later when Eliot slipped out—or as John put it, sneaked out—of the flat they had shared for nine years, got married to Miss Fletcher in the darkness of a winter morning, and never came back.

The separation was swift and all but absolute. I did not know this when, sending a note to Eliot in the following July, I asked him to convey my greetings to his housemate.

"I have not seen John Hayward since he came to lunch with my wife and myself to meet Robert Frost," he wrote, "but I am sure he will look forward to meeting you in August. I expect to be here during that month and so hope to see you also."

We did meet in August, twice on the same day.

"Do you have any notion of the furor your book about Dylan Thomas caused over here?" he asked. We were sitting in his office, the same white mugs on the tea tray beside us, the same glossy buns.

I'd seen press clippings in my publisher's office, I told him. His eyes were piercingly bright, his smile no longer bony and thin but broad and easy. Had he put on weight? "Since I've been accepting social engagements at a rate rather unusual for me," he said, "I can tell you that for a good week or so you all but succeeded in pushing our visiting Russian dignitaries out of the limelight."

"You've been well, then?"

"To the point where I can even contemplate some fairly distant travels," he said. "My physician recommends warm weather and I've been surprised to find that even the heat of the tropics is thoroughly agreeable."

"Under the bam," I said, "under the boo?"

A kind of harumphing noise—a stifled spasm almost approaching laughter—started in his chest, and stayed there.

"Hitherto," he said, "I'm afraid my tropics have been a purely theatrical reality."

A few hours later, during dinner with a friend at the Hotel Connaught, I took a moment between courses to visit the men's room. There, washing my hands, I looked into the wide mirrors above the row of basins and recognized the figure who had just walked in, and was now standing at one of the gleaming white urinals. Waiting to speak until I decently could, I pretended to go on washing my hands. Without taking my eyes from the mirror in front of me, I spoke into it.

"Mr. Eliot, I presume?"

Joined in ablutions, we toweled our hands and stepped out into the lobby. There, waiting, was the same young woman who, hugging a sheaf of manuscript, had led me into his presence seven years before.

"You've met Miss Fletcher," he said, "but not Mrs. Eliot. You'll join us in the lounge, for a brandy?"

As I took the hand she offered, her mink cape slipped, revealing a delicate circle of pearls about her neck. Quickly restoring the cape to her shoulders, Eliot kept his arm around her while she gazed up at his face with the mischievous petulance of a little girl about to tease her father.

"I must finish my dinner," I said, and bowed myself out.

Acknowledgments

For counsel and encouragement, I owe particular debts of gratitude to Merloyd Lawrence and Emily Morison Beck. For permission to publish materials in their control, I thank Valerie Fletcher Eliot, Francis Sitwell, Edward Burns (for the Estate of Alice Toklas), and Truman Capote. Through the good offices of Magnum Photos, Inc., Henri Cartier-Bresson made pertinent photographs available to me; for other photographs I am beholden to Rollie McKenna and Christopher Cox. For editorial insights rendered informally, I have counted upon William Abrahams and Howard Moss. Others whose generous attention, support, or comfort has been all to my advantage are Dennis Brown, Cristina Franchetti, John Hohnsbeen, Gay Jacobson, Kay Kuhn, Alice Methfessel, Rhoda Sheehan, Sylvia Putziger, Grace Stone, and Carol Todd. To the kindness of Patricia Curtis Vigano I owe the opportunity to complete this book in the Venetian light and shade of the Palazzo Barbaro.

—JOHN MALCOLM BRINNIN

The dates, seriatim, of my letters from T. S. Eliot are: page 258, Oct. 10, Oct. 14, 1951; page 263, March 18, 1952; page 267, Sept. 22, 1953; page 270, Jan. 21, 1955; page 274, July 17, 1957. The letter from Mrs. Eliot on page 268 is dated June 1, 1954.

The dates of my letters from Alice B. Toklas are: page 236, Feb. 8, March 28, 1947; page 237, Dec. 1, 1947 and July 27, 1950; page 238, August 7, 1950; page 239, Sept. 8, 1950; page 244, Sept. 22, 1950; page 247, Aug. 26, 1953; page 248, Nov. 14, 1959.